Age of Democracy

Age of Democracy

THE POLITICS OF POST-FORDISM

John Mathews

OXFORD
UNIVERSITY PRESS

Melbourne Oxford Auckland New York

OXFORD UNIVERSITY PRESS AUSTRALIA

Oxford New York Toronto
Delhi Bombay Calcutta Madras Karachi
Petaling Jaya Singapore Hong Kong Tokyo
Nairobi Dar es Salaam Cape Town
Melbourne Auckland
and associated companies in
Berlin Ibadan

OXFORD is a trade mark of Oxford University Press

First published 1989

National Library of Australia
Cataloguing-in-Publication data:

Mathews, John, 1946– .
Age of democracy: the politics of post-Fordism.

Bibliography.
Includes index.
ISBN 0 19 554913 6.

1. Socialism. 2. Industrial organization (Economic theory). 3. Mass production. 4. Trade-unions — Political activity. 5. Social movements. I. Title.

335.5

Edited by Vivienne Broadhurst
Designed by Pauline McClenahan
Typeset by Setrite Typesetters Ltd
Printed by The Book Printer
Published by Oxford University Press,
253 Normanby Road, South Melbourne, Australia

CONTENTS

FOREWORD

In this book John Mathews continues his work of challenging the social democratic and labour movements of the West to develop policies and structures suited to the politics of the 1990s.

His challenge is to step beyond, but not away from, the struggles of the past; to move towards a politics of inclusion—where the state's role is no longer limited to that of regulator and redistributor but rather where the state is an active agent in enabling all people to participate in the shaping of their world—at home, at work, in their community through to environmental and strategic issues of global concern.

He points to the fundamental weaknesses that undermine the future of 'New Right' approaches to politics—a politics that ultimately cannot cope with rapid changes in technology, or with the new and emerging roles of women, ethnic and other hitherto excluded groups in our communities; a politics that must ultimately rely upon organized force and suppression or collapse.

The principles of associative democracy described by Mathews provide cause for optimism, but simultaneously challenge the labour movement to rethink its goals. The seeds of associative democracy are to be seen in Australia today: the Accord between Federal Labor and the Australian Council of Trade Unions and the proliferation of tripartite and multipartite planning and consultative bodies provide mechanisms for the re-enfranchisement of all Australians. Economic, wages and industry education and training policies are now developed through processes of open consultation and dialogue.

The role of the social wage in development of the Accord has taken wages policy beyond the sectional interests of particular industries and industrial organizations. As we enter the 1990s we see emerging processes through which the union movement, in conjunction with Labor in government and employers, is reshaping not just the working environment of its members but also the whole career structures and training options to be open to workers into the future. Mathews insists that extension of democracy provides the framework for understanding and shaping these developments.

The challenges of associative democracy as described by Mathews are immense. We need the maturity as a labour movement to address our organizational structures and our methods of dialogue to provide within the organs of the movement the vehicles through which groups such as women, ethnic and peace groups, and environmentalists can participate fully. We need to develop a politics that goes beyond regulation and redistribution to address the ways in which our social organization and physical planning can build and support communities rather than isolating families and individuals. We must do this without sacrificing the gains we have made in the fairer distribution of economic and social resources. John Mathews's work provides a conceptual framework for the labour movements of the West, and the individuals and groups within those movements, to develop our thinking processes and structures for the 1990s, building on but not limited by the politics of the 1970s and 1980s.

The Hon. Brian Howe, MP
Minister for Social Security
and Minister Assisting the Prime Minister
for Social Justice

PREFACE

The social order of the twenty-first century, if there is to be any future at all for this planet and its inhabitants, will be shaped by the political interventions of the organized labour and social movements. Against the destructive trends of community erosion, spoliation of the environment, exterminist arms races, and the pollution of our cultures and imagination, these movements have the capacity to bring a perspective of social responsibility and to instil a sense of our collective destiny, into mainstream political processes. Yet as they face up to this colossal task of shaping the future, these movements find themselves burdened with a miscellany of doctrines, principles and ideas inherited from their past. While every social movement needs to preserve its heritage in order to provide itself with a culture, and to enhance its sense of identity, it does not follow that the heritage need dictate the future strategy of the movement. The organizing principles and strategies of any movement that is to survive and flourish, need to be subjected to constant review and revision; this is an elementary insight gleaned from the science of complex viable systems.

Such a review, it is argued in this book, needs to start with the recognition that the social and political order of the twentieth century, while being shaped by the organized labour movement, has been dominated by a Fordist vision of standardization and mass production. Social democracy itself, which began as a workers' creed for mutuality and self-sufficiency in the nineteenth century, was shaped by the Fordist vision to become a political engine of efficient economic growth and equitable distribution.

And it is the weaknesses, or internal contradictions, within the Fordist mass production system that are now opening up a space for industrial and social innovation. The challenge of the 1990s, it is argued, is to renovate the politics of social democracy around a vision of production efficiency that effects a rupture with Fordist standardization. What such a post-Fordist politics might look like is the subject addressed by this book.

Democracy, with full adult franchise, was won around the turn of the century, paving the way to mass participation in politics for the first time in history. Mass production, and the mass consumption it gave rise to, was not long in following. By the early years of the century, the elements of the mass production system were all in place, in core sectors of the US economy.

Standardization lay at the heart of its phenomenal success: standardization of parts, processes and products; standardization of labour through Taylorization, breaking work down into standard fragments with time and motion study, and divorcing conception from execution; and mechanization of assembly, thus standardizing the pace at which work was to be performed. This system, with its long production runs and huge capital investments, was able to produce goods at such low cost that it swept before it all competition and paved the way to the rise of giant multinational corporations. It is this industrial/technical paradigm that has had such a pervasive effect, imposing itself as the only feasible model of productivity and efficiency. Hierarchies, division of labour, surveillance and control: these terms became synonymous with efficiency and therefore with consumer well-being.

Mass producers soon found that mass consumer markets were required to absorb the expanded output of goods. Enormous marketing efforts were launched to shape and uphold consumer demand. Commodities that had been luxuries were essentially democratized. But as the Great Depression showed, corporate efforts on their own were not enough to sustain spending, and there was gradually erected an apparatus of government support for high wages and income maintenance. It was this combination of mass production and organized mass consumption that we now call Fordism—in honour of Antonio Gramsci, who first glimpsed the significance of these developments from his prison cell in Mussolini's Italy.

Whatever chance the nineteenth century socialist movement

may have had to reshape industry with its ideals of mutuality and co-operative ownership was lost with the rise of mass production which was utterly intolerant of any worker input or innovation. In turn, this vision was adopted by the nascent Bolshevik state in Russia where it was allowed to govern a new round of industrialization, as hostile to worker involvement as any enterprise in the West.

It was out of the crucible of despair created by the First World War, the Great Depression and the rise of Fascism—all calamities that democracy was powerless to prevent—that the Social Democracy/Labour (SD/L) project emerged in reconstructed form in the years following the Second World War. It was now completely subservient to the requirements of Fordism. The hegemony of visions of efficiency based on mass production, and the spread internationally of mass consumer markets, was complemented by the SD/L post-war projects of managing the economy with Keynesian fiscal and monetary tools, and the construction of a welfare state that went beyond poverty relief to become a system of genuine income support and maintenance.

Thus it may be argued that it was what we call 'Fordism' that generated the 'golden years' of the post-war boom, providing unheard of mass prosperity, but at the price of standardizing the world of consumption, politics and culture in its own image. Fordism regimented the army of labour in a machine of gigantic proportions. The agenda for negotiation between labour and capital was systematically narrowed. Aspirations for industrial democracy that had been expressed so forcefully by workers in the munitions and mining industries during the First World War, were swept away. Industrial relations settled into a ritualized confrontation between mass unions and employers over the distribution of productivity gains in the form of wages—with the 'rank and file' of the industrial army being called on to play a support role when industrial hostilities broke out.

A similar regimentation was imposed, or rather self-imposed, on the mass political parties of labour, and likewise the political agenda was constrained by the Fordist hegemony. Politics in the post-war era eschewed all questions of ownership and control of industry, and focused instead on questions of income distribution and the decommodification of labour, through collective provision of 'social wage' goods and services utilising the public resources of the State. But intervention in the productive apparatus was taboo, even in the industries that were nationalized. The SD/L parties could rearrange the accommodation on the ship, as it were, but they were sensible enough not to tamper with the engine room.

The essential expression of this brand of Fordist social democracy, with its threefold base of Keynesian macro-economic management, institutionalized collective bargaining and welfare statism, was Tony Crosland's *Future of Socialism*, issued in the UK in 1956. It buried, seemingly forever, any notion of socialism going beyond goals of redistribution to engage with the fundamentals of production.

But the longevity of Fordism was more apparent than real. So secure did the system seem, with all the talk of the 'end of ideology', the coming of a 'post-industrial society', the rise of the 'affluent worker' and a new post-war 'youth culture', that its unravelling came as a major shock, not least to the SD/L movement itself that had become so much a part of the system. This unravelling came about through a series of distinct but interconnected developments.

- The system reached its internal social limits, as workers rebelled against further intensification and fragmentation of labour, and students rebelled against the fragmentation of knowledge and its harnessing to massive systems of war and degradation.
- More fundamentally, mass production generated its own external limits through the rise of competitors in Japan and then in South East Asia. Exports from these countries made major inroads into the mass markets of North America and Europe, placing great strains on domestic industries and destroying the myth of full employment.
- The international regime upholding the Fordist system collapsed under these trade pressures. The Bretton Woods system of managing exchange rates fell apart, while the rise of OPEC placed further strains on metropolitan industries, and inaugurated a new era of 'funny money' as petrodollars washed through financial institutions, leading to the disengagement of the financial system from the processes of production, and underwriting endemic inflation.
- Most fundamentally, as new market conditions required rapidity of response, and as new technologies offered gains in productivity based on flexible worker input, the mass production giants found themselves unable to compete. Their vision of efficiency was no longer a guarantee of market success.

This eclipse of the hegemony of Fordism has been a turning point of enormous historical significance—what Piore and Sabel have termed a 'second industrial divide'. One paradigm of industrial response has been in the same mould as Fordism, but intensified—more intense Taylorization of work, utilizing the surveillance and control capacities of computerization, out-sourcing of production, more intense protection of markets. This neo-Fordist strategy generates a greater polarization of the workforce into a skilled elite and a mass of semi-skilled and semi-employed peripheral labour force; it is associated with enhanced authoritarianism in the workplace, and frequently with union-busting, with a move towards less overt regulation and greater reliance on 'pure' market forces. This is the strategy pursued by the New Right, under the political protection of neo-conservative regimes in Britain and the United States.

But an alternative paradigm has emerged, based on a model of efficiency that effects a sharp rupture with Fordism. Throughout the 1980s, claims that core sectors of industry have been dispensing with production strategies associated with Fordism, have been the focus of intense debate. 'New production concepts' have been identified which seek the achievement of flexibility, productivity and efficiency through a new focus on quality, on skilled worker input, on product innovation. It posits new productive relationships between work organization, skills formation, industrial relations and computerized technologies. The essence of this post-Fordist vision, which is being pursued as an industrial strategy in firms throughout the advanced industrial world, lies in its break with the rigidities and standardization of Fordism. It harnesses aspirations towards workers' direct involvement in production decisions, or direct industrial democracy, to the commercial success of firms deploying the strategy. In this way it maps out an area of 'co-operative accommodation' between labour and capital, on the assumption that their interests are not utterly irreconcilable (ie of an exclusively zero sum kind) but that on the basis of maintenance of their respective strengths, they can agree to co-operate in certain areas. But this triggers a dynamic for labour that has far-reaching implications—for workers individually, for workers collectively, and for the SD/L movement. Individually, workers experience a sense of empowerment and responsibility at work that was denied them under the conditions of mass production. This can be expected to translate into a further awareness of the economic conditions in which their enterprises operate, and to further demands for involvement in management decisions. Men and women who command respect for their opinions at work, can be expected to take more than a passing interest in the affairs of their community and the wider society—and so the problem of political apathy so widespread now may be contained and reversed. The role for unions under these circumstances will be enhanced, rather than diminished — but in a manner that is very different from the mechanical exercise of mass strength under Fordism. Unions will be driven to support the active interventions of their members at workplace level with resources, guidelines, channels of accountability, and a facilitating political framework negotiated with other interested parties, such as employers and political lobbies for various interests.

It is my contention that this provides the clue to a successful reconstruction of a politics of social democracy, utilising a broadened base of the labour and social movements. SD/L politics needs to break with the monolithic assumptions which it has inherited from its socialist antecedents and from its immediate Fordist past. The SD/L parties played their last Fordist cards in the 1970s, trying to maintain the Crosland vision with programmes of big government, big spending and high taxes. (Examples were the Common Programme between the Communists and Socialists in France; the 1974 UK Labour Platform; the Whitlam government in Australia; or the Carter presidency in the US.) They faced intractable odds, as Keynesianism collapsed in stagflation, the welfare state started to sag under the weight of rising levels of unemployment, and industry itself regrouped for its neo-Fordist offensive. By the 1980s, the loss of confidence of the SD/L parties in their historic mission, and their inability to contain the economic problems of late Fordism, opened the way for their neo-conservative successors. The post-war political consensus was well and truly over.

Meanwhile, the bills incurred during the post-war boom had to be paid. The environmental costs of growth came to be sharply identified, fuelling the rise of new environmental and conservation movements that came to play an ever more prominent political role. The social regimentation of Fordism was contested, as social, ethnic and gender groups began to forge their own identity, and brought a new set of social movements into the political arena. The insane threat of exterminism that had sustained the nuclear cold war, was openly contested by new mass movements that have shaken the SD/L parties to their foundations.

I claim that the renovation of social democratic thought and practice must start by learning the lessons from this experience. The statist illusions of the past must be shed, and a new respect be forged for the capacities of unions and social movements to intervene directly in the process of production and in wider social spheres to liberate our socio-institutional structures from their Fordist shackles. It is the self-activity of these organizations that will bring the SD/L movement back to life.

A post-Fordist political vision breaks with the mass conformity and unitary illusions of Fordist SD/L politics, and instead provides a favourable environment within which associations of workers and citizens may negotiate the direct democratization of industrial, economic and social life. It comes to terms with, and bases its practice on, an associational mode of social organization and a pluralist mode of political co-ordination. The illusion of rule is dispelled. The political arena is perceived instead as the locus of 'political exchange' between associations, which are encouraged to formulate wide-ranging 'accords' or agreements which further their respective interests through the formation of political coalitions, e.g. between unions and conservation groups over agreed forest management programmes. As Paul Hirst insists, there will still be a need for a form of public authority to regulate the negotiation and implementation of such accords, and to regulate the associations themselves—but in an associative order the State will not deploy a mystical 'sovereignty' that places it above and distinct from the society it regulates, but will instead play the role of the 'association of associations'.

My thesis is that the only social and political force that is capable of fashioning such a polity is the SD/L movement, harnessing the energies of unions and social movements which *in toto* can command an overwhelming majority of the population. But to undergo the change in outlook and practice that is needed if it is to play this role, and to elevate the relations between associations above that which obtains already (but informally) in all democracies, a new ingredient is needed. This ingredient is a vision, a framework—in short, a paradigm, that can integrate common concerns, that can marry present campaigns with a future social order, that is in tune with pluralism, yet is radical enough to facilitate the innovations needed in industry and the economy if our planet is to have any future at all. It must be a paradigm that goes beyond the unitary illusions of socialism, but is based on mutuality and co-operation; it must go beyond the sphere of production to reflect wider social and cultural concerns, yet reflect and complement the innovations achieved in industry through post-Fordist direct democratization. It must provide a vision of the future and a set of values that large numbers of people can subscribe to, and which will underwrite the reforms needed to correct the present self-destructing course on which the planet is headed. It must above all insist on the priority to be accorded to the general or public interest, expressed most eloquently in the phrase 'only one earth', over the individual interests that are catered for most efficiently by markets.

It is the central contention of this book that such a paradigm already exists, in the fragmentary visions and innovations already produced by associations of workers and citizens. It is not a question of inventing some grand new idea, nor of conjuring up some new historical force that will save us all from destruction. We have to work with what we've got. Our paradigm must emphasise the role that workers and citizens themselves can play, when combined in their associations, through direct negotiations in the workplace and in the community, thus building on but extending our notion of democracy from its hitherto narrow political conception. Hence my suggestion that the paradigm be called Associative Democracy. It does not have a given and immutable content; this must be worked out by the associations themselves. What it does is provide the guiding framework within which this constructive activity may best be carried forward. We can expect the struggle to be long and bitter.

For a decade the political initiative has rested with the resurgent Right. Under the banner of monetarist productivism, it has rolled back the gains of social democracy, and underwritten industrial restructuring along neo-Fordist lines. Some SD/L governments in Australia, New Zealand and in Europe, have stood their ground, and especially in Australia have made real headway in encouraging and facilitating the activities of unions and social movements. But they all demonstrably lack a coherent vision of their future. I argue that it is visions and values that will determine political outcomes in the 1990s. Even the neo-conservative governments are themselves coming up against political limits in the form of renewed demands for social responsibility, not just in the face of rampant polarization and generation of inequities, but to deal with problems of survival that are seen, correctly, to be global in character, overriding the pursuit of sectional and individual interests. These are aspirations that a renovated SD/L political order must respond to.

This book is informed by my twenty-one years of political activity, dating from the student rebellions of 1968, through the major social campaigns of the 1970s (around questions of energy use and lead-free petrol) to working with unions and Labor governments in Australia in the 1980s. I have experienced for myself the limits of influence that a social movement on its own can exercise, and how its role can be transformed when integrated with political activity and a negotiated alliance with other movements. On the other hand, I am directly familiar with the limitations imposed on the exercise of power by unions and labour governments in a pluralist democracy. Through all this, I am hostile to a politics which is radical but not responsible, expecting working people to take risks with their lives that defy rational calculation but I am equally hostile to the timid form of pragmatism that characterizes so many examples of SD/L governments that fail to sustain any transformative momentum by their retreats and evasions in the face of organized resistance. I have framed the paradigm of Associative Democracy in the light of this experience—as calling for radical but responsible innovations in the economy, industry and community, and as insisting that the momentum must be maintained by vesting primary responsibility for action in people themselves, organized in their associations as citizens and workers. I do not believe that there is any other viable way forward which may deliver us all safely into the twenty-first century.

Melbourne, June 1989

ACKNOWLEDGEMENTS

This book, more than most, owes its existence to the ideas and imagination of a host of colleagues and friends with whom I have collaborated in political campaigns over many years. In particular, for their encouragement or assistance, I wish to thank the following: Dennis Altman, Richard Badham, Stafford Beer, Peter Beilharz, Mike Berry, Peter Botsman, Stewart Carter, Barbara Champion, Peter Christoff, Ken Coghill, Mike Cooley, Richard Curtain, Alastair Davidson, Ed Davis, Kim Dovey, Jim Falk, Lyndsay Farrall, Boris Frankel, Steve Frenkel, Alan Greig, Richard Gillespie, Dick Gross, Winton Higgins, Stephen Hill, Phil Hind, Barry Hindess, Paul Hirst, Ron Johnston, Stephanie Key, Ben Kiernan, Jenny Lee, Alain Lipietz, Barbara Lepani, Stuart Macintyre, Freya Mathews, Race Mathews, Paul Matters, Rudolph Meidner, Kent Middleton, Jeff Minson, Carla Mumme, Claus Offe, Max Ogden, Cassandra Parkinson, Jan Powning, Belinda Probert, Geoff Pryor, David Rankin, Peter Rawlinson, Linda Rubinstein, Michael Salvaris, Ric Sissons, Bernie Taft, Mark Taft, David Turnbull, Bryan Turner, Birger Viklund, Rob Watts, Chris White, and Evan Willis. A special thank you to my father, Alwyn Mathews, for his painstaking review of successive drafts of the manuscript. And to Dale Rostron, Jan Martorana and Jill Shineberg, many thanks for their prodigious typing and word processing efforts on my behalf.

To the students of Tienanmen Square, Beijing
who died in the name of democracy

ONE

INTRODUCTION

In this text we are concerned with the organizing principles of the labour and social movements (L/SMs), ranged in their associations of citizens and of workers, and with the strategies of their dominant political arm, the Social Democratic and Labour (SD/L) parties. Of course this in itself is a controversial choice: there are many voices maintaining that the SD/L traditions are now bankrupt and are becoming part of the problem rather than of the solution. In my view, such dismissals are premature. The movement that shaped the modern world can, if armed with an appropriate vision, continue to shape a sustainable and civilized future.

The Social Democratic and Labour parties have always had an uneasy relationship with democracy. It was not 'their' system, but one which they inherited, and have adapted to their own ends. There has always been a hard core within the movement that rejects the trappings of 'bourgeois democracy' outright, following Lenin in favouring the more direct and authoritarian relations that have traditionally ruled industry. Yet the truth is that virtually all the gains won by the SD/L movement this century have been achieved under the protection of democracy. The creation of a public sector, the establishment of universal social security and health, education and welfare services systems, the upholding of economic activity and employment through Keynesian fiscal and monetary policies—all this has been achieved by SD/L parties wielding influence through a democratic state.

However it was readily taken for granted. It was easy for radicals to describe democracy as merely the 'shell' of an unchanged capitalist order. Now there is no excuse for such illusions. This century has witnessed the horrors of fascism and nazism unleashed when democracy gave way before armed thuggery. A World War had to be fought to remedy those mistakes. More recently we have witnessed the collapse of democracy, including elected socialist governments, in one Latin American country after another—with grievous results for the labour movement at the hands of unprincipled police states and death squads roaming the streets. We have seen how ultra-leftist terrorism in West Germany and Italy (courtesy of the Baader-Meinhof group and the Red Brigades) has achieved nothing but a loss of civil liberties on the part of all citizens and a disturbing increase in the influence of the military and paramilitary forces in those countries.

But in the 1980s the tide seems to have turned. The Latin American dictatorships have gone the way of their Greek, Turkish, Spanish and Portuguese brothers. The labour movements in all these countries now enjoy the freedom to organize that is all the sweeter for having been denied for so long. The emergent industrial powers of Asia and the Pacific region are going through their democratic revolutions (as Britain, France and the US did centuries ago)—as testified by the stirring recent events in the Philippines, South Korea, Burma and Thailand. The fashionable appeal of ultra-leftist terrorism in Europe has vanished. And most astonishingly of all, democracy is emerging as the driving force for change in the communist bloc. The Soviet Union is leading the way, as perestroika and glasnost become the watchwords of a revolution in expectations. Upheavals follow in Eastern Europe and in the Baltic states. In China, the Communist Party is frantically seeking to modernise along openly western lines. This is truly the 'age of Democracy'.

Yet the political agenda is in a constant state of flux. Against these favourable trends must be set the rise to power of the New Right, and its consolidation in the populist regimes currently governing the UK and the US. World-wide, the trends to the Right are all too clear, and very powerful.

There is the hard business agenda. This is represented at one extreme by the New Right and monetarist ideologues, with their insistence that all economic and, ultimately, social questions be settled by the 'democracy' of the market; from them comes a relentless depiction of the unions and the public sector as sources of inefficiency. At the other extreme it is represented by a new corporatism, where big business is prepared to do deals with big 'business unions' that are now so common in the US and the UK—deals exemplified by Rupert Murdoch's agreement with non-print electricians in his print headquarters in Wapping, London. In this agenda, from either extreme, there is precious little scope for workers to express their values and sense of social responsibility, for participation, consultation or co-determination. These trends are backed by the new found dominance and mobility of finance capital; and by the power of multinational enterprise to purchase labour and materials, and supply markets, by playing off State against State.

There is the hardening of bureaucratic decree, and the losing struggle of democratic organs like Parliament to keep on top of the government machine. Those who favour secrecy and cronyism thrive under such circumstances. The goal of democratizing public administration and ensuring freedom of information as a basic civil right has never seemed more distant.

Linked to this bureaucratization of State power is its quasi-permanent militarization. There is the hardening of military and para-military forces in response to the threat of terrorism, and the suspension of hard-won civil liberties under the pretext of containing this threat. Terrorism appears to have become entrenched in the modern world, fed by the contradictory elements of an expanding global armaments market, a series of intractable political situations (such as in the Middle East, Northern Ireland, and parts of Africa), and the relative vulnerability of civil and commercial organizations. The reckless export of violence to the Third World by the western democracies (notably in Africa and South-East Asia) has created a legacy that we shall have to live with for a long time to come. Meanwhile the blind pursuit of sectional ends by trade unions can be used as the pretext for further repression, as in the ill-fated miners' strike against the Thatcher government in the UK. The longer the period that New Right governments stay in power, the more time they have to build these formidable surveillance and repressive machines.

Fuelled by the firestorm of technological change and industry restructuring, there is emerging a yawning gulf between the employed and the unemployed; between the few educated youngsters who can hope to get a job and the majority who may be condemned to permanent marginality; between the workforce in full-time employment and the growing army, largely female, on part-time and out-work contracts. These divisions and polarizations all contribute to a growing violence and nihilism in social and cultural life. They are all fed by the other heads of the New Right—the fundamentalist, obscurantist and openly anti-rational movements like the 'Festival of Light', and the ugly street mobs like the neo-Fascists.

There is the awesome trend towards a uniform and strident illiberalism in printed and electronic media, as these come under increasingly global network control. The popular imagination, strong resource that it has always been, is now threatened with mass anaesthetization, if not annihilation, by the entertainment and leisure industry consortia that have colonized our media. If it is true that a movement must exercise power in imagination before it has any hope of exercising it in reality (as I believe it is—this being the essence of Gramsci's notion of hegemony) then this dominance of the realm of the imaginary by the trivial, the cruel and the pornographic must cast serious doubt on our ability to recover a sense of our own identity and power.

Finally, there are the omnipresent threats of environmental catastrophe and a nuclear holocaust, together with the deadly nuclear arsenals that need constant military supervision. The nuclear technology that feeds them requires a level of surveillance and control that is totally incompatible with the political and civil liberties won this century in the wider economy and polity. This spills over into a case for controls on trade unions and a further strengthening of the apparatus of public surveillance.

And this is just to speak of the problems of the OECD countries! Beyond them, the world is torn by war, by civil strife, by famine, by the spoliation of forests and environment on an unprecedented scale. New fundamentalist ideologies, such as those based on Islam, Sikhism, and other religions, are fuelling wars on a scale that makes Marxism-Leninism look tame in comparison.

It is of course all too easy to see these as the dominant threats and trends of our time (as indeed they are) and to see little scope for any counter initiatives, particularly from the Western labour movement and its potential allies in the various social movements for peace, conservation, civil liberties and the rights of the individual, and for an end to discrimination on sexual, ethnic or other grounds. But the power of human intervention in what seems to be a programmed course of destruction, should not be under-estimated.

The mere cataloguing of the groups and organizations that are potential allies in meeting the challenge of the New Right, shows that here is the basis of a coalition commanding an overwhelming majority of the population. The essence of a democratic strategy lies in the harnessing of this majority, utilizing a numerical superiority in the (parliamentary) political arena in order to legislate and co-ordinate the extension of democratic procedures into broader economic and social spheres. It embodies a simple precept of building a structure of economic and social democracy on the strong foundations of political democracy.

1.1 DEMOCRACY AND CITIZENSHIP

Democracy is our great cultural possession and political asset but it appears to be a thin, civilizing veneer in a world that is probably more violent and barbarous today than at any time in recent history. Despotism is everywhere. Whereas torture has always been practised in one form or another, today it is practised systematically by over half the governments that are members of the United Nations, simply in order to keep one elite in power at the expense of the rest of the population. Whereas famine has always been with us due to agricultural calamities or over-population, today we find famine occurring in one part of the world while agricultural surpluses elsewhere are disposed of down mineshafts. Whereas armed rebellion has always been a feature of political change, today it is practised systematically by armed forces overthrowing popular political leaders, or by one junta replacing another. In all of this, the veneer of western democracy seems thin indeed. What gives us heart and prevents us from capitulating to political despair, is the consideration that the industrial jungle created by emergent capitalist forces in the nineteenth century—a process repeated everywhere capitalism has been transplanted—has been tamed and civilized to some extent by the collective pressure of workers and citizens, organized in their unions, their Social Democratic or Labour (SD/L) parties, and their social movements. Against the claims of the market principle, the counterclaims of the citizenship principle have made some slight headway. This gives us some grounds for optimism.

The notion of citizenship has been most clearly formulated by T H Marshall in a series of lectures first given in 1949, and later elaborated on in his essay *The Right to Welfare.*[1] Marshall took a broad historical sweep, and argued that the notion of citizenship embodied three separate rights won over a period spanning two hundred years in England. The eighteenth century saw the expansion of civil rights concerned with legal status (e.g. habeas corpus); these were established and defended in the courts. In the nineteenth century there was an expansion of political rights, particularly extensions of the franchise, which were won in Parliament. The twentieth century has seen an expansion of social rights, such as the rights to education, to health care, and to social security. Marshall argued that capitalism was only possible once a developed system of civil rights had been established, for this protected private contracts; the expansion of political rights moderated capitalism to some extent; but it is the expansion of social rights which is at odds with the market and with the class structure of capitalism. Marshall viewed the working class struggle for regulation of the labour market and for an expanded public sector, which underpin the expression of social rights, as being in a 'state of war' with the capitalist market order.

This conceptualization is extremely fruitful, for it focuses attention on the arena in which the great battles have been fought this century by the SD/L movement, namely those of government and the public sector, based on the leverage obtained by the winning of universal suffrage at the close of the nineteenth century. It carries with it a strategic implication, namely that the political domain should be viewed as the site where the electoral or political superiority of the SD/L movement may be utilized to enhance or consolidate the social rights of the citizenry. This perspective is elaborated on explicitly by various SD/L movements, particularly the Swedish, which has long argued that workers' demands could not be met solely through negotiations with employers, but that their satisfaction must involve a measure of public provision won through numerical control of the political domain.[2]

In seeking a way forward, in expanding the influence of the citizenship principle, or in extending the domain of democracy from the political to the economic or industrial, there are some ideological factors of historical significance that give grounds for believing that our task is not hopeless.

Firstly, in most western countries there is an extremely significant ending of the historic Social Democrat/Communist split that dates from the 1920s, or of splits fomented by it, such as the formation in Australia of a Catholic anti-Communist faction within the Labor party in the 1950s. The two major streams of the movement, which had become solidified into 'reformist' and 'revolutionary' trends, have finally made their peace with each other—either through the institutional decline of the CP and its ultra-left opponents, or through the CP becoming a Social Democratic party itself (i.e. the Eurocommunist turn).

This means the end of the road, finally, for the Bolshevik seizing-State-power-by-force strategy, which was totally destructive of any set of positive or constructive proposals within democratic conditions. It acted as a brake on all transformative initiatives. It siphoned off the best militants, and it helped turn the SD/L parties themselves into those conservative, red-baiting organizations of the 1950s. Its collapse is welcome, and it frees energies for a more radical SD/L alternative.

Secondly, there is the exhaustion of the SD/L Keynesian project of seeking to control the economy externally, via fiscal and monetary policy, rather than seeking any internal intervention. A Keynesian approach remains viable as a means of technically regulating certain limited aspects of the (internationally dominated) economy, but it cannot lay claim to having any transformative potential. Nor can it cope with newer problems of structural unemployment. It was essentially a strategy that had mild redistributional effects in a full employment economy, and mild counter-cyclical potential in an economy in recession—but it never addressed the structural issues that are now high on the agenda.

Because of the dominance of this Keynesian paradigm, through most of the post-war period and right up to the present, socialists have been reduced to 'progressive Keynesians' in calling for higher budget deficits to prime the economic pump and to get national economies back on to growth trajectories. But external regulation of the economy has never been an adequate substitute for transforming the economy from within, and this is what is now on the agenda.

This brings us to the third of our ideological factors—the end, or at least the beginning of the end, of socialist illusion. It is no longer heresy in the radical wings of the labour movement to demand that policies be realistic and feasible, and to insist that vague formulations of goals such as a 'free society of free producers' are essentially meaningless in any real, complex society. Nor is it heresy to argue that an SD/L government may act as the umbrella under which social change occurs, but cannot and will not 'deliver' a legislated socialism; nor that the working class cannot and will not be the emancipating force for the whole of society. This new sense of realism is the essential precondition for any serious work to be done in bringing the policies of the movement into line with the needs of the 1990s.

The time for simple, mechanical formulae is long past. Marx's philosophical insight that dialectic logic could be applied to capitalism as a total system, with capital identified as thesis and proletariat as antithesis, and that this would generate in time an historical synthesis of the two, is breathtaking in its scope, and subversive of the existing order, but utterly irrelevant to any real political programme of transformation. In Marx's later work, he expounded an economic theory of capitalism predicting periodic crises and irresolvable contradictions between the forces and relations of production. These formulae, even if they contain a kernel of truth, have done irreparable damage to a socialist movement which saw its role as 'waiting for the crises' and building up its 'class strength', while waiting for the economic system to collapse. In predicating their political work on these notions, the early socialist parties condemned themselves to inaction, or to using Parliament as a mere gallery where the sins of capitalism could be paraded. This militancy in word but quiescence in deed brought the movement to the point of destruction during the First World war, when, ironically, the capitalist system really was in disarray.

Since 1917 a new dogma has held sway, formulated principally by Lenin. This is that the working class is potentially capable of controlling its own and society's destiny, but in practice it is confined to an economist consciousness through its autonomous trade union practice, and therefore it needs the external intervention of a disciplined party to guide it to the conquest of State power. No strategy could be less well adapted to the democratic transformative project in the West. It ignores the political democracy that workers fought so hard to obtain, and it ignores the radicalizing influence of struggles to change worklife—and all in favour of a narrow, violent conception of State conquest (treating the State meanwhile as a capitalist stronghold and therefore not to be tampered with). These simple formulae—the view of capitalism as a total system subject to contradictions; the role of the proletariat as the grave-diggers of capitalism; the revolutionary party as representing the true interests of the working class, if only they were not blinded by capitalist propaganda; the endless debate between strategies of revolution or reform; the notion of capitalism as a disease that must not be allowed to 'infect' the working class; the notion of the 'capitalist State' that co-opts and contains working class advances—all these and many more such formulae represent a ticket to nowhere for a transformative political project. They are socialist illusions. They must be dispensed with, and in my view buried once and for all.

The final ideological factor in our favour is the strength of the social movements, and the liberating effect they have had on political discourse. The narrow concerns of the trade unions and of the SD/L parties, making up the traditional labour movement this century, have now been broadened to encompass concerns about the quality of life, gender and ethnic issues, and the long-term survival of life on our planet. These concerns, coupled with a new understanding of the sophisticated tools needed to intervene in a complex economic system, provide the basis for a genuinely universal programme of political transformation, appealing to general and not just to sectional interests. Of course, such a programme has to be created as a conscious political act, through the negotiation of alliances based on commonality of interests; it does not fall mechanically into place as part of some supposed 'logic of history'.

1.2 RENOVATION OF SOCIAL DEMOCRATIC AND LABOUR THEORY

Thus there are some guarded grounds for optimism. But the renovation of ideology and principles is long overdue. The problems to be faced, and solved, by the SD/L movement in the 1990s and beyond, are of a quite different order from those faced during the 'long boom', when SD/L orthodoxy was last overhauled.[3] And they are utterly different from the conditions that obtained last century when the basic goals and strategy of the SD/L movement were formulated.

As examples, let us take three issues which we shall deal with in some detail in this text.

Social control of investment

It is at the point of investment, where the economic order is being changed at the margin, that social criteria have been most lacking in the past, and where they will need to be imposed in the future. But the instruments of control available to orthodox SD/L parties are wholly inadequate. External regulation of the economy utilizing Keynesian fiscal and monetary tools, even when combined with incomes policies, cannot be relied on to 'shape' the investment environment; and direct intervention via nationalized industries, which have tended to be as bureaucratic and hierarchical as their private sector counterparts, has not realised the hopes entertained for it. But new instruments are available in the form of collective funds under social control, such as superannuation and pension funds, employee investment funds, and national development funds, all financed in one way or another out of profits and payroll taxes. These instruments differ from those used in the past in that they offer a direct role to trade unions and associations of citizens—rather than their having to see their concerns mediated by governments or boards of nationalized industries. The price of failing to resort to these new instruments is likely to be high. Investment will then be generated on the terms acceptable to the New Right: no unions, free markets, less social expenditure and enhanced military expenditure.

Industry restructuring

Industries are having to drastically restructure as they move out of the certainties promoted by a regime of mass production, to a new and rapidly changing competitive environment. Computerization and management reorganization promise big productivity gains, provided the changes are introduced in a way that builds on workers' skills and reverses the now outmoded principles of Taylorism.[4] But how is such an approach to be imposed on industry? All the important economic conditions—relating to appointment of managers and, through them, to production levels, trade, marketing and promotion, investment, research and development and relations with employees—are made in the Boardrooms of a nation's leading companies. Reforming governments have sought in the past to influence these decisions, via overall fiscal and monetary policy; via regulation (for example, by providing health and safety standards and setting up an inspectorate to enforce them); via subsidies and tax incentives; via anti-monopoly (anti-trust) activity; and by providing a framework in which industrial relations can be conducted without undue disruption. But all these measures come up against the problem of their being imposed from without; they attempt to create an environment within which certain socially responsible decisions will be made. But they stop short of requiring that such decisions be taken directly, through internal reforms within the enterprises themselves.

The limitations of this approach should be evident by now. New interventionist industry policies are needed, at both the macro- and the micro-level, established through what could be an historic pact between industry and unions to bring about change on the basis of co-determination. In this text, we shall discuss a range of approaches to democratization of firms, which go beyond the agenda normally encompassed by the term 'industrial democracy'. They include: amending the company law to broaden the accountability of Directors; opening up Boards to worker and public representatives; inclusion of social and economic goals in the aims of firms which apply for and receive public subsidies; and involvement of workers collectively, through their unions, in job design and the carrying out of work.

Social policy

It can be argued that social policy, consisting of welfare payments and services, was thought of in the post-war period as being marginal to economic and industry policy, smoothing out the creases in the process of the economic growth that financed it. But now economic growth has faltered, while the demands on the system from the unemployed and from those not living as a conventional nuclear family are growing. This structural, fiscal crisis is the material basis for the relentless attacks mounted by the New Right on all social wage expenditure. The only viable response is to reconceptualize social policy as providing the framework for accommodating rapid social change, and finding new means of financing these services, for example from taxes on profits, and new means of delivering them, such as through a guaranteed minimum income scheme. In this way, the sectionalism that has dogged the labour movement is likely to be overcome, and an economic foundation laid for political alliances to be forged with social movements.

* * *

I argue in this text that the elaboration of the new instruments, strategies and principles needed to cope with these and other problems, requires a new perspective, or paradigm, of democratization.[5] But time is running short. The small democratic political arena that the labour and social movements have carved out this century is visibly shrinking . Apart from the relentless ideological assault by the New Right, there are authoritarian trends at work in technological and business developments which are steadily eroding the margins of choice. The challenge is to use what is left of this democratic political arena, and of the apparatus of social and civil rights that constitute citizenship, to stave off these authoritarian trends by extending democratic procedures into economic, social and industrial life. Such measures are also called for by the apparent failure of policies that have sought to control investment, industry development and social welfare.

Our narrow 'political' conception of democracy will either be consummated by this extension, or consumed. This I see as the great political contest of the next decade.

1.3 TOWARDS A POST-FORDIST PARADIGM OF ASSOCIATIVE DEMOCRACY

This text is dedicated to providing the labour and social movements with the intellectual tools needed to win the coming contest. It is argued that a drastically different perspective is needed, organized around the following points:

- The highest priority must be given to democracy, at all levels, and a strong ideological offensive mounted to democratize economic and social life, as the only viable alternatives to New Right policies.
- The emphasis needs to be on collective activity, via existing associations of workers and citizens, to release the energy and imagination of the membership, while bringing their collective strength to bear on political issues.
- The State needs to be seen as supporter and co-ordinator of the process of change, with the SD/L party in office, and not fetishized as the 'deliverer' of social transformation, nor theorized as being the omniscient agent of the cunning capitalist class.
- The movement needs to shift ideologically from a culture of protest to a culture of the responsible exercise of power; it must exercise power in imagination before it can hope to do so in reality. Formulation of constructive goals of productivity and efficiency will help to marginalize the New Right.
- Policy needs to be formulated around the notion of trans-

forming the economy from within, rather than regulating it from without. This means being prepared to establish radical new institutions within the economy, such as profit-financed investment funds that draw on a constructive, collective response from associations like trade unions.

- The break with the rigidity and standardization associated with Fordism, promoted by unions and social movements in post-Fordist industrial strategies, needs to be translated into a respect for a pluralism of associations at the political level, conceiving the role of the State as orchestrator of the process of 'political exchange' between associations.
- Programmatic goals need to be agreed in wide-ranging 'social contracts' that provide the framework for tactical responses to events, but stem any tendency to 'pragmatic evasion' on the part of governments.
- Goals need to be formulated to appeal to as many of the social movements as possible, furnishing solutions to the problems they identify, and thereby carving out the common ground on which a broad political coalition can be built that will sustain the electoral process.

This is the perspective that I propose be called the paradigm of associative democracy—because of its emphasis on democratization, and on associations of workers and citizens as the agents of democratization. Such a perspective provides a clear alternative set of goals and procedures to those espoused by right-wing Labourist pragmatism or by left-wing revolutionism and its heritage. It also clearly demarcates our goals from those of the New Right.

I argue that there is no point in confusing this perspective with that of 'socialism'. Socialism has traditionally provided the set of goals and values that has guided the labour movement, but increasingly it has done so in rhetorical terms only. It now provides a set of values that the movement must continue to draw on (such as mutuality and social cooperation), but it is incapable of generating a clear and unambiguous programme to meet the challenge of the New Right. It is in this sense that I describe the associative democratic paradigm as being 'post-socialist'. I should emphasize that I am a socialist, and will continue to call myself a socialist, but this identification should not blind us to the need to specify clear medium-term goals and imaginative new procedures and institutions for reaching them.

The associative democratic paradigm quite consciously addresses the same issues as those called up in populist fashion by the New Right. The paradigm builds on deeply held and respected values of liberty, independence and sense of property. It builds its practice on the key existing agencies and organizations of the labour and social movements, equipping them with a new and constructive theory rather than denigrating them and focusing only on their inadequacies. In this sense the paradigm forges a new deal between theory and practice, and equips the movements with a mobilizing vision of a new social and economic order.

For this, in my view, is what the labour and social movements critically need—a set of living and attainable goals, and a strategic conception of how those goals may be realized with a reasonable prospect of success, within a reasonable period of time (say, within the next decade). These movements need a paradigm that links policies to form a coherent vision of the future, in order to guide practical concerns and interventions in the present. Alternatives to 'associative democracy' exist. For example, some favour a term like 'social justice', but to my mind this is a weak label which can be made to mean almost anything one wants it to, and which moreover is devoid of any strategic or programmatic content. The term 'associative democracy' has the advantage that it describes a coherent set of policies tied together by their common emphasis on the goal of democratization, and a common strategy that calls on people to achieve change collectively, through their own organizations. It explicitly counters illusions that a new social order can be 'delivered' by a political party or leader acting on our behalf.

The elaboration of this paradigm occupies the greater part of this book. This is a task that is at once large in scope but limited in intention. I seek to establish general principles, and not to intervene in policy debates, nor in specific issues like conservation or peace. My aim is to provide a framework, or paradigm, within which these specific issues may be linked.

It needs to be said that a paradigm is not the same as an ideology. Ever since the Second World War, political philosophy has been searching to regain its authenticity and legitimacy, and throw off the spectre of ideology. The sight of groups rising to political power on the back of such abstractions as *Volk*, *Geist*, and *Reich*, has undermined confidence in the foundations of political philosophy. Henceforth, any ideology claiming to be all-embracing, has to be suspect. Over-arching abstractions led, whether the philosophers liked it or not, to fascist street gangs, prison camps and the gas ovens; these horrors all expressed, in one way or another, the seamy underside to the grand notion of the will to power. Politics thereafter has had to be more modest in its aims.

This present paradigm then, is applicable in all western countries where a Labour or Social Democratic party exists and is in power, or is about to take power. It is, in other words, a paradigm adapted to an advanced democracy with a high level of technology and industry, and strong labour and social movements. If these conditions are not met, the paradigm is not applicable. I should also emphasize that the paradigm of associative democracy is not offered as a substitute for any existing party, movement or platform. It is offered as a framework to guide actions within existing political forums, and to stimulate further detailed theory and practice which engages with the complex reality of the current social and economic order.

Above all, the paradigm presented in this text is one which is swimming with the tide of democratization: it is at one with the 'age of democracy'. There is now a strong consciousness amongst the thinkers of the SD/L movement that democracy in its widest interpretation provides the key to further advance.[6] No other form of political order can offer such a broad basis for the integration of communities and the 'associative concertation' of social organizations. Democracy is linked indissolubly with cybernetic notions of stability, resilience and flexibility of the social order. No matter how frustrating it may seem at times, the democratic way is always preferable to the authoritarian, the dictatorial or the market-driven alternatives.

A choice of strategy in favour of democracy must be conscious of the fact that much of the attack of the New Right is actually directed against democracy as a valid organizing principle for a social order, in favour of a pure market model of social co-ordination.[7]

So democracy is under attack—or rather, a form of democracy that favours the self-expression of organized associations of workers and citizens. The future of democracy will be bound closely to these questions of definition and interpretation. We have witnessed the astonishing spectacle, during the 1988 US Presidential campaign, of the public denigration of the word 'liberal' as standing for everything that is dangerous in republican eyes. That the Republican Party itself traces its origins to nineteenth-century liberal thought regarding the rights of the citizen *vis-à-vis* the State, seems to have mattered not a whit in this exercise of cultural and terminological vandalism. (It is not my brief to argue in this text that the peculiar American usage of the word 'liberal', denoting anyone who stands for even vaguely progressive notions is worth saving; my concern is with the wholesale write-off of a whole national political tradition.) The conclusion I draw from this experience is that 'democracy' will be the next term singled out for abuse by conservatives, if the SD/L parties do indeed pick up the notion of associative democracy as an all-embracing paradigm expressing their philosophy and values.

I would welcome the prospect of the SD/L movement having to make its stand against the combined forces of authoritarianism, individualism and untrammelled market forces, in the name of democracy. It is on this ground that the SD/L movement has the capacity to mobilize its strongest defenders and win its widest basis of support. But as I argue repeatedly in this text, an overly narrow conception of democracy, as confined to the 'ballot box' and electoral domain, is too weak a notion to survive the New Right attack. I argue that a stronger conception, extending the domain of democracy to encompass participation in the economy and industry, is essential to the survival of the very notion of democracy itself.

TWO

THE SOCIAL DEMOCRATIC HERITAGE

2.1 ORIGINS OF THE LABOUR MOVEMENT

The labour movement was born in the indescribable conditions of early industrialization within Europe and its colonies and former colonies—in the violence of the establishment of the early factories; of sweated child labour and indentured black labour; of the social discipline of the workhouse; of boom and slump, with desperation and starvation facing those thrown out of work; of laws of contract that bound workers to employers, like chattels. Workers and their families fought these conditions with the few remedies available to them. They resorted to the power to combine, and to enforce their collective strength through a ferocious discipline imposed upon themselves, in order to set collective conditions; and if all else failed, to riot. There was no one to help them but themselves. It is still moving today to read, for example, of the plight of the early nineteenth-century cottage weavers who were being ruined by mill-produced textiles.[1] Nothing was done to help them, even though they and their families were starving. They took their grievances to Parliament in a series of petitions—but were ignored. What else were rational people to do in such circumstances, but take up arms to defend their rights as human beings?

It is important to realize—for they did so in the nineteenth century—that these armed rebellions achieved very little in the long term. Countless uprisings in the nineteenth century such as the 'Captain Swing' rebellion in the North of England, the Newport rising in Wales, the Eureka Stockade on the Ballarat goldfields in Australia are recorded, but few are remembered. Most ended in repression and arrests; some in bloodbaths like the Paris Commune of 1871 or the Turin uprising in 1917. Insurrection was clearly not the road to long-term power for the emerging labour movement, but its heroic images remain as part of our culture.

Workers had already formed themselves into 'trade unions', at first encompassing only skilled workers, and then in the 1870s and 1880s, bringing in waves of unskilled workers as well. They had fought their early battles to remove the gross impediments, such as outright repression (the anti combination laws, Tolpuddle Martyrs), but more commonly, punitive sanctions imposed for 'breaking contracts' by collective action. The first great victory of the labour movement, then, was that of securing its right to exist, and to bargain collectively with the master manufacturers in that early, raw capitalist period. This victory also created the first strategic tension in the movement, between those who saw the future in terms of securing a legal framework to protect the interests of workers, and those who regarded such a course as self-defeating (for example, the 'physical force' Chartists of the 1840s). The more perceptive of the labour leaders realized that there had to be a better way than insurrection—and the legal administration of the economy and society, particularly the parliamentary system with the suffrage won by the bourgeoisie (but limited to land holders) represented the obvious arena into which to take their campaigns.

And so at different points in the nineteenth century we find the nascent workers' movement attempting to adapt this social, administrative, judicial and political machinery—in short, the State—to its own ends. There were the Chartists in Britain in the 1840s, calling for universal suffrage; there were the great campaigns for factory legislation to limit the length of the working day;[2] there were the campaigns by trade unions in alliance with the liberals in Parliament to have repressive legislation (e.g. anti combination laws) lifted; and finally there was the great invention of the workers' own political party, linked with a new drive to achieve universal (male) suffrage to enfranchise these parties—which took their place in the heart of the capitalist beast, in Parliament itself.

This was the cauldron out of which emerged the great political creeds of our time: socialism, liberalism and democracy. How were they defined and seen by their originators?

Socialism

Socialism emerged as a workers' doctrine in the early nineteenth century.[3] It was born in those horrendous conditions of early capitalism, to contest the vision of beneficence held out by the doctrine of liberalism. It promised a social order where all would share in the major decisions regarding labour and production, instead of these decisions being monopolized by mill-owners who, as a group, were manifestly incapable of allowing moral and social criteria to impinge on their decisions. In place of angry but futile rebellion against the harshness of individual mill-owners, socialism substituted the organized attempt to change the system as a whole.

It was this vision that sustained the early attempts to form trade unions, followed by socialist political parties. Conveniently enough, it was utopian, and quite beyond the reach of the nascent workers' movement. Early attempts to install socialist principles in a practical way, by such figures as Robert Owen, came to nothing.

The term socialism made its first appearances in the 1830s, particularly in Paris where it was developed into a systematic vision of the future. But it was the German theorists Karl Marx and Friedrich Engels who took it over and made it the lynchpin of their 'world historical system', dominating debate on the topic in the mid-nineteenth century. It was Engels who coined the term 'scientific socialism' to distinguish his and Marx's work from that of their 'utopian' predecessors such as Fourier, Owen and Saint-Simon. Until very recently, little was done to elaborate further on the Marxist synthesis of French socialism, English political economy and German philosophy, as the guiding vision of the labour movement.

The achievement of socialism in the real world was another matter altogether. This is the issue that has launched more rivers of ink and rivers of blood than perhaps any other doctrine in the modern world.[4] The story is well known and need not be repeated here. Sporadic attempts to form socialist parties were made in the nineteenth century. By the turn of the twentieth century, parties of labour had been formed, claiming to be able to deliver this long sought goal. As Adam Przeworski puts it, in his masterly survey of this period:

> In spite of all the ambivalence, in spite of the pressure of short-term preoccupations, socialists entered into bourgeois politics to win elections,

to obtain an overwhelming mandate for revolutionary transformations, and to legislate the society into socialism. This was their aim and this was their expectation.[5]

But these aims and expectations, we all know now, remain far from being fulfilled. There have been successive attempts to approach something akin to socialism, via nationalizations, via the creation of social security systems and social services financed out of public taxation, and via the post-war efforts to regulate the economy and maintain employment levels using monetary and fiscal control. All these have clearly had some effect in changing the social and economic order, but they have obviously not created 'socialism' by any reasonable definition of the term.

Liberalism

Liberalism was the great rival doctrine to socialism and for this reason is still widely misunderstood or misrepresented by the SD/L movement. For example, in his *Short History of Socialism,* George Lichtheim unfavourably characterizes liberalism as the ideological cover for the callous acts of early factory owners, encouraging them to pursue their selfish interests in the face of widespread social concern. Even Raymond Williams, in his estimable *Keywords,* finds it hard to say anything positive about liberalism, noting that it is a doctrine based on individualist theories of man and society and is thus in fundamental conflict not only with socialist but with strictly social theories.[6] This completely misses the point that liberalism arose as a progressive defence of civil liberties against encroachments by the State—marking out a sphere of 'civil liberty' where individuals would be free to pursue their own interests and devotions. It was in this sense that liberalism became the creed of an emergent economic order based on private initiative—capitalism—for it was merchants and early factory owners who had most to lose by State interference, and most to gain from its dismantling. Liberals stood, then, for free markets—against the entrenched regulation of trade through privileges and prerogatives dating from feudal times; and they stood for civil liberties and individual rights—against the arbitrary actions of authoritarian absolutist regimes that recognized only their own 'divine right' to rule. The history of the seventeenth and eighteenth centuries rings with the victories secured by political forces organized under the banner of liberalism, from the triumph of Parliament over the Stuarts in England, through the granting of civil rights such as habeas corpus, the development of contract law, the lifting of taxes on the press, to the American and French revolutions.

Liberalism as a political doctrine did not take its definitive form until well into the nineteenth century, although it drew from a rich pantheon of writers and thinkers as diverse as Locke, Kant, Montesquieu and Adam Smith. Its principal exponent was undoubtedly John Stuart Mill, through such classic texts as *On Liberty*.[7]

From the modern perspective, liberalism appears to be an unsatisfactory and unfinished doctrine, upholding individual rights without ever seeming to develop a coherent account of the forces and balances that are needed to maintain a complex social order, nor to develop a perspective on the claims of the collective and social over those of the individual. My own generation that came to political maturity in 1968, with all its heady utopianism, found so much more in socialism and particularly in Marx, with his strong brew of a theory of history, with class struggle as its engine, and his powerful critique of ideologies as the masks worn by historical actors with different material interests. Liberalism, from this perspective, was castigated as the facade behind which capitalists could accumulate their wealth while drowning the proletariat, as well as overseas indigenous peoples, in a sea of blood. But my generation has also lost all patience with the dull and conformist heirs to Marxism, in its various guises of Leninism, Stalinism, Maoism, not to mention deviations like Titoism, or even Kim Il Sungism. Tedious repetitions of tired slogans is not the way to capture people's political imagination.

Fidel Castro has nailed this depressing characteristic well, in observing:

> There are times when political documents called Marxist give the impression that you go to the archives and ask for a form: form fourteen, form thirteen, form twelve, they are all alike, with the same empty words, which logically is a language incapable of expressing real situations . . . And many people are told this is Marxism . . . and in what way is this different from catechism, and in what way is it different from a litany, from a rosary?[8]

With this heritage, and its contempt for the rights of the individual, it is little wonder that there is renewed interest in the roots of the doctrine of liberalism. The ideas expressed by Mill—such as the need for limits to be placed on the power of government; the beneficial effects of competition, particularly between parties; the praise for pluralism and diversity and the condemnation of all notions of corporatist conformism and enforced consensus; the absolute necessity for freedom of opinion and for this to be embodied in a free press—these all resonate now in a period when the technologies of surveillance and control available to the State dwarf the capacities of anything that Mill could have known or conceived of.

It is this emphasis on the protection of the individual from the arbitrary behaviour of governments, political parties, or other associations such as trade unions, that underpins the current relevance of liberalism, and shows up a grave weakness in the doctrine of socialism as it has been interpreted by its numerous exponents. It is this which dictates the need for an accommodation between these two great streams of political thought—a point which is now widely recognized.[9]

2.2 THE DEMOCRATIC ROAD TO POWER

The modern Social Democratic or Labour (SD/L) tradition dates formally from the foundation of the German Social Democratic Party and its Erfurt programme of 1871[10]—but beyond that it drew its inspiration from socialist, anarchist and other ideologies, seeking to distinguish itself from the doctrines of liberalism.

It spread rapidly thereafter, with socialist parties of one sort or another being formed but frequently disappearing again within a year. The impetus to form parties of labour came after the defeat of mass strikes, as for example in Belgium in the 1890s and 1902; in Australia in the 1890s; in Sweden in 1909. These experiences made it clear to perceptive leaders that the machinery of the State could be used indefinitely to frustrate any further gains of labour, in the absence of any counter-moves.

The SD/L tradition was not, in itself, a turn to electoralism. After all, for a good part of the Bismarck era, the German SPD was an illegal party. And running through the entire tradition there has been a constant tension between 'electoralism' (that came to be associated with 'reformism') and 'revolution'—a tension that exploded into open warfare after the Russian revolution and the rise to power of the Bolsheviks.

Despite the scorn heaped on it by revolutionists, the turn to electoralism was anything but easy. There were no concessions from the political parties of capital. In the first place, mass strikes were needed to win 'universal' suffrage (i.e. universal for men), as for example in Belgium and Sweden. But with the suffrage won, key choices were thrown up.

Three of these can be singled out for discussion. Firstly, there was the issue as to whether the emergent parties should act as mobilizers and educators, awaiting the day when their strength was sufficient to mount an assault, or get involved in the bourgeois 'game' of parliamentary politics, putting up candidates for election. Secondly, there was the issue as to whether they should campaign on the difficulties faced by their members, and seek to achieve immediate concessions, or aim for the dismantling of the capitalist system in toto. Finally, there was the question of alliances: should the SD/L parties attempt to win power electorally on their own, based on their own class strength, or should they recognize their numerical weakness and attempt to forge coalitions with other groups, such as farmers and small business people? There were theorists like Karl Kautsky, who argued that the development of capitalism would inevitably bring with it the development of the proletariat as the majority of the population—and so he argued vehemently *against* any policy of alliance.[11]

But more practical parties, like the Swedish, forged an alliance with small farmers in order to win the suffrage in the first place, and found this to be a successful means of isolating the class enemy. Similar deals were made by the early labour movement in Australia.[12]

So the SD/L road to power was defined by the answers given to these questions: the SD/L parties opted to participate electorally, to seek alliances, and to struggle for immediate reforms. As Adam Przeworski puts it:

> The reason why involvement in representative politics of the bourgeois society has never ceased to evoke controversy is that the very act of "taking part" in this system shapes the movement for socialism and its relations to workers as a class. The recurrent question is whether involvement in electoral politics can result in socialism, or must strengthen the existing, that is capitalist social order. Is it possible for the socialist movement to find a passage between the "two reefs" charted by Rosa Luxemburg: "abandonment of the mass character or abandonment of the final goals?"[13]

As it became clear that the forward march of the SD/L movement would be based on electoral participation, the seeking of alliances and the implementation of reforms, the necessity for a specific programme in addition to the 'social objective' asserted itself. At the outset this was not the case. The first Swedish SD programme, for example, specified that 'Social Democracy differs from other parties in that it aspires to completely transform the economic organization of bourgeois society and bring about the social liberation of the working class . . .'.[14]

But these goals could not be achieved overnight. What then were to be the tactical and strategic measures that it was hoped would lead eventually to the attainment of these goals?

With hindsight, we can see that the SD/L parties tackled this question with astonishing naivety. They either evaded it altogether by referring in general to the 'advancement of the most immediate needs of the people'[15]; or they formulated elaborate 'maximalist' and 'minimalist' positions, like the Italian Socialist Party, but did little in practice to implement such platforms.

Underlying these positions there lay a gross mechanistic conception of the social and economic order, linked to a deep belief in the notion of progress towards some desirable goal, namely socialism. This was implicit in the work of Marx, but it was brought to the fore by Kautsky, who, as we saw above, argued vehemently against the workers' party (the SPD) entering into any political alliance with other parties which represented different class interests. In Kautsky's view the strength of these parties was bound to decline as that of the SPD rose, in line with the expected steady expansion and 'maturation' of capitalism. In his *The Class Struggle,* an extended commentary on, and exposition of, the SPD's 1891 programme, Kautsky argued that socialism was to be the inevitable outcome of the internal development of capitalism.[16] Economic tendencies, he argued, using his mechanistic model, were creating a proletariat whose interests were irreconcilable with those of the capitalists. The aim of the party was to secure the conditions—such as freedom of speech, of assembly, of the press—for open political competition, in order to capture 'the State'. Power could only be won if the proletariat maintained its political unity, and hence alliances were ruled out.

Kautsky's views were challenged in the 1890s by Bernstein, in his *Evolutionary Socialism,* for which he earned the label 'revisionist'.[17] Bernstein was at least able to see reality. He argued against inevitability on the grounds that:

1 Economic tendencies were in fact creating a middle class faster than a proletariat;
2 Votes for the SDP did not necessarily mean votes for socialism, given that immediate issues were part of its platform;
3 The working class had not been prepared by the trade unions for the running of production.

These points resonate in our own time. It is remarkable how modern Bernstein seems today, and how dated Kautsky.

Furthermore, Bernstein argued that democracy has to be accepted on its own terms, and not merely as a tactical accommodation, and for this reason he argued against the term 'dictatorship of the proletariat'. In view of the nebulous nature of the long-term goals, Bernstein argued that the immediate demands were everything.

Rosa Luxemburg waded into this debate in 1900, with her text *Reform or Revolution,* a passionate defence of the revolutionary option. At her most sarcastic, she noted:

> Fourier's scheme of changing, by means of a system of phalansteries, the water of all the seas into tasty lemonade was surely a fantastic idea. But Bernstein, proposing to change the sea of capitalist bitterness into a sea of socialist sweetness, by progressively pouring into it bottles of social reformist lemonade, presents an idea that is merely more insipid but no less fantastic.
>
> The production relations of capitalist society approach more and more the production relations of socialist society. But, on the other hand, its political and juridical relations [have] established between capitalist society and socialist society a steadily rising wall. This wall is not overthrown, but is on the contrary strengthened and consolidated by the development of social reforms and the course of democracy. Only the hammer blow of revolution, that is to say, *the conquest of political power by the proletariat, can break down this wall.*[18]

This sudden exorcism, the magical effect of the proletariat's entry into history, has been the leitmotif of revolutionists ever since Luxemburg's seminal polemic. While from our perspective today we can sympathize with her impatience, knowing that it eventually cost her her life when she was brutally murdered in 1918, we must nevertheless resist such 'easy options' as appealing to a 'world historical' force to seize its hour and transform the political-economic system. This tendency was amplified immensely by the victory of the Bolsheviks in Russia in 1917.

The Bolshevik epoch

The Russian Revolution in 1917 was surely one of the key events of the twentieth century. It showed that a determined group of Marxist inspired revolutionaries could seize State power—an outcome that had become a matter of extreme doubt since the bloody collapse of the Paris commune forty-six years earlier. Of course the Bolshevik seizure was of a State machine reduced to rubble by a devastating war; of course it occurred in a country which was totally innocent of any democratic traditions at all; of course it was seen at the time, and especially by the Bolsheviks, as merely the first in a series of revolutions that would detonate all over war-ravaged Europe. Of course it was more of a coup than an insurrection, although it did involve genuine popular participation of which the storming of the Winter Palace in St Petersburg will forever remain the symbol. Of course it was all these things—but still its influence on SD/L strategy in the quite different conditions of Western Europe was immense. The Bolsheviks exercised a profound appeal to western socialists, fed up as they were with the carnage of the war and the seeming inability of the SD/L parties to extricate themselves from the nationalist fever that had gripped them. It was an appeal that was to have devastating consequences.[19]

The Bolsheviks were, above all, professionals in the matter of State power. But they shared the same sketchy approach to the building of socialism as the other SD parties of the time, resting their case on the delightfully simple but effective slogan 'Bread, Land and Peace'. Lenin himself swayed alarmingly on key issues in the immediate aftermath of the February 1917 revolution, in the few months' interregnum leading to the October coup. He advocated at one time 'all power to the Soviets', or popular councils, but withdrew such a slogan as the prospect of seizing power drew closer. Once in power, the Bolsheviks shifted their policies in desperate bids to stay afloat and to retain a modicum of popular support during the terrible years of the civil war. War communism—virtually complete nationalization of enterprises, requisitioning of agricultural produce, military discipline in the factories and suspension of all political representation—was quickly seen to be a disaster. It gave way to its opposite in 1921: the New Economic Policy, involving a loosening of state controls, and a return to market operations, immortalized in Bukharin's famous exhortation to the peasants: 'Enrich yourselves'.

It has been observed that Lenin took a 'censorious attitude towards discussing future problems. He preferred Napoleon's advice, "On s'engage puis . . . on voit".' (one engages, and then . . . one sees.) As Howe put it: 'Alas, we have seen'.[20]

Bad as the anti-democratic turn by the Bolsheviks was in the USSR, with its outcome in the Stalinist tyranny, and the subsequent misery and dullness of that country, the effect in the West was disastrous. The appeal of the revolution in 1917 to western intellectuals and socialist militants was profound. Lenin's approach to 'smashing the State' and instituting the 'dictatorship of the proletariat' (a convenient cover for the dictatorship of the Bolshevik party) was seen as an attractive option for socialists who were getting impatient with the parliamentary game. Although there were western Marxists who took public issue with Lenin over his anti-democratic tactics—Rosa Luxemburg and Karl Kautsky, for example—they were swept aside in the drive to form new 'revolutionary' communist parties in the west out of the floundering SDP. The best militants were creamed off, and the stage was set for the split in the western labour movement that has lasted the best part of sixty years, and is only now coming to a close. This was a wrong turning of enormous magnitude, leading so many dedicated socialists up the blind alley of disengagement from democratic political activity which ended in single-minded but futile concentration on the conquest of State power, to the neglect of all the immediate social and industrial issues that urgently needed attention. It also had the effect of closing ranks and minds within the SD/L parties, and locking them into a defensive anti-communism that they have thrown off only relatively recently. It is the ending of this bitter era that I see as one of the important ideological factors pointing to the likely success of a new associative democratic reconstruction guiding the SD/L movement in the 1990s.

Social Democratic governments

The great debates between Kautsky, Bernstein, Luxemburg and other social democrats had taken place in opposition. After the carnage of the First World War, with the international labour movement split and the Bolsheviks clinging to power in Russia, the social democrats found themselves exercising a degree of political power they had not expected to embrace so suddenly. They were riding a wave of militancy, expressed through factory occupations in the metals and armaments industries, in Britain, Italy, France and Germany; there were mutinies within the armed forces; and the old order appeared to be tottering behind the pomp of the treaty negotiations of Versailles. What all this exposed was the lack of serious thinking within the SD/L leadership about a relevant and viable transitional strategy.

Armed as they were with a theory of exploitation stemming from private ownership of the means of production, and with a general goal expressed as socialization of those means of production, their programme, simply enough, called for legislation taking these productive resources into State ownership (i.e. nationalization) as a first step. Even this turned out to be beyond them.[21]

In spite of the prevalence of SD/L governments in the inter-war years, up to the Second World War, not a single company or industry was taken into public ownership in Western Europe, with the sole exception of the French armaments industry nationalized by the Popular Front government in 1936.[22]

This failure stemmed partly from a theoretical confusion over whose interests the nationalized sector was supposed to represent—those of the workers concerned, or of the whole of society—but more immediately from a lack of practical knowledge as to how to effect the transfer and to indicate how the State-owned sector would be managed. This issue came to a head with the Depression in the 1930s. It revealed that where SD/L parties were in power, or formed part of a coalition government, they had no economic tools to call on, short of 'socialization'. With the exception of the Swedish SD party, which under the guidance of such theorists as Ernst Wigforss pioneered a counter-cyclical policy to deal with unemployment, utilizing public works and government spending as a stimulus, most SD/L parties found themselves lining up with the bankers and liberals calling for wage cuts.[23]

This was probably the nadir of social democracy. Mercilessly attacked by the Moscow-aligned communists as 'social fascists'; struggling to find a means of coping with the emergence of real fascism in Italy and Germany; watching their movement being shattered by the Depression—what did the social democrats have to offer the labour movement?[24]

Out of this crucible, and during the Second World War, there emerged a new ideological and theoretical alignment within the SD/L movement. Theoretically, it took its inspiration from Keynes, who in his *General Theory* provided macro-economic tools for the management of a capitalist economy; and from Beveridge, who in his 1944 White Paper laid the foundations for the post-war welfare state. This charted a new course for the future.

The labour movement emerged from the Second World War holding political power in a majority of western nations. For the first time, SD/L parties were armed with a distinctive ideology: full employment, Keynesian fiscal and monetary management, welfare transfer payments and services, and nationalization of the 'commanding heights' of the economy. The mistakes of the inter-war years were not going to be repeated; the parties and the unions had benefited from sharing power during the war effort; there was a new sense of hope in the air.

And yet within a few short years the movement was again on the defensive. With few exceptions, governments were defeated and unions were paralyzed by the impact of the cold war and anti-communism. These defeats, directly attributable to the communist-anti-communist split, constituted a catastrophe for the labour movement. Confidence in the socialist project started to wane. The absence from government bred factionalism and extremist policies. The political initiative was retained by conservative parties. As a result, the SD/L post-war programmes were not carried through to completion. They were picked up by conservative governments who were more inclined to stimulate economic activity by letting large defence contracts than by judiciously expanding the public sector. Inflation started to become a major economic issue, and SD/L governments were forced to accommodate it in their plans, sacrificing social expenditure in the process.

The Scandinavian countries, particularly Sweden, were alone in showing that it was possible for a SD party to hold office continually, and to do so on the basis of radical policies that explicitly favoured workers' social and economic well-being.

In the 1970s and 1980s, new SD/L governments have been elected, bringing with them the fervent hopes of their supporters. In several cases, they have successfully held their conservative opponents at bay, and presided over far-reaching structural changes in the economy. They have modernized their electoral tactics, and their management of the public administration. But one has to ask: is that all there is? Has the century-long political tradition outlined above come to mean in the 1980s no more than a thirty-second political commercial in an election campaign?

2.3 A STOCKTAKE OF THE SD/L TRADITION

It is my conviction that there must be more: that there is scope for radical transformation to be effected by and through the democratic system. As a prelude to setting out the elements of a new paradigm, let us take stock of this SD/L tradition, to evaluate what it has achieved and where it is constrained by its own burden of past ideologies and visions. The major features we shall focus on are:

- democratization as a process
- the dynamics of reform
- economic strategy and performance
- social contracts and party programmes
- the rise of social movements and electoral alliances
- the role of government.

Democratization of politics

Firstly, we have learnt that the process of democratization is open-ended, with a momentum of its own. This means, as a corollary, that there is no 'ruling class' which has 'allowed' the labour movement to enjoy a degree of freedom up until now, but which will step in and 'restore order' (by suspending democratic procedures) if the movement pushes its luck too far.[25]

There are, of course, only too many examples of this occurring in the twentieth century, and these collapses of democracy into fascism stand as grim reminders of the limits of reform, or rather of the pace of reform. But my point is that there is no 'logic' in the system that necessarily calls up these forces of reaction. They are pragmatic responses by disaffected elements, normally from a stratum that has long enjoyed power. The fact that such elements have rebelled and brought down an elected government in the past means that any prudent SD/L government will take steps to isolate such elements, and force them into illegality (so that they can be arrested) earlier rather than later. Recent examples of fledgling democratic governments that have protected themselves against attempted coups include that of Spain and, more recently, the Philippines. I cite these as evidence that the cause of a democratic government is not hopeless, even when confronted with lawless reactionary elements.

We have come to understand how fragile a democratic constitution is, and how hard the SD/L movement has to work to maintain it. We need to recall that a genuine political democracy based on universal suffrage was achieved in the metropolitan countries only at the turn of the century. It is the supreme political achievement of the labour movement, from which all else has flowed. And it is the achievement which must be protected as the highest priority, for it provides the framework within which workers can organize open political parties, policies and platforms; can contest and win elections based on these platforms; and implement the policies to change the economic and social order. Any retreat to pre-universal suffrage strategies for achieving social change, such as the insurrectionary model of the Bolsheviks, is futile.

Commitment to democracy entails abandoning once and for all any notion that an 'insurrectionary' option could succeed in a democracy. It is an illusion to believe that there is a constituency for insurrection, in the working class or anywhere else, that is prepared to throw overboard all the constraints and protections of the political process for the wilderness of 'armed struggle' and for the hazardous prospect of the 'dictatorship of the proletariat'. The shadows of Mussolini, Hitler, Stalin and others loom too large over this century for such fantasies to be taken seriously. But even if such a constituency could be conjured into existence (as the Red Brigades in Italy imagined was the case) the only possible outcome of their launching their terror campaign in a democracy would be the suppression of democratic liberties for all, and the appearance on the streets of counter-groups, like the roaming 'death squads' in Central America. It is the labour movement which loses first and most heavily from such a collapse of democracy.[26]

Dynamics of reform

Second, it is essential to acknowledge that the social order is amenable to politically-inspired intervention. The economic and social system that operates today is heavily influenced and shaped by the SD/L activities of the post-war period. This is to contest the widely held view that there is a transcendental 'logic of capitalism' which, in the end, renders futile all attempts to transform the system. It is a theoretical illusion to view the capitalist system as a 'total entity' subject to internal contradictions, such that these contradictions will work themselves through in time, leading the proletariat to take charge. Every step of this proposition is misleading. Capitalism is not an organized but a disorganized system, held together, if one can call it that, by a myriad of intersecting private interests.[27]

One can see 'contradictions' between forces of production and relations of production at every one of the intersections: it is these contradictions that provide the leverage or space for collective intervention. But this intervention is not one which changes the total system, holus-bolus, but one which in practice democratizes it one part at a time. Hopes of changing it *in toto* are mere intellectual fantasies. (Even where indisputable political revolutions have occurred, as in Russia in 1917, China in 1949 or

Cuba in 1958, the social and economic changes have come much more slowly.) Hence a totalizing conception, and all the abstract formulations that flow from it, such as 'the capitalist system', a 'bloc' of capitalists, 'the State' as defender of the capitalist bloc, and others, establish a theoretical framework which is a positive hindrance to real world intervention.

However, it has been found through bitter experience that to change the world by collective action is a far harder task than any reformer anticipates, or than any latter-day revolutionist dreams of. The real world of business and finance turns out to be more resilient, more complex and more adaptable than the early SD/L theorists could possibly have imagined. I say by 'collective action', because of course the world is constantly being changed by capital, which moves restlessly from one site to another, introducing new technologies, labour processes, or trade patterns as it sees profitable opportunities. But over the past century some real and effective techniques to contest the actions of capital have been learnt by the labour movement, all premised on collective action and solidarity—from protests, strikes and labour withdrawals, to political campaigns and pressure brought to bear on particular targets, to more recent techniques of intervention in the world of finance via pension and superannuation funds and Swedish-style wage earner funds (discussed in detail in chapter 3). There is a momentum here which can be harnessed to enable the labour movement to effect more sophisticated and transformative interventions, each one building on the previous changes, in a dynamic of reform. But there should be no illusions as to the difficulty of the task, nor as to the design skill needed to fashion the instruments of intervention.

Despite it being clearly demonstrated that associations of citizens and workers are fundamental instruments of democratization, orthodox SD/L theoreticians have shied away from such 'open-ended' strategies, and have formulated as a convenience the doctrine of the 'primacy of parliament'.[28] Departure from this doctrine, and the placing of a renewed emphasis on the activities of social movements and trade unions outside Parliament, is in my view a precondition for further development of the SD/L project.

Economic strategy and performance

Through all their intricacies, the economic policies pursued by SD/L governments in the post-war period can be characterized as falling into two broad areas:

- the pursuit of distributive justice (income support and 'social wage' services) increasingly through public expenditure and the 'welfare state', rather than through wage bargaining between unions and employers;
- the maintenance of employment and general regulation of the economy through the operation of macroeconomic fiscal and monetary controls, rather than through direct intervention or planning mechanisms.

These represent the limits of SD/L economic intervention, and provide the context for current debates over the efficacy of reformism.[29]

Distributive goals

The Danish theorist of social democracy, Gösta Esping-Andersen, argues that the ultimate foundation of labour movement solidarity is public provision of resources, via public expenditure on services such as education, health and welfare, and income security. The political strength of the movement, then, depends on the reformist measures obtained, and on how well they can be defended against attack (for example, from the New Right).

This is the dynamic, feed-back element that simplistic critiques of 'reformism' fail to grasp. The attainment of 'social rights' is not at all predetermined, but is the outcome of a process dominated by strategic issues, by questions of political choice. Esping-Andersen argues that this process is not an end in itself, but provides the foundation of economic security, of universal entitlement, for the overcoming of sectional differences, and that this enables the movement to proceed to its next historic task: the democratization of economic life.[30] This, he claims, is a desirable development in itself; but it is also necessary to provide sources for welfare support that are not dependent on taxation, thereby getting around the tax resistance that is being manifested in all OECD countries. Esping-Andersen claims that this is where the SD movements find themselves today: the social citizenship state is at once attained, but is exhausted.

The other side to this is the issue of targeted versus universalistic benefits. The more particularist that benefits become, the less they contribute to solidarity—and the reformist dynamic could go into reverse. The most straightforward means of securing universal benefits is to institute a Guaranteed Minimum Income Scheme—towards which hesitant steps are being taken by the French and New Zealand SD/L parties.[31] But these are hampered by continuing trade union insistence on wages remaining the prime component of family income. The two principles—income secured through employment, and income generated through public expenditure—are clearly at odds. This represents one of the chief contradictions in orthodox SD/L policies, and one which will have to be resolved if the movement is to progress further.

Economic regulation

It is now widely agreed that the macroeconomic regulatory apparatus of Keynes has been utilized to the maximum extent feasible. We have seen how SD/L policy by the middle of the century was founded on a combination of Keynesian economic policies and social welfare programmes, the former offering economic growth and the latter economic security. While it looked like a universal policy, it was in fact crucially dependent on a rather bizarre and special set of circumstances: a regime of fixed exchange rates (Bretton Woods system) restricting the international market in money; an expanding export market for manufactured goods from the west in the Third World, financed by credit; and the economic growth from this arrangement paying for exchange rate control and the social welfare benefits. All this came to an end with the collapse of Bretton Woods (itself a response to the rise of Japan and West Germany as industrial powers), the rise of OPEC, and the tide of protectionism in world trade. In the confusion all this has given rise to, the intellectual vacuum on the left has been filled by the snake-oil nostrums of monetarism and the New Right.

Keynesian macroeconomic control promised to square the circle—to deliver economic growth and full employment without requiring any 'political' intervention in the economy. Such a perspective was enthusiastically endorsed by orthodox SD/L Treasurers in post-war governments. But the essential underpinning of a successful Keynesian programme (assuming the world remained stable enough) soon came to be seen as a political framework of wage determination. This was recognized most clearly in northern and Central Europe—in Scandinavia, Austria and Germany—where Keynesian policies were judiciously employed within a politically negotiated 'social contract' encompassing wage determination and positive industry and labour market programmes. Such a strategy entailed a conscious policy of 'cooperative accommodation' between unions and employers—something that Anglo-Saxon SD/L parties recoiled from.

The relative success of the Scandinavian and Austrian approach to economic regulation is not just a matter of argument. Empirical work based on cross-national comparisons reveals how wages, unemployment and inflation have been kept in check in these countries, better even than in places where conservative governments have pursued tight monetary controls.[32]

Lessons from the past

It is now clear that the success of the Social Democratic political project depends on the maintenance of economic buoyancy. This lesson has been learnt at dreadful cost. Consider just one historical example : the movement for workers' control. This reached a high point in the munitions industries during the First World War, and it became central to the labour movement project of constructing a new social and economic order. Yet within a few short years it was nothing but a memory—defeated by economic recession, or by fascism, or by Bolshevism.

Economic recession

The movement for workers' control in the era of the First World War, was defeated primarily by economic recession and depression. This certainly accounted for the shop stewards' movement in Britain losing much of its steam in 1920. When workers' jobs are threatened, the defence of those jobs becomes, understandably, their highest priority. Gains over the control of work will be jettisoned if these are seen to threaten continued employment.

There is a clear lesson to be learned from this. A labour movement that is constructing a new social order has everything to gain by the economy remaining healthy (i.e. profits remaining steady) and everything to lose by its plunging into recession. Hence it is the role of a Social Democratic or Labour government to so manage the economy that it remains healthy. If employers are unco-operative in this endeavour (for example, by withholding investment) then positive steps need to be taken by the SD/L movement, such as mobilizing funds through profits and taxes. The alternative is to see the drive for democratization wilt, as it did in the 1920s.

Fascism

Where the movement for workers' control went farthest, it was physically broken by an armed takeover of the State. This achieved its clearest form in Italy, where a liberal government managed to maintain its neutrality during the period of the factory occupations (i.e. siding neither with the workers nor with the factory owners) but crumbled before the armed bands of *fascisti* organized by Mussolini, who took over State power after the march on Rome, with the full support of the industrialists. He lost no time in showing where he stood by dissolving the trade unions, using physical force where necessary, and establishing tame fascist organizations, together with corporatist councils, in their place. This scenario took longer to unfold in Germany, where the Weimar republic tottered from putsch to aborted revolution, eventually succumbing to Hitler and his Nazi brownshirts in the early 1930s. (It is notable that Taylorization of work in Europe went to the farthest extremes in fascist Italy and Germany.) There was also a certain amount of repression in Britain (such as the arrest of leading shop stewards' leaders in Glasgow in 1917) and in the United States (the jailing of IWW activists). The attractiveness of the fascist solution was such that it was taken up in Spain and Portugal, then, after the Second World War, in Greece; and it has since become endemic in Latin America, Africa and Asia.

The lesson is clear for countries that have Social Democrat/ Labour governments in power and a union movement actively seeking reforms directed towards industrial democracy: the role of the State must be primarily and fundamentally that of safeguarding democracy. It must retain the power to seek out and destroy any attempts at illegality on the part of employers or their agents, or on the part of workers. Without such a defence, it is certain that, when the going gets hot and it appears that the unions and workers are starting to exercise real influence in the workplace, there will be a group of employers who will break with legality and place their faith in a national leader, over-riding democratic or constitutional norms. We know well that the repression unleashed by such a collapse of democracy, can lead to a dark age and set back the movement for decades.

Bolshevism

Finally, the movement for workers' control was deflected and, in a sense, 'captured' politically by Bolshevism. This was the converse of being broken by fascism. The appeal of the Russian revolution in 1917 was profound, and Lenin's approach to 'smashing the State' and instituting a dictatorship dubbed 'of the proletariat' was seen as an attractive option by industrial militants who were becoming impatient with 'gradualism'. When the new Communist Parties were set up in Western Europe in 1920 and 1921, they inevitably creamed off the best of these militants, and in line with Russian practice (where the worker-controlled Soviets did not last long) turned their backs on a workers' control strategy, aiming instead for the conquest of State power. As argued above, this was a wrong turning of enormous historic magnitude for the western labour movements, and, in a sense, we are still recovering from it. It is certainly one of the factors involved in the long delay in getting workplace democracy firmly back on to the political agenda of the labour movement.

Social concertation

Through its various political and economic vicissitudes, the SD/L movement has come to understand that influence can be exerted at many levels, and not just at the level of parliament and government (through the Party) and the level of the workplace (through the union). Intermediate forms of social co-ordination have been invented, going under such titles as 'social pact', 'social contract', 'accord', or 'tripartism'. As these structures grew more common in the 1970s, they became the subject of sustained theoretical investigation, using analytical concepts such as 'neo-corporatism', 'political trade unionism', or in more neutral terms, 'social concertation'.

The role of social contracts, indeed the necessity for them in providing a framework for a process of transformation, is now firmly on the labour movement's agenda. This is one of the 'flashpoints' where the movement is most bitterly divided—between those who see such contracts as 'political trade unionism', with potential to overcome the sectionalism that dogs trade union practice, and those who see them as 'corporatism', as a framework for holding back, containing and demobilizing the movement.

This is a difficult issue to discuss because of the fog of competing terminology and the biases that are consciously or unconsciously revealed by the terms used, and because it carries with it no developed theory or even self-recognition as a species of political process.[33]

The essential feature of these phenomena is the generalization of agreements between unions and employers at the level of the firm, to industry and economy-wide level agreements backed by or endorsed by the administrative machinery of the State. These go under a variety of names, and have been promoted for very different social and political ends. In Scandinavia and Austria, for example, a highly developed structure of such 'political trade unionism' has been developed and promoted on behalf of the trade unions by the SD/L parties in government; whereas in Britain, and to some extent in West Germany, such developments have been promoted by conservative governments with a clear aim of containing inflationary wage demands, in the establishment of 'tripartite' state mechanisms that attempt to lock union leaderships into positions favourable to employers and to use them to discipline their own membership.[34]

A penetrating study by Claus Offe, *The attribution of public status to interest groups,* written in 1977 as a reflection on the West German experience, explores this issue. Social contract modes of government are seen as providing public status to interest groups, notably trade unions. Offe describes this development as stemming from a widespread sense, in the wake of the 'long boom', that the bargaining power and political influence of organized interests, particularly trade unions and employer organizations, was undermining responsible parliamentary government based on political parties; conflicts between the powerful interest groups were being settled at the expense of social groups that were poorly organized (such as consumers).

According to Offe, a wave of 'post-pluralist realism' led to steps being taken to establish new structures and institutions in which organized interests could be represented; indeed, Offe argues that without such structures the State would have become paralyzed because it lacked the information, held by these interests, which was essential for the formation of public policy. Offe sees a trade-off for both sides in these developments:

> Modern conservatives find themselves forced to acknowledge the irrevocable reality of mass democracy, the welfare state, and collective representation of the working class in wage and other negotiations, although their ideologies of an organicist order or a world of free competition may leave no place for such phenomena.
> Social democrats, however, find themselves forced realistically to recognize the non-transformability of essential premises of the capitalist political economy, in spite of the socialist visions of their individual or collective past.[35]

Offe identifies two 'gaps' or 'instances of malfunctioning' in the institutions and procedures of liberal democratic government, which have provided the impetus to develop social contract structures. One is the 'erosion of party identities' (meaning the loss of a close relationship between unions and SD/L party, on the one hand, and between business organizations, and conservative parties on the other) due to the demands of consensus politics. The other is a typical 'impasse in bureaucratic design' and implementation of policies—meaning an inability to develop and implement policies without the active co-operation and participation of the major organizations.

Offe's analysis has been borne out by events. From the perspective of the 1980s, it is clear that the principal site of class conflict in all capitalist countries, since the 1973/1974 recession, has been over macroeconomic policy formation (aimed at ensuring growth and maximizing employment) and industry restructuring. Where the labour movement has demanded effective institutional channels for the resolution of these conflicts, as in the Scandinavian countries and Austria, it has been most successful in keeping its broad social and economic goals intact. But is this a contingent phenomenon, or can a pattern be discerned here?

Theory of social concertation

As it becomes clear that 'social contract' arrangements are becoming a permanent feature of advanced industrial societies, whether governed by conservative or SD/L parties, so the theoretical claims made for them grow in significance. The most remarkable treatment is given by Schmitter and Streeck, who characterise such arrangements as a fourth form of social coordination. In a most original and arresting contribution to social and political scholarship, they identify three models of social order in the form of markets, the community, and the State; these correspond to the three principles of social coordination: dispersed competition, spontaneous solidarity, and hierarchical control. They posit the 'association' as a fourth model, corresponding to a principle of 'organizational concertation'.[36]

Schmitter and Streeck discuss an 'associative model of a social order' as a stable and distinctive 'pure form' of social coordination. This is a remarkable theoretical development. With it comes sustained and serious attention being given to associations as important political entities capable of negotiating stable political arrangements between themselves. While this may appear obvious to the participants in tripartite structures, it remains the case that in mainstream social science, 'associations' (such as unions) are seen as extraneous and intrusive, sapping legitimacy from more established social institutions.[37]

Intriguing as these developments are, our interest must be in the dynamics of social contracts.

Dynamics of social contracts

The really interesting question concerning this form of penetration by trade unions to the political level, is the potential it holds for bringing employers into binding agreements and interventionist industry strategies, thus socializing the process of investment. Or, on the contrary, must this form of articulation demobilize the unions and their membership?

Offe argues that three outcomes are possible. One is a stabilization of the structures in such a way that they favour capital over labour. This arises from what he calls the asymmetrical impinging of associational modes on their organizations. The organization of labour actually creates, by its formation, the collective interests of workers; whereas the organizations representing employers and investors do not create an interest, but merely articulate a pre-existing interest and sanction (e.g. of withdrawal of investment). Therefore restrictions on internal procedures of 'organizations' in general, mean restrictions on unions in practice.

On the other hand, a second outcome could be an unstable associational structure resulting from a development towards an institutional core (unions and employers) and a margin of social groups, community interests and single-issue campaigns which grow increasingly hostile to 'the system' and generate social unrest, violence and repression.

Interestingly, Offe speculates that this unstable formation could precipitate a third outcome, which is favourable to labour. He argues that the institutionalization of the capital-labour conflict, but the non-institutionalization of other conflicts, could precipitate a process 'in which, in order to maintain the loyalty and allegiance of their rank-and-file members, union leaders would insist on demands and strive for accomplishments that are impossible to achieve unless the inherent bias of corporatism is overcome'. By this, Offe means making commitments binding not just on unions, but on investors as well, whether or not they find it individually profitable to comply with such programmes. Offe recognizes that this is in fact a major incursion into the property rights of capital, and would be fiercely resisted; it would 'shake the economic system at its foundations'.

Offe therefore posits an interesting logic of corporatism that leads unions involved in the process to demand more radical and equitable commitments in order to keep peace with their membership.

A similar logic has been developed by Gösta Esping-Andersen, who has argued that the associational mode brings 'class struggle' into the heart of the State, and that the outcome cannot be predicted in advance. In a similar way to Offe, he argues:

> Corporatism is an internally contradictory mode of incorporating the working class. The premise of a corporatist strategy is that the inclusion of . . . working class organizations in formal state planning processes will reduce working class opposition to state policies without requiring massive concessions to popular demands. If however, the leadership maintains close ties to the working class and remains a legitimate instrument of real working class organizations . . . [this will] undermine the planning function of corporatism and bring class struggle into the administrative heart of the state apparatus itself.[38]

Offe and Esping-Andersen were still arguing from the premise that corporatist structures are imposed as a means of containing trade union power; but that they have subversive potential. The stage has now been reached where the argument can be taken further: unions in many countries are now demanding such structures in order to enhance their political influence, to overcome their sectionalism, and to open up the potential that is there for greater and greater co-determination. They view the SD/L parties as the vehicles for assisting unions to make these gains.

This issue has come to prominence recently in Australia, with the development of the ACTU-ALP Accord in 1983, acting as the lynchpin of the Hawke Labor government's economic strategy. The Accord is interesting because it goes beyond the unhappy experience with a 'social contract' in the UK in the 1970s, and gives an explicitly broad range of industrial and social issues to be developed in return for wage moderation.[39]

We shall discuss the Accord, and social contracts pursued explicitly as a strategy of 'political exchange', further below.

Rise of social movements: electoral alliances

Trade unions are certainly not the only countervailing associations formed within the current social order. They are merely one of a host of movements, organizations and campaigns formed around issues to espouse values that have frequently been neglected in SD/L politics. Since the 1960s and 1970s, when many of the current crop of social movements developed a mass base, these issues and values have come to exercise a dominant influence on the political agenda, and are being taken up by parties to the Right as well as to the Left. Since many of the movements are spontaneously anti-capitalist, this is a conundrum, one of many thrown up by the new forms and practices of these groups. Any political paradigm that ignored them, or failed to generate a means of linking their concerns with those of the labour movement, would be worthless. Hence we must investigate how social movements fit into current SD/L practice, and what changes are needed if they are to take their rightful place within it.

The social movements include such groups, organizations or campaigns as:

- women's organizations, centres and clinics;
- peace and anti-nuclear groups;
- sexual politics groups, such as gays;
- anti-racist groups;
- aboriginal and indigenous peoples' rights groups, e.g. land rights councils;
- anti-apartheid and anti-imperialist groups;
- consumer rights groups;
- legal, civil and social rights groups;
- housing action and tenants' groups;
- transport, energy and alternative technology groups;
- environmental and conservation groups;
- ethnic organizations;
- community organizations;
- self-help groups;

as well as various single-issue campaigns (e.g. for abortion rights, lead-free petrol, and many more).

Such groups generally arise from people's experiences of injustice perpetrated within the current social order, and span the gamut of issues and experiences outside the workplace. They can be oriented towards immediate and local issues such as poor housing, inadequate transport or insufficient child-care facilities; or aimed at longer-term and global issues such as conservation of the earth and nuclear disarmament. Groups can be formed explicitly to influence the political agenda, and adopt a campaigning, lobbying and mobilization stance; or they can be formed more as a collective act of self-esteem in order to better confront oppressive attitudes, as in the case of many anti-racist groups, gays' groups and ethnic groups. Social movements can also have long histories. In a sense, the oldest and best organized social movement is the Church; and the way in which it has generated heresies and schisms, forms the paradigmatic case emulated by all ideologically-based social and political movements ever since. The newer social movements, particularly conservation and environment groups, and women's groups, have been forced to confront their long histories as part of their own process of self-discovery. The attempt to forge a political link with groups formed before them, such as Societies for the Prevention of Cruelty to Animals, has become a major issue for these groups.

This miscellany of groups and campaigns can conveniently be referred to collectively as *social movements*. They will be just as important as trade unions in advancing a social order based on Associative Democratic principles. Most activists start in these groups, myself included, and they are a constant source of renewal of intellectual and political energy.[40]

The existence of the social movements signals a healthy pluralist culture of dissent in the community, but it also signals a failure on the part of SD/L parties to articulate the immediate issues and concerns that move people to action. This is probably an irreversible phenomenon; there is no point in making rhetorical gestures calling on these parties to 'heed the grass roots' and abandon their single-minded pursuit of power through the electoral process. These SD/L parties have become, and will remain, political machines, and the tangled tissue of 'grass roots' concerns will be articulated through *ad hoc* campaigns and activist organizations, seeking remedies through a variety of methods: direct action; demonstrations; media campaigns; and lobbying of other organizations; as well as working through the more narrowly interpreted political process.

The response of the orthodox SD/L parties to these developments has been ambivalent. On the one hand, a willingness has at times been manifested to secure a political alliance with a movement, through the SD/L party adopting its policy as a platform commitment, and looking to legislate such a policy when in government. In this way, progress has been made on such issues as abortion, homosexual rights, and conservation issues. This is a 'half-way' alliance, for it fails to integrate social movements' policies with the SD/L economic and industrial strategies. What such an arrangement ignores is the fundamental dynamics of social movements, SD/L parties and trade unions, and how they can complement each other. It ignores the fact that protest movements remain wedded to effects, rather than causes; that they draw attention to symptoms rather than to cures. For example, the Green movement opposes industrial pollution, but it opposes it as if 'industrialism' were the cause, rather than an economic system that fails to force firms to account for externalities. What the SD/L parties are starting to learn is that it is up to them to supply the cures for the symptoms that the protest movements oppose. This is what provides the grounds for a commonality of interests between the SD/L parties of the labour movement and the social movements.

To date the SD/L parties have tended simply to adopt an environmental policy which repeats the concerns of such groups as Friends of the Earth or Greenpeace (but fails to back them up with campaigning drive)—a politics of pure opportunism. A rather more constructive approach is one where the SD/L party attempts to demonstrate how its economic and industrial policies are going to achieve the goals campaigned for by Friends of the Earth and Greenpeace.

On the other hand, there is still a widespread belief, both within the SD/L parties and outside them, that the working class remains as the 'grass roots' of the parties, and that it must be the dominant agent in any social transformation; the claims of other social groups such as women, blacks, ethnic groups and social movements organized around specific issues like peace and conservation taking second place. This orthodoxy was the core of any Marxian theorization of the socialist project until the new 'revisionists' like Ernesto Laclau and Nicos Poulantzas suggested that the socialist project could only be constructed at the level of politics and ideology.[41] But the orthodoxy dies hard, and has recently been forcefully restated by Ellen Meiksins Wood in her *The Retreat from Class: a new 'true' Socialism.*[42]

The problem with the 'orthodox' position is that it is grounded in an unreconstructed version of Marx's account of exploitation in the process of production; this is seen as the ultimate 'contradiction of capitalism' from which all the social struggles viewed at the surface ultimately derive. But this perspective is no longer tenable given the dynamic nature of SD/L transformative effects, and the role that the public sector now plays in offering a basis for collective action beyond the ranks of workers proper. In any case, it ignores the contradictions in the cultural domain—between racial and ethnic groups, or between men and women—which give rise to the various social movements, and which cut across issues of class.

This orthodox class position is linked to the 'objective' perspective on exploitation which assumes that the 'exposure' of the exploitative nature of capitalism will lead people to reject it. Such a position can be expressed in the view that there is a potential majority for support for socialism, which only has to be tapped to deliver overwhelming support for a political programme of democratization. This is simply false. Far from there being a 'latent support' for an alternative social order, there is in fact a strong and all too obvious support for the status quo. This support is both material (economic) and ideological. Almost everyone has an economic stake in the system as it is. People own land or a home; workers have a job; shopkeepers have a small business; even the unemployed have the prospect of a job if only economic conditions improve. The expansion of debt means that virtually everyone owes money and has repayment commitments, so that they run the risk, if their payments lapse, that assets will be seized. This is the panoply of pressures that Przeworski calls the 'material basis of consent', to a system that is quite openly unequal and exploitative.[43] The idea of an alternative can only take root if it is alive to these existing private interests, and meshes with them. The SD/L movement has not yet managed to come to terms with this issue, other than in a rhetorical fashion. A paradigm of associative democracy would identify values that are held in high esteem, and elaborate a means of protecting those values by extending them in the face of threats to destroy them. This must surely be the essence of any viable SD/L strategy: to build on the economic dependence and freedoms already won in order to defend a more adequately grounded economic independence and range of liberties.

If in fact there is no latent majority support for change, then the constituency for change needs to be constructed at the level of politics. This again brings SD/L parties back to the real concerns of people, and forces them to formulate programmes that broaden and generalize their support, based on a concern to provide a framework in which people can organize effectively for themselves. I agree with Esping-Andersen that the SD/L parties are at a crossroads, and will have to organize their programmes around the notion of economic democracy if they are to avoid decomposition. But I would argue that this term needs broad interpretation, for it must accommodate not only the means to intervene collectively in the firm and the wider economy, but also take into account the legitimate concerns of city dwellers about the state of their environment and services as well as wider concerns about eliminating gender, racial and ethnic stereotypes and inequities. Experience to date shows not only that the SD/L parties need to accommodate these issues, but that SD/L parties need to understand that their role is simply to provide a means of enabling people to resolve these concerns more effectively. The old idea that a political party could 'deliver' a new social order, in or out of government, seems finally to be dead.

The task of politics, then, may be conceived as the process of formulating the grounds for an alliance between different organized social movements, including the labour movement, and then working through these movements and SD/L parties to cement alliances in practice. This implies that the social transformation desired will not occur mechanically, through the maturation of some supposed 'logic of history', nor will it occur as a result of citizens entering into struggle and having the 'ideological veils' which mask capitalism miraculously removed from their eyes. On the contrary, transformation requires a mass base of support to be forged through alliances, and these need to be constructed at both a political and membership level. This is one of the fundamental lessons taught by the experience of SD/L parties to date.

Role of government

It is through the active maintenance of a broad alliance that the SD/L party may expect to retain control of the democratic political arena, while it facilitates and orchestrates the extension of democracy into the social and economic domains. Rather than viewing the State as some supposed embodiment of capitalist interests, combining paternalist with repressive characteristics, the SD/L movement has come to see 'the State' as an important sphere of economic and social as well as political life, and one where resources are available to the party that mobilizes popular support to claim them. The State is viewed as the guarantor of the civil, political and social rights that constitute our notion of 'citizenship'—and it provides the platform and the resources needed to extend these rights into the economic and social domains. This is why extensions of democracy are feasible only with an SD/L government in office.

For much of the twentieth century, the labour movement has been obsessed by the conquest of State power, via the 'parliamentary road' or by other means, in the quite mistaken belief that this was the means of 'delivering' a new socialist order. We now appreciate the rather more demanding complexities of any such transition, and the rather limited role that government and public agencies can play in this. It is now understood that the election of an SD/L government is needed to orchestrate the processes of negotiation and agreement involved in developing such matters as 'social contracts'—but not as 'deliverer' of any new social order. This perspective is in fact neutral on the question of public/private mix in any economic democracy, and on the level of regulation involved. What is needed is a shift of emphasis away from these concerns, towards the more important issues of democratization, in the political domain as much as in the economic and social (and the State could encompass all three)..

A positive role for the State

It took the labour movement a long time to wake up to the potential for utilizing the various levers of public power available in Parliament, public administration and the judiciary—and having done so, it has tended to fetishize these instruments as the only legitimate organs of power. We need to have a clear-eyed perspective, seeing through the pomp and circumstance of the State with its ancient lineages, to the real powers and liberties that are available for use. In my view, the most fruitful perspective is to see these institutions as 'soft technologies' of co-ordination and control and, as such, amenable to analysis, design, and experimental testing. This is in fact the oldest branch of science, as witness Aristotle's masterly discussion of Greek city-state constitutions, enumerating their good and bad points, in his *Politics*. Classical constitutional theory recognizes three 'arms' of government, namely:

- Legislature—the law making institutions, including parliaments and the array of regulatory authorities accountable to parliament;
- Executive—the 'public service' and statutory authorities that give effect to the decisions of the legislature;
- Judiciary—the courts and tribunals that oversee the legislature and executive, settle civil and administrative disputes, and punish criminal offences, with their apparatus of coercion.

But in the modern period the SD/L movement has initiated three further lines of development that contribute to our current concept of the State and citizenship. It is these further lines that have been specifically targeted by the New Right.

Regulation of the economic system This development stems from demands made on public authorities to shape the behaviour of firms in the market-place, all in the name of the public interest. This line traces its origin back to the Factories Acts of the mid-nineteenth century in Britain, and has achieved an enormous development in the US in the form of a series of federal regulatory agencies, such as the Food and Drug Administration, Federal Communications Commission, Federal Securities and Exchange Commission, or the Environmental Protection Agency. This is the line of development which the New Right seeks to halt and roll back under the slogan 'deregulation'.

Provision of 'social wage' goods and services This is a line of development which stems from demands made on the public sphere for social resources. It started with the public provision of monetary pensions, and then became the full-blown welfare state with provision of health, education and community services, sometimes with public housing and other services added, as well as the range of monetary transfer payments and disability compensation schemes. This is the line of development which the New Right seeks to halt and roll back under the slogan 'privatization'.

Public sector productive enterprise Complicating this picture is the existence of the public 'productive' sector, comprising transport, energy provision, telecommunications, postal service, water supply, sewerage systems, road construction and other large public utilities, all in different proportions in different countries depending on their specific histories. The New Right seeks to curb this sector also under the slogan 'privatization'.

It is astonishing how the New Right has breathed new life into old controversies, and in this way has brought the fundamentals of social organization to the top of the political agenda. The drive for privatization and deregulation, major threat that it is, is also a drive to fundamentally redefine the role of the state in a modern capitalist society—and through this, to throw open the question of the nature and purposes of public authority, public power, public administration and public provision of services. This is a debate which the labour movement should welcome. (We shall pursue these questions of privatization and deregulation in chapter 4.)

Whereas Marx in the nineteenth century envisaged an eventual 'withering away' of the State, we have seen how the SD/L movement has come to rely more and more on public resources, controlled through government, in achieving its goals. The Swedish theorist Walter Korpi has expressed this in terms of a notion of the 'power resources' of the SD/L movement being enhanced by holding government:

> With more extensive organizational power resources, the political arena will become increasingly important for labour. To the extent that labour is successful in acquiring control over political institutions, it can exercise its power through these means and will not be limited to the industrial arena. On the other hand, the possibilities for employers to exercise political power well decrease.[44]

The terminology 'power resources' is introduced by Korpi to dispel any notion that a strategy of 'cooperative accommodation' between labour and employers, under the auspices of an SD/L government, is in any sense a strategy of weakness. On the contrary, it is a sign of a new maturity and sophistication on the part of the SD/L movement, which augurs well for its future.

2.4 ELEMENTS OF A NEW PARADIGM

This brief survey indicates what a rich tradition there is to draw on in formulating SD/L policies for the future. It shows that there are strategic options to choose from which have the potential to lead the movement forward, towards a genuine transformation of a complex social and economic order, or backward, to decomposition and decay as the SD/L parties lose any distinctiveness from their erstwhile conservative opponents.

This text contends that if the SD/L movement is to regain control of the political agenda from the New Right, then it must develop a coherent alternative vision to the 'small government—low tax—market forces' model that is so assiduously promoted by free marketeers. This alternative vision cannot rely on a return to the 1960s identification of the Left with 'big government—big spending' reforms, i.e. nationalization and social programmes involving huge federal or national government expenditures (leaving to one side the extent to which the policies of the Left really amounted to this). The vision for the 1990s must be at once radical and responsible in hinging such programmes to national self-reliance, to reasonable levels of taxation, and to a pace of change that is not overly disruptive to community ties. Such a vision is in my view politically attractive and feasible, and capable of stemming the rightward drift in western democracies in a way which goes beyond the SD/L right-wing, pragmatist policies of 'holding the centre', 'steady as she goes', and refraining from initiatives for fear of offending the international money markets. Such centrist responses, I fear, will simply be swept away by a resurgent Right.

The temptation to moderate policy in order to hold the middle ground of politics; to appease the New Right by accommodating moves towards lower taxes and smaller government; to seek coalition partners to the right of the SD/L parties—this will always seem to be attractive in short-term tactical terms. It is the course that will be argued by the pragmatists and conservatives in the movement.

But there is already much experience to show that such a policy leads nowhere in the longer term. The dithering and lack of direction of the Callaghan Labour government of 1974–79 in the UK, stands as a permanent reminder as to where such policies take the movement. They play into the hands of stronger forces from the Right who will never be satisfied with the 'sacrifices' made by a moderate SD/L government, and who will find their champion in a Thatcher or a Reagan to sweep the moderates from office. What this brief excursion into the SD/L tradition has shown, is that there is no inexorable logic of reformism that compels the political party of labour to compromise with capital and demobilize its supporters. This has happened, and will no doubt continue to happen, but it is not a situation that is *determined* by the nature of electoral and industrial politics. Moreover, this glimpse has revealed that, at times, SD/L parties have taken steps that contest the power of capital, and have utilized their majority support in the political sphere to curb the power of capital in the economic sphere. Such steps are practicable and politically feasible.

It is now clear that the economic and industrial policy of the SD/L movement needs to be based on a notion of intervention and democratization which does not simply regulate from the sidelines, but seeks to transform social relations through the dynamics of the social and economic system itself. It needs to build on people's skills and confidence rather than on their sense of injustice. Change is demanded then, at the political level, to remove irrational constraints on people's creativity—constraints such as despotic and hierarchical management systems in the workplace. This is a reconceptualization of Marx's famous dictum, stated with such oracular brevity, that the 'forces of production' would come into contradiction with the 'relations of production', and burst them asunder. These words come to life when applied to people's skills and confidence being frustrated by systems of control in the workplace that fail to draw on, and actively frustrate, these skills.

* * *

Any political paradigm stipulates a theory and practice, and a relationship between them. Let us be rigorous, and formulate a set of four criteria that any such paradigm should satisfy.

- The paradigm must offer a clear vision of a medium term future, that is a clear alternative to the vision advanced by the New Right.
  This is the integrative function of a paradigm, that shows how struggles and campaigns, and constructive acts in government, are related to each other, forming a coherent set of goals and practices.
- The paradigm should be linked to the current agenda and express the essential features of current campaigns. This is the engaging function of a paradigm, that meshes it or engages it with present realities. This is the hardest point for any design of a future social order to achieve—to link the design with what exists. For we have to start where we are, and with people's genuine, current concerns.
- The paradigm should be founded in an understanding of the dynamic forces and relationships within the capitalist economy, and provide an explicit means of modifying or transforming them. This is the programmatic content of a paradigm, which can be varied and adjusted as economic conditions change. Reforms that are advanced without reference to the dynamics of the system that they are supposed to be reforming, are a sham.
- The paradigm should provide a means of making a strategic or tactical choice of policy from the options available. This is the discriminatory function of the paradigm. I claim that the notion of 'socialism' is now too vague to provide this function, and some more explicit strategic goal is needed.

In this text we seek to show that a paradigm of Associative Democracy, to be elaborated below, is able to satisfy these four criteria of integration, engagement, programmability and discrimination. The elements of the paradigm emerge from current initiatives being taken by the labour and social movements in many countries. Our task is to systematise these disparate initiatives into a coherent vision.

In terms of the Associative Democracy (AD) paradigm, we can view existing associations of workers and citizens as the agents of change, and hence of practice—provided they are mobilized by a theory which sets them to work in new ways in order to achieve specified medium-term goals of democratization. The AD programme departs from alternative paradigms which seek to demonstrate the inadequacy of trade unions and SD/L parties and set only vague long-term goals of socialism.

The AD paradigm does not specify a final state of society. On the contrary, it sees democratization as the precondition for people being able to make some rational and informed choice over how their society is to be shaped. Such a discussion is not feasible today when citizens and workers are allowed to effect so little collective leverage over social and economic life.

The AD paradigm has the virtue that it engages with the existing social reality. We start from where we are, and with what we've got, and seek a feasible and practicable strategy for effecting a democratization of the social and economic order. This in turn provides the framework within which social decisions can be taken regarding future social evolution.

Furthermore, in engaging with the existing social reality, the AD paradigm provides a means of discriminating between different strategic and tactical options, bringing an informed perspective to bear on our political choices. It avoids making oracular and vague pronouncements about what might be the 'correct' way forward.

In these ways, the AD paradigm dispenses with an old and conservative theory of knowledge, namely that there is a single 'truthful' way of describing or accounting for phenomena, including social phenomena. The open and constructive approach to theory adopted by the AD paradigm is founded in a pluralist or relativist epistemology.[45]

2.5 A POST-MODERNIST POLITICS?

Before embarking on an elaboration of the AD paradigm, there are some preliminaries that need to be attended to. In this postmodern era, we need to be textually self-aware. What are the basic assumptions of the enterprise we have embarked on?

A first and fundamental assumption we are making is that the idea of a coherent social strategy designed to achieve certain defined aims, actually makes sense. We are assuming that we can talk sensibly about 'associations' having aims and developing strategies—as a sort of shorthand for the people constituting these associations sinking their individual differences in order to achieve common purposes. Such common purposes are of course an abstraction: individual members have their own particular interests, as do the leaders of the association. In a sense, our enterprise could be seen to fall victim to the post-modern doctrine of incredulity in the face of all the grand 'narrative traditions' such as rationalism or humanism, socialism or liberalism.[46] But only in the sense that any political treatise must engage with these traditions—or be inaccessible to its potential readership. Our project of renovation of SD/L thought must be predicated on the view that coherent collective action is possible and, more to the point, can succeed in achieving expressed aims. This view flies in the face of much contemporary theorising of a dispersal and disintegration of social coherence, which is evident as much in the cultural domain as it is in the economic. In a slightly old-fashioned way, such a view upholds the importance of the public domain, where individuals and organizations contend and engage their differing definitions of what constitutes the 'public good'.

Of course, our assumption leaves open the question of what sort of policies these individuals or organizations may be pursuing. They might be from the traditional Left—but, equally likely, they might be from the Moral Majority, the Right to Life, or some other movement identified with the traditional Right. Our basic framework of politics must lend legitimacy to their interventions as much as to those of the SD/L movement. In the end, there can be no confirmation or refutation of our conjecture as to the 'possibility of coherent social action': we assume such a coherence as soon as we embark on any definition of the 'public good' that is abstracted from the daily clash of individual interests and values.

A second assumption of our paradigm is rather more subtle. It asserts that coherent social action is not only possible, but that it can be mounted in a constructive fashion in order to shape a future social order. Such an approach must be at once critical of the status quo, and constructive in its proposals, and optimistic that they will have a favourable effect. This requirement is surprisingly onerous. It sets the literature on social democracy apart from the two great traditions of the human and social sciences. On the one hand, there is the (dominant, mainstream) tradition which views society as ordered in a functional and homogeneous fashion, and therefore perceives social problems as departures from some desired norm. On the other hand, there is the critical tradition which adopts the perspective that societies are cleft by irreconcilable and opposing interests. In this tradition, problems are simply interpreted as manifestations of those contradictions; they are therefore ultimately irresolvable. The discourse of social democracy finds a home in neither of these camps. For the mainstream, it is too critical and too prone to emphasize differences (e.g. differences in income, or in power) rather than shared goals or values. From the critical perspective, it is too ready to identify areas of common interest, and to place reliance on the institutions of a flawed society: it is rejected because of its refusal to make the 'grand refusal'.

In the face of such resistance, it is difficult for the discourse of social democracy to make much headway. Yet the effort must be made, and without apology. The stakes are too high to quit this game. For in fact the two great traditions of thought offer no clear solutions to the present global impasse. The main streams of dominant thought, in economics, in sociology, in the study of technology, are either too general and abstract to engage with the specifics of problems, or too compliant with dominant interests to effect sufficiently radical change. On the other hand, the streams of critical thought, as exemplified by the Frankfurt School, structural marxists and others, defeat their own best endeavours: they highlight the contradictions in the current order, but refuse to 'legitimate' any existing institutions or organizations which must, in practice, engage with these contradictions.

It is only the discourse of gradualist transformation that can avoid these twin problems. Yet the variety of intellectual traditions opposed to this approach is prodigious. It is worthwhile identifying some of these traditions for they represent serious obstacles to the success of any renovation of social democratic thought.

There is, for example, a range of positions that have in common an impatience with gradualism and a distrust of the organs of the labour movement. Two sets of approaches can be identified and described as *theoretical immobilism* and *capitalist essentialism*. They function in my view as a theoretical deadweight on the SD/L movement, occupying space that could otherwise be fruitfully used. It is therefore worthwhile spending a little time in examining them, to see how they differ from the approach advocated in this text.

Capitalist essentialism

There is a line of criticism that goes, for example, in paraphrased form: 'Don't these gradualists realize that the logic of the capitalist system will eventually defeat all their precious reforms through the sheer force of the law of value, the hegemonic dominance of the ruling class, and the appropriation of all forms of opposition?'

I characterize this perspective as 'essentialist' because it is based on a static view of the current social order as being 'essentially' capitalist and therefore immune to any political action. According to this view, if workers organize in any constructive fashion, they can expect to be met by the full force of the 'capitalist state', or are bound to be misrepresented in the 'capitalist press', or in any case will not be able to overcome the iron effects of the fundamental 'law of value'. The press misrepresents them because it is capitalist; just as the State blocks them because it is a capitalist state, and, by definition, serves the interests of capital, and so on.

An example of this sort of argument is to be found in the interesting book by David Selbourne, *Against Socialist Illusion*. In one of its chapters, this text takes as its target progressive reformers of the educational system who have sought to make it more egalitarian and open to working-class children. They are castigated by Selbourne for their failure to understand that inequalities are part of the capitalist order; that they are 'organic and functional to it'; and it has been a 'major folly' of socialists to believe that these inequalities could be removed by welfare measures.[47] Whatever the virtues of the case against 'welfare socialism', it is not advanced by this sort of argument that resorts to timeless 'essences' and attempts to refute initiatives by definition.

In his view, the very idea of seeking to establish new institutions that depend on and cohabit with the capitalist/market system is the source of all subsequent error. Facing up to these dilemmas would entail abandoning the gradualist project. Here Selbourne is at his most disarming in virtually declaring a priori that any proposal short of overthrowing the 'capitalist market system' will be doomed because it will have to 'depend on and cohabit with' that system. This is to preclude any option of practical political involvement in presently constituted—and any future—society.

A similar example may be found in the criticisms made by Panitch and others of social contracts or 'political trade unionism'. Criticisms of failed initiatives, like the ill-fated social contract of the Callaghan Labour government of 1974–79, are fused with dogmatic statements about the eternal nature of capitalism.[48] Any form of trade union intervention at the level of the State is ruled out, and anyone who advocates such a course is held to be betraying an 'insufficient appreciation of the role corporatist structures necessarily play, as arenas of top-level bargaining, in forestalling or constraining working class mobilization'. For Panitch, 'corporatism must be seen as a system of state-structured class collaboration. As such, its extension poses not an opportunity, but a danger to working class organizations'. For him, writers like Esping-Andersen who emphasize the positive gains that can be made by unions in these structures, are lost causes because they fail 'to understand that corporatist political structures ... are a form of capitalist domination'.[49] This *ex cathedra* statement comes after a long debate that was never a real debate at all because in the end Panitch has defined corporatist structures as a form of 'capitalist domination'.

Panitch thereby dismisses all the co-determination achievements of trade unions within these associational structures, and in particular the gains made by Scandinavian unions in the 1970s, by resorting to a breathtakingly simplistic endorsement of industrial militancy. What counts is the number of strikes, sectional wage gains, industrial class struggle unfettered by any social or political perspectives.

Panitch, in my view, is held to these positions because of an extremely static view of the world. He seems to see no *dynamic* in associational structures, but only *essences* to be slotted into his world picture. This is a medieval view of things, more in tune with Thomas Aquinas than with a modern progressive.

We see here the sterility and barrenness of the 'essentialist' position. Any advance that gives workers greater control over their own lives, in the workplace and beyond, is seen as threatening the project of mobilizing the working class as an industrial army. Hence any form of autonomous advance is denounced as collaboration, and the structures of co-determination established as 'corporatist', which, as we have seen, is defined as meaning a form of 'capitalist domination'. The circularity is perfect—we are in a fantasy world where the only way out is via some unspecified successor to the SD/L party.

I have argued that a more fruitful line of advance is to accept the associational mode as a valid means of advancing the cause of the labour movement. It is, above all, a means of broadening the movement's concerns in order to transcend sectionalism (but not an end in itself) subject to an informed theory of the *limits* of its validity and of the *criteria* governing its application. Such an approach engages with the history of social contracts, and provides the movement with guidelines for the future, rather than merely dismissing this history and abandoning the movement to its fate. Within such a perspective we are led to ask: What are the theoretical foundations of 'political' trade unionism, within a new 'associational' framework? (And we attempt to answer such a question in the section 4.5 on trade unions below). It is in encouraging us to ask such constructive questions that the AD paradigm reveals its superiority over 'essentialist' perspectives.

Theoretical immobilism

Another line of criticism focuses on the 'cultural contradictions' of capitalism, but it, too, ends up as the prisoner of its own assumptions.

Let us take as an example the notion of 'hegemony'. As is well known, Antonio Gramsci introduced the notion of hegemony as a corrective to the simplicities of Leninist political assumptions.[50] Gramsci theorized in the wake of the defeat of an insurrection (Turin 1919) that seemed to have everything going for it—a militant working class, a seizure of the means of production, a developed notion of working class democracy, and strong political leadership. But this clearly was not enough. The weak Italian State was able to mobilize an army to contain and crush the insurrection, with minimal civil disturbance elsewhere. In particular, the countryside was unmoved by what was happening in the urban industrial quarters around Turin. This led Gramsci to formulate the notion of the 'hegemony' of the dominant classes in securing the 'consent' of the subordinate class, and to postulate that the subordinate classes had to wage an 'ideological struggle' to neutralize that hegemony before they could hope to bring about a successful social and economic transformation. This was a dramatic departure from the mechanistic conceptions, derived from Kautsky and Engels, that prevailed in socialist circles at the time. It established that any political party seeking to lead workers and citizens in a process of transformation, would have to engage with people where they are, with their existing ideas and institutions and practices. This became in the 1970s the theoretical foundation for the strategy of the Italian Communist Party and of Eurocommunism. In a sense, it is also the underlying philosophy of the associative democratic paradigm, in that it encourages engagement with the actual institutions of the economy in place of a detached approach to their external 'regulation'.

But theorists like Adam Przeworski take the notion of hegemony and, in my view, subvert Gramsci's original intention in introducing it. They succeed in turning 'hegemonic strategies' into part of the 'logic of capital', and thereby undermine the legitimacy of a counter-hegemonic gradualist strategy. Przeworski argues that:

> Force, permanently organized physical force, is for Gramsci a constitutive element of consent, in the sense that any breakdown of consent activates the mechanisms of coercion which are inherent in all realms of social life and which remain latent as long as consent is sufficient to reproduce capitalist relations.[51]

What does this phrase 'activates the mechanisms' really mean? It seems to imply that there is a ruling bloc which 'allows' people to fool themselves that they consent to their subordinate status, but that if they 'see through' this illusion then this bloc turns towards other means of keeping the populace in check. Surely this is the very *opposite* of what Gramsci meant. For Gramsci, there was no omniscient ruling bloc, but a group who held power in the State and who used all the influence at their command, including notions of hierarchy and of 'God's will', that reinforced their position against the constant restlessness of those denied a voice in proceedings. Gramsci argued that to contest these ideas was the first step to claiming a place within the organs of the State. In other words, a social group had to be able to exercise power in imagination prior to its being able to exercise power in reality. It had to believe in its capacity to govern.

These are potent ideas, but in my view Przeworski turns them on their head arguing that the hegemony of the 'ruling bloc' is actually part of the logic of the system that keeps the workers subordinate.

Where does Przeworski leave the labour movement? It seems that as workers 'see through' the illusions planted for them in one institution after another, they merely 'activate' the more repressive or coercive apparatuses (police, army) that lie behind them. This is why I call this line of argument a species of 'immobilism', because in the end it counsels despair: there is no way out of the trap laid by these cunning capitalists. What is Przeworski's 'solution'? He provides a rhetorical gesture, a vacuous, evasive formula:

> Unless the capacity to institute socialism is organized economically, politically and ideologically within the capitalist society, wage earners are better off avoiding crises and co-operating in the reproduction of capitalist accumulation.[52]

We are left in the dark as to what this 'economic, political and ideological' programme might look like, but we are left in no doubt that in Przeworski's view a 'gradualist' programme would fail this test.

The point I am making is that the theorist Przeworski has taken Gramsci's notion of hegemony and used it to argue against the efficacy of any programme of action taken by unions or a political party of labour. Theory is used here as a weapon against action.

In my view, to cure people of these intellectual delusions there is no better medicine than a dose of real world involvement. A spell working in a trade union, in a Minister's office, in a government department or in business, will quickly reveal that the real world is far more complex than that envisaged in simple models of the economy or of the State; that it is immensely resistant to change; but that it can, nevertheless, be changed by the right politics and theory.

Let me emphasize most strongly that I am not arguing against the need for theory. Without a theoretical perspective, without a sense of direction, the labour movement finds itself cast adrift in a sea of opportunism. What I am arguing for is more emphasis on useful theory: theory that makes sense of people's collective experience and projects this into a future that may contain many possibilities. The striking feature of Gramsci's thought lay in its conception of theory as seeking to empower people as they confront the intractabilities of the given order.

2.6 THEORETICAL SOURCES FOR THE AD PARADIGM

What the AD paradigm draws on is the best in social democratic and socialist traditions in order to meet the new challenges. Within Europe, over the past decade the Swedish Social Democrats have led the way in the formulation and implementation of radical initiatives in economic and industrial democracy. In West Germany, the SPD has been involved in a far-reaching debate to replace its 1959 Bad Godesberg programme, and has brought to the fore many of the concerns outlined in this text in the report from its Economic Commission, *Renovating the Economy on the basis of Social and Ecological criteria*.[53] Similar fundamental debates are being pursued by the Left in Italy and France, where an openness to new strategies and institutions is evident.

Gone is the concern with a single, world-historical, epochal transition from capitalism to socialism. One hopes we have more respect now for the intractability of the social order; for the status of existing organizations; for the necessity to intervene strategically and not simply wait for contradictions to mature; and for the mobilizing appeal of specific and concrete proposals rather than vaguely formulated goals.

Democratization is also the key concern of the foremost SD/L theorists in the US. Michael Harrington, in his study of socialism published in 1970, coined the term 'democratic collectivism' which is very close in spirit to our term 'associative democracy'. He said:

> One need not any longer ask whether the future is going to be collective—if we do not blow ourselves to smithereens, that issue has already been settled by a technology of such complex interdependence that it demands conscious regulation and control. The question is: what form will twenty-first century collectivism take? Will it be a totalitarian, a bureaucratic or a *democratic collectivism*?[54]

Harrington's transition programme encompassed such measures as: socialization of investment (e.g. through socializing a portion of profits); democratic planning of investments; and social ownership of corporations, via structural reforms. This was put forward as a sophisticated alternative to nationalization and primitive socialist notions of 'expropriation'. As he put it: 'The gradualism of this strategy is derived not from any abstract principle, but from the actual experience of socialist governments over half a century—as well as from a sense of what might be acceptable to the (American) people' and, one might add, to people in other western democracies.

More recently, the political economy movement in the US has generated the impressive 'Economic Bill of Rights', formulated in 1983 by Bowles, Gordon and Weiskopf in their book *Beyond the Wasteland.*[55] This, too, shares many of the features of the paradigm advocated here, in that it draws away from nationalization, heavy taxation and external regulation policies in favour of democratization, reliance on associations, and intervention within the dynamics of the economy. The big difference, of course, between a US strategy and that to be pursued in other western social democracies is the absence of an SD/L party in the US—and so it is no accident that the Economic Bill of Rights does not include a 'social contract' between unions and such a party.

Within Italy, where the fascist legacy and chronic weakness of the State make his views resonate more than elsewhere, the political theorist Norberto Bobbio has been pursuing the theme of democratization. Bobbio advocated the renovation of traditional SD/L ideology in his controversial 1976 text *Which Socialism?* In his latest writings he has re-examined the liberal tradition, with a view to effecting a merger between the best in socialism and liberalism.[56] He seeks to adapt the institutions of democracy, and extend them, by asking not 'Who can vote?', but 'Where can you vote?' By this he means that democratic principles need to be extended into other locations in the economy and society, such as the workplace, school and hospital boards, bureaucracies and technocracies.[57]

It is interesting that this fusion of socialism and liberalism has been discussed before, particularly in Italy. For example, Carlo Rosselli, a contemporary of Gramsci, coined the term 'liberal socialism' as an alternative political goal to that promoted by the Bolsheviks and Communist International. He contended that the two streams of thought complemented each other; this point of view became particularly relevant under Fascism.[58]

There is now a healthy stream of literature on democracy itself, and its prospects. In his comprehensive review, David Held identifies a series of 'models of democracy' (classical, protective, developmental and direct), and concludes that if democracy is to survive it must become a 'double-sided process'—by which he means, it must be concerned on the one hand with reform of State institutions, and on the other, with the restructuring of civil society.[59] He asks how state policy might be made more accountable, and how 'non-state' (i.e. civil society) activities could be democratized. While opting for constitutional guarantees and a bill of rights to uphold an extended notion of 'government', he discusses novel initiatives in the fields of investment (Meidner plan), reorganization of social welfare provision, and democratization of industry through trade union rights as supporting its extension in the non-state area. Like myself, Held wishes to break with the conventional view that 'state economic planning plus the nationalization of industry advances citizen economy'. He calls this model of state and society, organized around a process of 'double democratization', a system of 'democratic autonomy' (or 'liberal socialism').[60]

Within this stream, a number of erstwhile 'pluralists' of the 1950s and 1960s who had no time for radical theories of democracy, are displaying an interesting evolution in their thought. Foremost amongst these, Robert Dahl has developed the thesis, in his recent *A Preface to Economic Democracy*, that an economic system of worker-owned and worker-controlled enterprises could provide a much better foundation, in theoretical as well as practical terms, for democracy, political equality and liberty than the present order of corporate capitalism.[61]

There is the stream of writing on social contracts between business unions and government, which has referred, in prejudicial terms, to 'corporatist' arrangements, but is also looking forward to an evolution of democracy along such negotiated lines. For Schmitter and Streeck, leading contributors to the literature, there in no corporatist 'master plan', but a loose set of arrangements that have emerged in most democracies as a result of conflicts of interest where neither side could impose a preferred solution on the others. As noted above, Schmitter and Streeck have coined the term '*associative model* of social order' as a generalization of corporatist arrangements, and contrast it with what they call 'community, market and state social orders'.[62]

There is Paul Hirst's work on industrial democracy and on a pluralist model of socialism that he calls 'associationalist'. He argues that Labour in the UK can only defeat Thatcher's equation of socialism with bureaucratic collectivism and authoritarianism by fully embracing pluralism and associationalism. As he says:

'Socialists must build on the pluralistic elements in society by pluralising the state. Socialists must commit themselves to reducing and eliminating the powers and functions of centralised and bureaucratic big government, transferring as many of them as possible to associations and co-operative bodies. These bodies must be democratically self-governing and regulated by law: they should also, where necessary, receive a share of the public revenue in order to carry out their tasks. Socialists must commit themselves to democratizing and associationalizing large-scale corporate enterprises as far as possible, promoting both self-management and associational ownership (for example, in the form of a trust representing various interests).'[63]

These revivals of a discourse focused on the non-statist role of associations represent a significant coming to terms with the pluralist realities of modern democracies, and with the necessarily pluralist character of the social and political goals that SD/L parties pursue. It comes to terms with the fact that associations of one kind or another already dominate political and social life—but informally, and with an inevitable bias in influence exercised by wealthy and professional associations such as those organizing the interests of barristers or medical practitioners. To bring the role of associations into the open, by acknowledging their central role in social concertation, is to open the prospect of a legal and political order that is concerned to regulate the behaviour of associations, and to insist on certain minimum democratic standards being complied with. Concentration on such issues is already resulting in the recovery of a lost history of 'associationalism' in the twentieth century.[64]

Complementing the concern with pluralism in the political domain, is the theorization of a post-Fordist industrial system that is coming to replace the standardization of the Fordist system that has dominated industry this century.[65] We pursue this theme in the next chapter. It is one of the basic contentions of this book that the political paradigm of associative democracy provides an appropriate pluralist framework within which the SD/L movement may pursue post-Fordist industrial strategies of flexibility and co-determination.

It is striking how, in their different ways, all these streams of thought concur on the fact that the organizations of citizens and workers in 'civil society' will play a key role in the development of a democratic order of the future. But they insist that the notion of democracy cannot be limited to this expansion of economic and social rights, and that it will take place within a framework of pluralist, representative or 'liberal' democratic institutions within the domain of the State. The paradigm of AD is conceived as a synthesis and extension of these promising and exciting lines of theoretical enquiry.

Similar tendencies can be detected within the field of marxist political economy. The 1970s saw a renewal of interest in developing the economics of socialism. One of the major contributions, which has since provided a framework for debate, is Alec Nove's *The Economics of Feasible Socialism.*[66] While taking the notion of socialism as given, this text in practice extends it to the point where it is indistinguishable from a democratized capitalism. I hasten to add that this is not meant as a criticism, but as an indication of the trend of serious work on future economic systems. We return to Nove's model, and others like it, in our discussion of the democratic economy in the next chapter.

Finally, let us draw inspiration from the courageous and successful actions of the Swedish SD party during the Depression years of the 1930s, and from the impressive theoretical and ideological contribution to this effort made by Ernst Wigforss. What we are seeking to construct with the AD paradigm is essentially a 'provisional utopia' in the sense that Ernst Wigforss gave this term in Sweden in the 1920s and 1930s. Wigforss, who attained adulthood and political maturity at the time of the great 'revisionist' debate between Bernstein and Kautsky, saw early on that a strategy of 'waiting for economic crisis', as espoused by Kautsky, was doomed to failure and, in any case, demobilized the party and its base; while a strategy of bland reformism, going just a little bit further than liberalism, was equally fruitless in the long term. Wigforss developed a clear notion of a socialist strategy as needing to combine a future vision with an immediate agenda. This is the implication of rejecting the Kautskyan-Marxist economic determinism that saw socialism coming as the inevitable supersession of capitalism, as the working class gained in numerical and material strength. The term he used for this linking of principles with policy was 'provisional utopia'.

According to Tilton, writing in 1979:

> A *provisional utopia* is a tentative sketch of a desirable future society. It serves as a critique of existing social conditions and as a guide to present action, yet it can be revised in accordance with future experience . . . By tying day-to-day political work to longer-term objectives, it seeks to avoid the dangers of bogging down in purely 'pragmatic' politics . . . the provisional utopia's emphasis on a political creativity that blends enduring socialist aims with immediate reformist measures characterizes not only Wigforss' thought but also the theory and practice of Swedish Social Democracy.[67]

Tilton sums up Wigforss' strategy, then, as: 'a policy of *permanent reform*.' Wigforss, he says,

> rejects the charge that successful reformism diminishes the prospects for more radical transformation. Through initiatives for social welfare policy, progressive taxation, economic planning, industrial democracy, and socialization, the party can simultaneously raise the employee's standard of living and restrict the capitalist's privileges. Each series of reforms sets the stage for new ones and weakens the capitalist's ability to resist ... Wigforss is unambiguous; through a process of gradual reforms, he wants to transform bourgeois society and to establish social control of the means of production.[68]

This is a quite remarkable theoretical outlook that is still barely known outside Sweden. Within Sweden during the turbulent decade on the 1930s, this approach was adopted by the SD party with spectacularly successful results, laying the foundation for the SD dominance of Swedish politics from 1932 (holding office continuously till 1976). This success was based on the SD party providing a clear and radical democratic alternative to the do-nothing, laissez-faire approach of other conservative political parties. Higgins, in 1985, states categorically that:

> Under Wigforss' leading influence, the Swedish SDP abandoned its politics of compromise and launched a head-on attack against the reigning *laissez-faire* orthodoxy, beginning with its application to crisis management in the depression of the 1930s. No other main reformist party of labour has mounted such a thorough challenge to *laissez-faire*... In other Western democracies, the labour movement has mounted no such challenge, and *laissez-faire* doctrine has guided the bourgeoisie's successful counter-offensive in the post-World War II reconstruction period, in its defense of private investment prerogatives and its containment of trade unionism during the "Keynesian compromise", and in its return to outright deflationary policies today.[69]

The parallel with our own time, and with the challenge posed by the New Right, is striking. Wigforss and the Swedish SDP showed that a radical philosophy framed in positive, constructive terms to aid economic recovery, could carry the day politically. It is a lesson that needs to be listened to now when the option of retreat in the face of New Right attacks seems so attractive to pragmatic SD/L parties.

The paradigm of associative democracy may be viewed as a Wigforssian 'provisional utopia' for our own times, in that it insists that radical democratization of the economy is the responsible solution to economic and social problems. It is ideally adapted to the notion that sees democracy as a constant adjustment by the social order to economic and industrial developments. It is to the specification of such a 'provisional utopia' for the 1990s that we now turn.

THREE

ECONOMIC, INDUSTRIAL AND SOCIAL DEMOCRACY

The purpose in formulating a paradigm of Associative Democracy is to guide the process of democratizing industry, the economy and social domain by the SD/L movement, utilizing existing associations of workers and citizens. The test is to be specific and concrete. In this chapter we look in detail at democratization strategies, and the prospects for their success, in the areas of: industry; capital formation; social programmes; and technology.

We complete the chapter by examining the coherence and political feasibility of the democratic economy that would result from such measures. Above all we seek to show that the AD paradigm is functional; that it generates strategies that take the SD/L movement forward; and that it lays the basis for a consolidation of the SD/L movement in power in the twenty-first century.

3.1 DEMOCRATIZATION OF INDUSTRY

The democratization of industry, to give workers a determining influence in the affairs of production, has long been a dream of the labour movement. In a real sense, this was the goal that motivated the first formulations of socialism as simply 'socializing' the production process, but the notion of worker involvement was lost as socialism came to be identified with State ownership. At different points in the nineteenth century a more explicit form of democratization was advocated such as that proposed by Sydney Webb in his *Industrial Democracy*. The goal seemed to come closest to realization at the time of the movement for workers' control, unleashed amongst munitions workers during the First World War. This astonishing period witnessed the rise of a shop stewards' movement amongst munitions workers in Britain organized around a programme of workers' control and, in 1918, militant opposition to the war; the appearance of factory councils in Turin in 1919, arising from internal commissions that were recognized in a national metalworkers' agreement; a shop stewards and factory committee movement in Germany in 1919; a movement of factory delegates organized by the metalworkers' union in France, following legislation regulating wages and mandating arbitration in January 1917; and the formation of Soviets of workers and soldiers in Russia in 1917, leading to a state of dual power after the February revolution, which was resolved by the Bolshevik takeover in October 1917. As Carmen Sirianni, writing in 1980, put it, in his lucid comparative analysis of this extraordinary period:

> For the first time the efforts of skilled workers to control their own jobs were transformed into mass struggles to wrest control of the production processes as a whole from the capitalist class and to lodge it in organs democratically constituted by the workers themselves. Those skilled workers who had previously been in the forefront of job control struggles began to develop organizational forms that promised to transcend the boundaries of craft and to include the mass of less skilled workers in the general project of democratic management. For the first time truly mass struggles were waged to give concrete institutional expression to the socialist project of expropriating the means of production and transforming the relations of production.[1]

This is not the place for an extensive discussion of the rise and fall of this movement. To account for the rise, let us just quote one extract from the testimony of William Straker, then secretary of the Northumberland Miners' Association, to the Sankey Commission of 1919 into the British mining industry. His words convey the aspirations of a generation:

> In deciding what is to be the character of mines administration it is necessary to remember that workmen are more than machines, or even 'hands' as they are so often termed. Industrial unrest is a question about which everyone is concerned, yet there is a general lack of appreciation of what is the real root of this unrest. In the past workmen have thought that if they could secure higher wages and better conditions they would be content. Employers have thought that if they granted these things the

workers ought to be content. Wages and conditions have been improved—but the discontent and the unrest have not disappeared, and many good people have come to the conclusion that working men are so unreasonable that it is useless trying to satisfy them. The fact is that the unrest is deeper than can be reached by merely pounds, shillings and pence, necessary as they are. The root of the matter is the straining of the spirit of man to be free. Once he secures the freedom of the spirit he will, as a natural sequence, secure a material welfare equal to what the united brains and hand can wring from mother earth and her surrounding atmosphere. Any administration of the mines under nationalization must not leave the mineworker in the position of a mere wage-earner, whose sole energies are directed by the will of another. He must have a share in the management of the industry in which he is engaged, and understand all about the purpose and destination of the product he is producing; he must know both the productive and commercial side of the industry. He must feel that the industry is being run by him in order to produce coal for the use of the community, instead of profit for the few people. He would thus feel the responsibility that would rest on him as a citizen, and direct his energies for the common good. This ideal cannot be reached all at once owing to the way in which private ownership has deliberately kept the worker in ignorance regarding the industry; but as that knowledge, which has been denied him, grows, as it will do under nationalization, he will take his rightful place as a man. Only then will labour unrest, which is the present hope of the world, disappear. The mere granting of the thirty per cent and the shorter hours demanded will not prevent unrest, neither will nationalization with bureaucratic administration. Just as we are making political democracy world-wide, so we must have industrial democracy, in order that men may be free.[2]

These hopes have not, obviously enough, been realized by the subsequent experience with nationalization of the mines. But the movement for workers' control was directly undermined by other factors that limited and eventually destroyed it. These included, as we saw in the last chapter: the influence of economic recession; the turn to Bolshevism; and the resort to Fascism.

The industrial system

The defeat of the workers' control movement in the 1920s, and the consolidation of employer dominance in all matters pertaining to production, paved the way to the development of a new industrial system of immense productive and competitive potential: the system of mass production.

In place of previous systems of batch production dependent on the input of skilled artisans, firms were able to standardize and lengthen their production runs, employing semi-skilled labour, and thus cutting costs and reaping returns to scale. Employers followed F. W. Taylor's lead and instituted new systems of 'scientific management', embodying time and motion studies, and also followed Henry Ford's lead in installing moving conveyor systems of assembly. Industry has never been the same since. Skilled jobs were broken down into semi-skilled components, and brought under a new form of bureaucratic control called 'management'. The whole transition took a half century to accomplish—from 1880 to 1930.[3]

Consolidation of mass production

The mass production system became the driving force of capitalist development globally in the twentieth century. Perfected in the US, where it drove out its artisan and workshop competitors, it was exported to Europe and Japan. There it was consolidated in the years following the Second World War, acting as the prime mover of the 'post-war boom'. In the 1960s and 1970s it has been re-exported to South America and South-East Asia, with the result that Brazil, Taiwan, South Korea, Hong Kong and Singapore are all dominant industrial producers in the 1980s. Mass production drives out its competitors because of the cheapness of its commodities, and it ushers in the dominance of large firms because of the high capital costs of entry. But mass production on its own is not a self-sustaining system; mass produced goods need mass consumer markets if they are to be sold. These in turn have to rely on the maintenance of mass purchasing power—which was the need that Keynesian instruments of monetary and fiscal controls responded to. It fell to SD/L regimes in the post-war period to usher in the system of economic regulation that has sustained and consolidated the mass production/mass consumption system globally. This is the system we now term Fordism.[4]

Fordism was the economic base on which the post-war boom was built. It was the mould that shaped post-war politics and ideology. It has been internalized as a system by all of us—as well as by SD/L parties and governments. Fordism was in fact the rock on which all dreams of industrial democracy foundered. For the essence of mass production is its inflexibility, its long production runs, its careful separation of design from the work organization producing goods—matters which are intolerant of worker input of any kind.

Unions for their part had to come to terms with Fordism, for it delivered reasonable wages to their members (a trend started by Henry Ford himself, with his famous $5 day), and promised continuing high levels of employment, at least during the post-war boom. The agenda for industrial negotiations was narrowed to fit in with Fordist requirements: questions of co-determination of production, which had seemed so urgent in 1920, came to be non-existent.

In this way, a characteristic Fordist labour process was shaped—not deliberately, as if by some conspiracy, but in response to a series of pressures we now discern as the elements of Fordism. Mechanization and standardization of tasks spread to all industrial branches, to the primary sector, and then in the 1960s to white collar work as well. Automation and computerization threatened to take the process to its ultimate conclusion: the elimination of all human worker input. This was the picture of industry in the 1970s described by Harry Braverman as 'the degradation of work in the twentieth century'.[5]

However, there was another side to this story. The Fordist system is riddled with contradictions. As mass produced goods were exported, peripheral countries could copy the techniques and set up in competition. Within the rules of the economic system, there was nothing US auto producers could do about lower-priced, better quality Japanese models—and now there is nothing that Japanese electronics producers can do about lower-priced better quality Korean products . . . and so on. Externally, then, the Fordist system runs up against the limits produced by its own dynamic, and the original Fordist heartland finds itself hemmed in economically by its own imitators. Internally, the Taylorist organization of production runs up against limits in the form of gross alienation of workers who are condemned to repeat endless cycles of meaningless tasks without any possible hope of job satisfaction or responsibility—an alienation which was translated in the late 1960s and early 1970s into outright rebellion, sabotage and wildcat strikes, aimed as much against Fordist unions as at Fordist managements. By the 1970s, then, the foundations of the Fordist system were beginning to crumble. The end of the Fordist era was looming. But what was to take its place?

Towards a post-Fordist industrial system

The last ten years or so have seen unprecedented upheavals in industry. New centres of competition have arisen, putting one industry after another in the metropolitan countries under severe pressure—steel was all but wiped out in the US; shipbuilding was completely rundown in Sweden; Britain declined to an also-ran in the motor industry. New technologies have changed the face of production—new computerized systems, robots, flexible manufacturing cells, CAD-CAM, and so on, are all changing what seemed to be permanent rules of the game. New management techniques, such as Just-In-Time inventory control and Total Quality Control systems, are calling into question traditional management hierarchies. Above all, the successful producers are now finding that they need to depend on skilled, reliable and flexible workers who can take initiatives and cannot be subjected to the punitive surveillance and supervision that prevailed under Taylorism. Piore and Sabel characterize these upheavals as a second 'industrial divide', as significant in its ramifications as the first divide which saw the rise of mass production at the turn of the century. Many of the responses of industry are in the same mould as Fordism, only intensified—more intense Taylorization of work utilizing computers; or more intense protection of markets utilizing tariff barriers. These are what may be termed *neo-Fordist* strategies. But other responses move in a new direction; they aim for quality rather than quantity; for flexibility of response rather than standardized long runs; for skilled autonomous worker input rather than the programmed input of de-skilled process operators. These then are the elements of a 'post-Fordist' strategy; it is taking shape principally in Scandinavia, West Germany and Japan, which are now the world's leading industrial powers.

Post-Fordism has, of necessity, to be a total strategy, encompassing marketing, design, innovation, management, as well as production. Within the sphere of production, it posits new relationships between computerized technologies, work organization, skills formation and industrial relations. The differences from the Taylorized workplace under Fordism are so great that commentators are still struggling to find an appropriate vocabulary with which to describe them. The Germans Kern and Schumann talk of 'new production relations'; the Britons Cooley and Rosenbrock talk of 'human-centred' manufacturing; Piore and Sabel talk of flexible specialization; Anglo-German research groups like that led by Arndt Sorge talk of the end of 'skills polarization' and a new strategy based on 'skills enhancement'.[6] Trade unions are responding with new and vigorous proposals for restructuring of industry and of work organization, and are searching for a new framework of 'co-operative accommodation' with employers in which to operate.[7]

It is in this context that proposals for democratization of industry are being revived. There was a flurry of activity in the 1970s, built on 'Quality of Work Life' programmes that were introduced largely by employers looking to blunt the excesses of Taylorized work systems. This activity was largely confined to the establishment of consultative and representative forums in the workplace, which were deemed to be structures for what employers called 'employee participation' and unions called 'industrial democracy'. But these forums tended to have limited agendas that excluded any matter having 'industrial relations' overtones, and in some cases were explicitly designed to over-ride union channels of representation (as was the case with many Quality Circles). Reforms inspired by the 'Socio-technical' school, with their focus on semi-autonomous work groups, attempted to go further, but they remained isolated as demonstration projects for as long as the logic of Fordism and neo-Fordism held sway.

In the late 1980s and 1990s, the situation looks to be very different. The post-Fordist production paradigm carries with it momentous implications for the organization of work and for the role of workers in the process of production. Now democratization of industry takes on new meaning: it is seen to be economically responsible. Indeed, it is an essential accompaniment of a post-Fordist reorganization of industry. Demands that seemed utopian only ten years ago are now seen as normal! Such is the pace of change in industry as it restructures to meet the challenges that lie ahead. We are entering an era of 'competing paradigms' of industrial efficiency—with momentous political implications.

Of course, to argue the case for industrial democratization is very different from seeing it implemented. There will be employers, and whole industries, who refuse to take the path of co-operative accommodation with their workforce; they may not survive, and take whole industries to oblivion with them. There will be unions who refuse to accept the new framework of co-operation that is needed to implement a strategy embodying post-Fordist elements, and who hark back to the days of militant posturing and refusal to get involved in the bosses' business—and again they may lead their members into oblivion. There will be employers who seek to restructure and make their operations more flexible by resorting to New Right tactics—union busting, sub-contracting, and use of financial incentives such as share and bonus schemes to promote employee loyalty.

The restructuring of industry along post-Fordist lines will present the SD/L movement with its greatest challenge to date. It will emerge from this experience, towards the year 2000, either strengthened politically, industrially and ideologically; or it will be swept away, to become historically irrelevant. The stakes in this game are high.

It is for this reason that I labour the point that the SD/L movement needs a vision of its future, in the form of a fresh and relevant paradigm, rather than be weighed down with projects that failed in the past and will fail again in the future.

Having liberated ourselves from the mechanical dogmas that saw history as an unfolding piece of clockwork, we now have to face the necessity of constructing a politics of democratization that is adequate to the emergent post-Fordist era.

The paradigm of Associative Democracy, I suggest, provides us with a starting point. Within this framework, what are the specific and concrete strategies that unions, SD/L parties and citizens' associations need to pursue in order to democratize industry?

Strategies of democratization

The traditional SD/L approach to bringing firms under wider social control (for all the reasons outlined above) has relied on external regulation through the auspices of the State. This has taken the form of companies legislation, anti-trust (or anti-monopoly legislation) and specifically-targeted bodies, such as Press Councils which oversee the affairs of the media. At the macro-level some tripartite bodies have been established to develop guidelines on industry development policies, but without any direct say over investment they are not very effective. However they can be used strategically by unions in global negotiations with employers. At the micro-level some progress has been made, particularly in Scandinavia and West Germany, in achieving an element of co-determination at the level of the firm between unions and management, from shop level committees to 'supervisory boards'. However this has normally been implemented via separate legislation; the task of amending companies legislation directly has apparently seemed too daunting. Other approaches have been developed via planning agreements negotiated with individual firms, in return for government equity—an approach spelt out in the UK 1974 Labour Manifesto (but not carried through) and since implemented on a small scale by Local Authority Enterprise Boards in the UK.

Consistent with the paradigm of associative democracy, our approach will be to examine feasible and practicable means available to unions and social movements to bring industry under greater social control via internal democratization. This is the essential departure in our paradigm from the more usual reliance of the labour movement on industrial policies of external regulation.

Reforms that need to be addressed include:

- incorporation of companies—reform of the company law and more flexible use of Memorandum and Articles of Association;
- worker and public representation on Boards;
- provisions for sharing of management information;
- organization of work.

The means available for democratization that we shall consider include:

- reform of company legislation;
- promotion of democratic public enterprise;
- negotiation of planning agreements with firms;
- negotiations between unions and employers of co-determination agreements and work organization agreements;
- promotion of worker co-operatives.

The broader questions of democratization of capital, and through this, of the economy as a whole, will be tackled in subsequent sections.

Democratic incorporation of companies

The rules for incorporation (called 'chartering' in the US) are laid down in the companies legislation of each country. They require a new company to establish a Memorandum and Articles of Association, which is the document that regulates the affairs of the company. Topics covered include meetings of shareholders, appointment of directors, allocation of shares and declaration of dividends. This is a classic example of a legal apparatus that is 'blind' to the real world of production, trade, and work. The company law registers only the rights and obligations of shareholders and their entitlements to profits, but remains blind to the source of those profits, and to the claims of other parties, particularly workers. Their rights are simply not registered in the company law—and so attempts at co-determination that are restricted to the industrial relations arena and do not amend the company law, are constantly frustrated.

Democratization in this case means bringing the rights and obligations of workers and the general public into the Articles of Association of companies, and then requiring the company to follow these wider rules under pain of sanctions imposed by the company law.

In the US, Ralph Nader has proposed a national uniform set of procedures (federal chartering) to regulate the internal affairs of corporations.[8] Nader's chartering bill covers such matters as: the board of the corporation to include mandatory consumer and worker representatives; strict controls on mergers to prevent conglomerates being formed; production of a regular social audit to identify the wider social, environmental and health impact of the company's operations; and rights of employees to due process when being hired, fired or disciplined.

Other matters that I would add include: increasing levels of public accountability and disclosure as the capital value of the company increases; procedures for consumers and the general public to make complaints and obtain a fair hearing, without having to sue the company in the courts; disclosure and reporting requirements to workers, board, shareholders, and general public; and general statement of the social goals the company is engaged in pursuing. Matters concerning recognition of trade unions and rights to be accorded to job delegates (shop stewards) are best dealt with in the industrial relations arena, and not in the company law.

Such a structure evades any New Right charge that it constitutes 'over-regulation'. On the contrary, it can be defended as possibly leading to *less external* regulation (for example, by a federal companies and securities commission) in favour of co-determined 'self-regulation'. Conversely, any campaign initiated on the part of industry for greater 'self-regulation', can be met effectively by the SD/L movement agreeing to such a move (provided a basic regulatory mechanism to prevent fraud and white collar crime is kept intact) in exchange for greater internal democratization.

It is most interesting to observe what Friedrich Hayek, known as the father of the New Right, has to say about management and control of the firm in a democratic society. Writing in 1960, he asks whose interests the corporation ought to serve. Hayek makes the telling point that 'if the management is supposed to serve wide public interests, it becomes merely a logical consequence of this conception that the appointed representatives of the public interest should control the management'. Thus Hayek would approve of public representatives on Boards, provided wider public interests were built into the firm's Articles of Association.

Hayek also had some very interesting things to say about the rights of property in corporations—remarks which tally remarkably well with those made by the socialist Harrington cited above. He proposed that while powers of individual shareholders should be increased, those of corporate shareholders should be restrained, to the point of being non-voting. His grounds are that one corporation having voting rights in another 'opens the possibility of the complete and perfectly legal control of large resources by persons who own only a small fraction of them, and of the use of such control in the interest of that group only'. With these words, Hayek anticipated the very problems that have occurred since 1960 with the 'corporate raiders' who manipulate the share-markets for their own ends. He traces the conceptual root of the problem back to the nineteenth-century invention of the joint stock company when it was assumed that 'if legal personality was conferred upon the corporation, then it was natural to confer upon it all powers which natural persons possessed'. But this seemed to Hayek to be by no means a natural or obvious consequence. Hayek was in effect calling for a social *definition* of the powers of property, on the grounds that it is a social construct with social effects.

He concluded that:

> The complete separation of management from ownership, the lack of real power of the shareholders, and the tendency of corporations to develop into self-willed and possibly irresponsible empires, aggregates of enormous and largely uncontrollable power, are not facts which we must accept as inevitable but are largely the result of special conditions the law has created and the law can change. We have it in our power to halt and reverse this process if we want to.[9]

These remarks by a conservative Free-Marketeer deserve to be taken very seriously. The freshness and robustness of his approach shows just how pussy-footed the SD/L parties have become when confronted by companies—trapped as they have been in their Fordist assumptions. Future development requires that companies be seen for what they are: the legal entities through which trade and production is carried on, and through which *social controls over economic activity* are best accommodated in a democratic fashion. This is what I mean by moving from a mode of *external* regulation to one of *internal* regulation (or 'self-regulation') called up by the dynamics of the economic system itself.

It is a big step for the SD/L movement to see the democratization of company structures as a valid strategy for the reform of working life. It goes against the grain, and stems from a long tradition of not wanting to get sucked into the 'capitalist system'. Such scruples stand in the way of further evolution of the SD/L movement. It is the fundamental reform of company structures that will allow the claims of employees to be accommodated—and also the claims of customers, suppliers and the host community, who make up the 'stakeholders' in any company's activities. The articles of association can provide for their rights to representation on the Board—or rather, following the innovations of worker co-operatives in Mondragon, on several boards, each with certain powers delegated to it under the articles. There is scope for the establishment of a 'corporate senate' within each company, acting as a body of review, and providing for the representation of stakeholders as well as smaller shareholders.[10] SD/L governments can facilitate this process by removing impediments from the company law. As elections to company boards, committees and 'corporate senates' come to be seen as matters of public moment, so a new field of active democratic organization and activity will open up. The endorsement of candidates for such office will come to be an important activity for unions, social movements and parties; indeed success at such elections will become a means by which associations can test their public credibility and standing. Beyond this, such innovations are likely to generate their own dynamic, and call into question such strange conventions as the doctrine of perpetual property rights, and the status of corporate shareholders as 'natural persons' which have become embodied as the unquestioned assumptions built into the company law, but which facilitate all the current problems of the concentration of power and wealth criticised by Hayek.

There is no need for the SD/L movement to court maximum resistance to these proposals by seeking to apply them across the board to all existing companies. A more sophisticated approach will rely on the fact that new companies are being formed all the time—and it is here, at the point of change, that the proposals can be applied. Over time, these more democratically incorporated companies will demonstrate their superiority—and it will become politically feasible to set sunset clauses on the non-democratic features of existing companies. This is an instance of a general strategy for seeking social change by intervening at the point where change is already occurring, and where the dynamic of the system works with the change rather than against it.

Expanding Board representation

Those members of the labour and social movements who think that the affairs of their country are dealt with by Prime Minister and Cabinet, have obviously not been privy to the proceedings in the boardrooms of the country's leading companies. This brute fact just cannot be ignored by the labour movement any longer. Firms cannot be allowed to remain islands of autocracy in an otherwise democratic sea.

Conceptually, as we noted above, it is a simple matter to require Boards of Directors of public companies to allocate places for representatives of workers and of the general public. Numbers of such representatives could conveniently be determined by a formula taking account of the size or assets of the company. The public representatives could be appointed via publicly contested elections. These would resemble current elections for municipal office, and no doubt the major political parties would wish to endorse candidates for these elections, at least for the major corporations whose operations have a significant effect on the economy. Elected representatives could be paid a small sitting fee, as are directors now, but there would need to be a limit on the number of directorships held by any individual at any one time.

Worker representatives could be appointed by workplace elections in which all employees would be entitled to vote. Candidates would be expected to be endorsed by their trade union. The conduct of such elections would become an important activity for unions, as well as for the firms themselves.

There is now considerable international experience with both public and worker representatives on Boards. Almost every country in Western Europe during the 1970s enacted some legislation placing workers on Boards of Directors. The longest experience has been in West Germany, where 'co-determination' was introduced in the iron and steel industries as early as 1950 and in all major companies from 1976 on. (Ironically, it was installed in order to prevent a resurgence of German militarism by the same Allied powers who rejected such measures in their home countries.) The German system has now been in operation for so long that it has been officially evaluated, by the Biedenkopf Commission. The impact of the worker directors, who have parity representation with shareholder directors, was found to be wholly positive: 'While participation of workers on the supervisory board did indeed lead to a stronger emphasis of the social aspects ... nevertheless the validity of the principle of profitability as the keynote of entrepreneurial initiative and planning was in no case called into question.'[11] In short, worker directors on Boards in Germany have not brought about an end to capitalism—but this measure, taken along with others, has had a democratizing effect on the operations of the economy.

In Sweden a series of measures were enacted in the 1970s curtailing managerial prerogatives and giving workers more influence in the running of their companies. Along with reforms of health and safety, rights of job delegates, job security, status of union officials and employment promotion, these measures provided for worker representatives on corporate boards. A law was passed in 1976 providing for two worker representatives to be elected to the boards of all firms with more than twenty-five employees—not just as a step towards parity, but also as a means of providing information to workers which could then be used in plant negotiations. This measure was complemented by the fundamental co-determination law which is discussed below.[12]

In Norway, the Labour government in the 1970s introduced radical measures giving Parliament the right to appoint a majority of members of the Boards of the commercial banks, with a minority being appointed by shareholders. This is an interesting alternative to the idea of public elections; it also implies that Parliament can remove Directors (in the same way that Parliament can appoint and remove judges in most Anglo-Saxon countries.) Involvement of Parliament can ensure that appointments will be of a cross-party character (e.g. five Parliamentary nominees could be specified, three coming from the government and two from the Opposition). This would lend the system greater robustness in the eyes of the public. Per Kleppe, the then Finance Minister who introduced this measure, characterized it as the 'de-privatization' of capital; I prefer to call it the *democratization of the firm*. The system was dismantled by the conservative government that came into office in Norway in 1981.

In Britain the role of worker directors in firms was canvassed extensively during the sitting of the Bullock Committee of Inquiry into Industrial Democracy, during the last years of the Callaghan Labour government. As the Committee's recommendations were not implemented at the time, nor by the incoming Thatcher government, this discussion came to nought.

Based on such wide experience, it may be concluded that the presence of worker directors is a *necessary,* but by no means a *sufficient* condition, for the democratization of industry. As advocated above, their presence on Boards should be complemented by representatives of the general public. But they would have to be *effective* representatives, with their own channels of accountability and resources. In a report commissioned by the Bullock Inquiry, Eric Batstone listed the conditions under which directors could exert some influence: parity of representation; provision of resources to analyze information required; accountability of worker-directors to plant committees; and full disclosure of company accounts to Board Directors.[13]

Each of these matters would have to be raised by the trade unions if worker directors were to function as a democratizing influence, rather than as captives of the management.[14]

Democratic planning agreements

Where SD/L governments have sought to influence the behaviour of individual firms, they have traditionally done so through external incentives, such as tax concessions, bounties, investment grants, and other measures.

We have already considered a more direct and democratic intervention in the form of opening up the structures of the firm itself. Now we shall consider how a government, in consultation with the trade unions, may impinge more directly on a firm's behaviour through *planning agreements.*

By planning agreement is meant any form of quid pro quo insisting on certain democratic and social objectives being met by a firm which is in receipt of public subsidies of one form or another. These objectives could be varied in character: they could, for example, be purely economic or industrial, requiring the firm to locate in a certain area, or to produce a certain mix of products; or they could be more social in character, such as requiring recognition of trade unions, full co-determination with employees, equal opportunity and equal pay for work of equal value. These requirements would be over and above general undertakings that the enterprise be competently managed according to a properly thought through business plan.

In the UK, the 1974 Labour Party platform envisaged the setting up of a National Enterprise Board (NEB) which would sign planning agreements with most major enterprises it dealt with. In the event, the Labour government found itself embroiled in an economic crisis, and it never seriously attempted to implement this aspect of its platform. The NEB was set up, but it has operated no differently from any other investment house.

The rationale for the planning agreements has been argued for most convincingly by Stuart Holland in his exposition of the 1974 Labour Platform, *The Socialist Challenge*.[15] The platform envisaged:

- the operation of a system of planning agreements, under which leading companies would be obliged to disclose their investment and other plans to the government and workers;
- the setting up of a state holding company, the NEB, with power to extend public ownership into profitable parts of the economy;
- public aid to a company to be matched by the right of the government to take equity in the company.

The fate of these proposals is worth considering. A new Industry Act was to be introduced which, according to Harold Wilson in 1973, would provide the government with powers which it would use . . . 'to seek agreement with companies over a wide range of industrial matters, including prices, profits, investment practices, overseas trade, industrial relations and industrial democracy, and if necessary in the national interest, to issue directives on any of these issues.'[16] An Industry Bill was presented by Tony Benn to the House of Commons in 1975, providing for: power to require disclosure of information by companies; equity to be taken in firms receiving government financial support; joint planning between government and firms; right to acquire firms, with approval of Parliament; power to protect firms from foreign takeovers; extension of the idea of receivership to cover defence of the interests of workers and of the general public; and safeguards against abuse of power by multinational corporations.

This represented a radical break with the past, when SD/L governments maintained a hands-off policy and sought to influence boardroom decisions solely by external measures such as subsidies and negative controls. It represented a means of intervening *internally*. It is now a matter of historical record that these proposals were defeated. At the height of the attack, Tony Benn, the then Minister of Industry, put the matter well in addressing a business audience in 1975:

> The violence of attacks upon our public ownership plans and on us for defending them, launched by big business and the media, confirm our judgment that these plans are a serious threat, as they are intended to be, to the unaccountable power they wield and the unacceptable privileges they defend with that power. We should all now have learned the hard way that you cannot bully and bribe businessmen into pursuing policies to meet our regional employment needs, our investment needs and our national interests, against the interests of their shareholders. *We have come to the end of that road.*[17]

Indeed we have. This is a political issue that remains to be fought out in other countries and in other times—but with the active support of the trade unions as part of a comprehensive paradigm of associative democracy.

Although not much came of the National Enterprise Board in the UK, the principles of the 1974 Labour platform have been carried forward by various Local Authorities, such as the Greater London Enterprise Board (GLEB), established as a job creation institution by the Labour-controlled Greater London Council in the early 1980s. The GLEB has been using its considerable budget to great effect ever since, channelling funds to enterprises which look capable of generating long-term employment in the production of socially useful goods and services, and negotiating planning agreements with the recipients of funds to ensure that they operate along sound business and industrial democracy lines. Similar Enterprise Boards have been established by other UK local authorities. An example is a body in Birmingham called the West Midlands Enterprise Board, established in 1982 by the West Midlands County Council. In its first year it invested 3.1 million pounds in ten local firms, creating 1500 jobs, and signing a comprehensive 'planning and investment' agreement with each recipient.[18] Although small, these Enterprise Boards have shown that it is possible to have an effect on the internal democratic structure of firms through this form of SD/L government pressure.

A variation on this theme has been practised successfully in the US, where the federal government and several State governments have inserted various 'social goal' clauses in contracts signed with providers of government goods or services. For example, contractors to the federal government are required to commit themselves to 'equal opportunity' employment practices.

This is the essence of the 'planning agreement' approach. Governments are powerful, indeed dominant players in any national economy, but they are not like any other commercial entity. Governments are special in that they have social as well as normal commercial goals. They should not be coy about expressing those goals where they have some real influence—such as in their economic dealings with firms. Conditions can be set on contractors, and on firms bidding for public subsidies or benefits of some kind, including tax concessions: such an approach can be justified as non-discriminatory on the grounds that no firm is *compelled* to bid for government contracts or public subsidies. SD/L governments which shy away from setting such conditions (whose ripple effects through the economy can be prodigious) are simply abandoning one of the principal tools available to them as holders of public power.

Democratic public enterprise

The terms of public and private enterprise are coming to acquire new ideological significance for the labour movement. Public enterprise is no longer associated with a notion of giant, State-owned bureaucratic monoliths, but instead with a range of efficient and frequently quite small public corporations, capitalized from public funds, and providing all manner of useful infrastructural and service functions. Private enterprise, too, is not necessarily associated with giant firms like IBM, Ford or GM, but with small businesses that are seen as being useful providers of employment, responding efficiently to local needs, amenable to democratic management and control, and providing a framework for dynamic technological innovation.

It used to be thought in the labour movement that the only way in which workers could exercise influence over the economy was through expropriation of the capitalists (i.e. major shareholders and owners of firms) with their assets being taken into 'public', i.e. state ownership. This view, of course, carried with it an implication of bloody pitched battles, for it could hardly be expected that capitalists would hand over their assets voluntarily. But there are democratic alternatives to such expropriation. Purchase by the State is one option. The use of collective investment funds, financed out of industry or profit taxes, is another one (discussed below) which has greater mobilizing potential. Another option is the channelling of public funds into newly-formed public enterprises run along industrial democratic lines.

The company law already provides the category needed for such ventures—it is the company 'limited by guarantee' (as distinct from the usual company 'limited by share'). Such a structure allows a group of people, in this case a government, to form a venture for a particular purpose, spelt out in the company's Articles of Association; form a Board of Directors; and capitalize it with public funds. The entity then operates in a commercial fashion, under the control of its Board, but not subject to the pressures of having to pay dividends to shareholders. In fact, all profits can be ploughed back to the enterprise, after taxes and charges have been deducted.

There is nothing particularly 'socialist' about such public enterprises: indeed many are started or cheerfully operated by right-wing governments. But they are decidedly *democratic,* and offer, when SD/L governments are in power, scope for establishing a democratic form of enterprise which can provide a model for the private sector, and also act as a market disciplining force in the area of its operations.

The mechanism of a public corporation whose shares are owned by government, provides an extremely efficient means of achieving the goals that SD/L governments have traditionally sought through grants, subsidies or pressures of various kinds. Moreover, they do not constitute a drain on public resources (i.e. taxes), since they interact with the private sector and obtain a return on their services. If such an enterprise goes bankrupt, this is an indication either of very bad management, or of a decline in the demand for the sort of services or products it is supplying.[19]

Democratic public enterprise that is commercially successful has another strategic value, and that is as a base from which to argue for a dynamic public sector, and against the more simple-minded of the 'privatization' initiatives that have been advanced, and acted on, in the past ten years.

Workers' co-operatives

Workers' co-operatives represent an advanced phase of social ownership and control of productive economic resources. In most OECD countries they have enjoyed widespread support in the 1970s and have become consolidated in the 1980s.

Workers' cooperatives are the living embodiment of the practicability of a democratic economy combined with workers' self-management. They are tender shoots in an extremely hostile competitive capitalist environment, and they need to be nurtured with all due care by the labour movement, particularly when SD/L governments are in office and can offer them public assistance in getting started.

The best example of worker co-operatives in action is provided by the Mondragon group in the Basque country of Spain.[20] There are strong worker co-operative sectors in France and Italy.[21]

But in most Anglo-Saxon countries—and in Australia—they have barely got off the ground. Perhaps their neglect is due to radical socialists having their eyes glued to the State (what I call *'fetishization of politics'*) to the neglect of the workplace; perhaps it is because of the hostility of trade unions to something they feared and misunderstood. In any case, there is evidence that the new interest in, and support for, worker co-operatives is better based than previous efforts. A whole new generation of such co-operatives has sprung up in the US and elsewhere since the 1970s.[22]

The support for workers' co-operatives (or 'employee ownership') is not based on the hope that the co-operative sector might one day grow to become the whole economy, for this would be to delude ourselves.[23] There is no such mechanism for expansion in the co-operative sector. Rather the reason for support is that it provides a living laboratory for the development of new, socially responsible modes of organization and management, and a demonstration that such innovations are compatible with commercial viability.

SD/L government support for worker co-operatives needs to be vigorous, but also appropriate. The life of co-operators is not easy; failures are all too common. Lack of management expertise can be just as damaging as lack of capital.[24] It is in responding to these issues that the SD/L movement can liberate itself from its somewhat primitive understanding of private enterprise and its potential for democratization.

Democratization of work organization

Ultimately, the best safeguard of a democratized workplace is a form of work organization that demands responsible, autonomous, skilled and group-based worker input to decision-making. In the absence of this, attempts to democratize the management hierarchy of firms will always be constrained. It was the dominance of Taylorist work organization under Fordism that stunted the development of 'industrial democracy' and 'Quality of Work Life' initiatives in the 1960s and 1970s. It is the relaxing of this constraint that has generated a series of post-Fordist initiatives that will become dominant in the 1990s.

The paradigm of Associative Democracy suggests that the reorganization of work is not a matter for government regulation, but for direct negotiation between employers and unions. Such negotiations are now actively taking place—but not without considerable resistance, for the formulation of restructuring and efficiency agreements takes both unions and employers into novel regions, uncharted by previous Fordist conceptions of industrial relations.

Workers are understandably suspicious of such initiatives. A system that has rigidly *excluded* their input in the past, cannot be reversed overnight. Confidence in their ability to contribute to decisions needs to be carefully nurtured, particularly by their unions. The process of democratization of the workplace needs to be taken one step at a time, and has to build, in the first instance, on workers' concrete experience of joint determination structures.

For example, the great gains made by unions in Europe and North America in the 1970s, and in Australia in the 1980s, in negotiating improved conditions of worker health and safety, provide just such a *concrete experience.* The union approach to this issue represents an abrupt break with the previous approach which focused on victim blaming (exhorting the 'careless worker' to work safely) and on the exclusive right of professional experts to determine objectively 'safe' conditions of work. Unions have forced a genuine democratization of the issue, through insisting on the principle that those who run the risks must be involved, collectively through their unions, in evaluating these risks.

In Australia, I have been impressed with the great progress made by unions in the 1980s in negotiating a consultative framework at workplace level within which health and safety questions may be addressed as a *collective issue,* between employer and workers organized in their unions. These agreements establish the principle that evaluation of risks to health and safety and the measures needed to control them, will be matters for joint determination and negotiation. Through them, employers recognize the legitimacy of union-appointed health and safety representatives, together with the rights and powers they need in order to perform their roles effectively (e.g. the rights to inspect the workplace, to receive hazard information, to prevent continuation of unsafe work). The agreements stipulate that all health and safety matters that would formerly have been raised by a worker individually with a supervisor, will henceforth be channelled through the worker's health and safety representative, ensuring that such matters are dealt with on a collective rather than an individual basis. Furthermore, the agreements establish joint union–management health and safety committees at workplace level, company level and industry level as appropriate. Their constitution and terms of reference are spelt out in the agreements. Their functions are stipulated to be those of review (e.g. reviewing any disagreements that may have occurred between a health and safety representative and a supervisor) and of initiating the development of codes of practice and standards needed to enable work to proceed safely. In this sense, they function in the same manner as Parliamentary committees with their power to review legislation. Health and safety representatives are accountable to defined 'constituencies' of workers exposed to similar hazards, again in the same way that Members of Parliament are accountable to their constituents.[25]

Health and safety agreements thereby represent an irreversible democratization of work organization. Evaluation of proposed technological changes with regard to their hazards to health, can be expected to evolve logically into wider evaluation of their effects on the labour process as a whole, and from there, to their effects on the economy and society.

The next step towards workplace democracy focuses on questions of work organization. It moves beyond what may be seen as a *defensive* initiative to protect workers' health and safety (something clearly in the workers' interest but not immediately in the employer's) to the joint determination on a collective basis of the way in which work will be performed. It thus encompasses questions of productivity and efficiency, and through these, profitability.

As in the case of health and safety agreements, the aim is not to *solve* the issues of work organization in a single written document, but to establish the workplace *structures* and *procedures* which bring the matters explicitly under joint determination. The issues can be tackled on a day-to-day basis by job delegates servicing a defined constituency of workers, and policy questions and review of disputes can be addressed by joint workplace committees meeting regularly.

The labour movement has taken this process farthest in

Sweden. A whole series of workplace democracy initiatives were enacted in the 1970s, mostly of an umbrella character, designed to establish a framework for plant level negotiation. The most far-reaching of these was the Co-determination Act of 1976, giving local trade unions the right to information concerning their company's production, finances, investment plans and personnel policies. Under this Act, unions have the right to request and review relevant books and accounts. The Act also provides for consultation and negotiation to take place prior to any change that will substantially affect working conditions or terms of employment. The Act is thus a legislative generalization of many technological change and industry restructuring agreements, and is designed to facilitate the negotiation of further such agreements. The Act was virtually the last passed by the SD government before falling from office in 1976, when it went into six years of opposition. Significantly, the Act itself was not withdrawn by the ensuing conservative government, but agreements under the Act's umbrella were not easily forthcoming in the new conservative political environment.[26] From this experience two points of general relevance can be drawn. Co-determination measures depend for their success on an SD/L government being in office; movements excluded from government rightly attach the highest priority to regaining it. Even more fundamentally, the Co-determination Act has revealed the limits to any process of reform that remains within the ambit of industrial relations, and does not seek to 'trespass' in the broader domain of the company law. This is why co-determination measures need to be complemented by the democratization of company incorporation procedures.

In my view, it is around the issue of union involvement that the politics of industrial democratization will be fought in the 1990s. There is likely to be a determined drive by elements amongst the employers, backed by the New Right, to achieve flexibility in the disposition of labour and autonomy of worker input through by-passing unions altogether, and encouraging the formation of a skilled elite who see themselves as having nothing in common with their fellow workers. This is the thinking behind the drive to form individualized company suggestion schemes, quality circles, and financial incentive systems such as share issues and productivity bonuses.

The challenge for unions in this new environment is to accommodate the moves towards greater flexibility, while continuing to provide a collective expression of workers' interests.

The trade unions that survive are likely to be oriented much more towards servicing their members through technical advice and assistance, rather than acting as a cash-box for the conduct of long drawn-out industrial warfare campaigns. With the new workplace comes, necessarily, a new union.

3.2 DEMOCRATIZATION OF CAPITAL

The oldest and most fundamental dream of the labour movement, going back to the time of the founders of socialism in the nineteenth century, has been to bring productive assets and resources which found their way into private hands, under some form of public control.[27] This was theorized as a process of 'socialization' of capital, and as such it appears as the basic goal of Labour and Social Democratic parties around the world.

For such a fundamental category, the process of socialization has been subjected to remarkably little critical discussion. In the period leading up to the Second World war, socialization seems to have been understood as a one-off 'expropriation' of capital assets (with or without compensation). Social control thus became identified with State ownership, which was to be achieved via nationalization.

It is now widely agreed that this route to socialization has turned out to be a disappointment for the labour movement.[28] Exclusive public control of enterprises and even of entire industries, via state ownership, has not been found to lead, necessarily, to greater worker influence, either at workplace level or at the level of Boards of Directors. This has forced a critical rethinking of the notion of 'socialization', and of the means available for achieving it.

An alternative approach is directed at the question of profit-sharing, and the accumulation thereby of capital funds under social control. This gets at the essence of nineteenth century dreams of socialization. Related approaches include those of collectivization of a portion of wages, or of some other economic category, such as rents. I would argue that these are the approaches which are compatible with our notion of 'associative democracy', and which are likely to secure greater social influence than did previous efforts via nationalization.

Internationally, the Social Democratic and Labour (SD/L) movement now has extensive experience of collective capital formation schemes of various kinds. Funds that fall within this general category can be said to include:

- pension/superannuation funds—financed out of wages and normally controlled jointly by unions and employers;
- wage funds—financed as forced savings out of wages, to be used for investments;
- development funds—financed out of taxes on profits or other economic categories (such as imports) and normally operated under tripartite control;
- wage earner funds—equity holdings accumulated through collective profit sharing, and under union control;
- training funds—financed directly by firms but with expenditure under joint control (e.g. Renewal Funds in Sweden);
- social funds—financed out of taxes or levies on specific activities or sectors (e.g. work environment research and improvement, press diversification, education).

These collective democratic forms of financial participation by employees need to be distinguished from individualized worker shareholding schemes. There is a long liberal tradition of fostering such distributed shareholding schemes, going back to the nineteenth century. It is a tradition which is very much alive in the current spate of Employee Stock Ownership Plans (ESOPs) which have swept the US; and in talk of the 'share economy' where workers take part of their reward in the form of individual shareholdings.

Collective funds, on the other hand, financed out of profits or by direct levies, can be viewed as case studies in the democratization, or socialization, of capital. They bring the investment process under some degree of social influence, not *indirectly,* via parliamentary or government influence, but *directly,* through membership of the Board controlling the Fund. It is in this sense that the democratization of capital takes its place within a wider paradigm of economic or associative democracy.

In this section, we provide a survey of the experience obtained to date in achieving structures of financial participation, to illustrate how widely the notion has spread, and how it represents a feasible alternative path to socialization. We examine the establishment of capital funds from first principles, looking at the options involved and the arguments for and against them. Finally we look at the political implications of opting for a strategy of collective capital formation.

Experience with collective capital formation

Collective funds can be established in different ways, depending on the short-and long-term goals guiding the initiative. Their operation, and their democratic potential, varies according to the options taken. Hence we need to identify the principal criteria governing the design and operation of funds, and establish some preferences, without becoming dogmatic.

Firstly, the goals for which funds are established are varied. Karlsson (1983) identified four quite clear objectives which unions and SD/L parties have pursued in Europe, as being:

- wage policy considerations—use of funds to ensure that excess profits generated by moderate wage policies are in fact channelled into productive investment;
- equalizing distribution of wealth—use of funds to effect a redistribution of capital in favour of employees;
- job creation—use of funds as an alternative means of maintaining employment levels;
- industrial and economic democracy—use of funds to enhance the influence of employees in the decisions taken within firms.[29]

In the way that I have defined the term 'collective capital formation', a fifth objective needs to be added to these:

- social policy considerations—use of funds to achieve social goals such as maintaining diversity in the press, promoting training and research, and underwriting costs of improving the workplace environment.

Secondly, a number of criteria may be identified which enter into the design of collective funds, and affect their operation. Eight such criteria may be listed as follows:

- *financing* of funds—whether they be derived from profits, wages, or some other economic category;
- *holdings* in the funds—as equity in firms, or as cash and securities;
- *scope* of the funds—limited to a single firm, sector or region, or national in scope;
- *ownership* of funds—shares owned individually or collectively;
- *expenditure* of funds' income—spent on retirement benefits, or for other purposes;
- *investments* by funds—according to prudential or social considerations;
- *control* over funds—whether this be tripartite, bipartite, union control, or public control via some other mechanism;

- *operation* of funds—according to the form of interventions in capital and securities markets.

Demarcation of these criteria illuminates the sometimes confused history of attempts by unions and SD/L parties to establish collective funds. We shall look briefly at this history, utilizing these eight criteria that we have identified.

Pension/Superannuation Funds

Historically, superannuation funds have provided the main vehicle through which trade unions become involved in the collective control of capital. Frequently they were established as an employer initiative in order to provide post-retirement income for employees; their capacity to democratize investment is a secondary, albeit important, characteristic.

Prior to being seen by the unions as an 'industrial issue', and therefore subject to negotiation, pension funds grew up in a haphazard way, covering some occupations and not others, and offering remarkably variable retirement benefits. Some schemes lacked elementary protection (inadequate portability or vesting) and some were little more than a cheap source of finance for an employer, funded out of workers' wages. The process of bringing these funds under some form of collective worker influence has been long and hard.

In the US, pension plans originated in the nineteenth century. In a comprehensive study, *Pension Funds and Economic Power,* Paul Harbrecht noted that:

> The early attitude of employers toward pension plans was [that] pensions were gifts to their workers in recognition of "long and faithful service" and that no legal rights were thereby given to employees who became beneficiaries of a plan.[30]

Funds grew, particularly in the 1930s after the Depression, when the new Congress of Industrial Organizations (CIO) unions pushed for retirement benefits, and the US Congress legislated to allow employers to claim their contributions to funds as a tax deduction. Widely publicized abuses occurred, such as at South Bend, Indiana, in 1964, when the Studebaker Corporation closed down and terminated the pension fund, leaving workers deprived of their contributions. On the other hand, the Teamsters Union used its own large pension fund to finance gambling casinos. Legislative protection of funds was enacted firstly in the Welfare and Pension Plans Disclosure Act of 1958, and then more comprehensively in the Employee Retirement Income Security Act 1974.

Ownership and control of pension funds in the US is still not settled, but the view of them as 'deferred wages' got a big boost by a 1949 decision of the Supreme Court, upholding a ruling of the National Labour Relations Board that 'this type of wage enhancement or increase, no less than any other, becomes an integral part of the entire wage structure'.[31]

Pension funds have grown to an enormous size; it is estimated that by the end of the 1980s, they will account for *one half* of all capital raised in the US.[32] This phenomenon has led some authors to talk erroneously of 'pension fund socialism' (Drucker, 1976). In practice, there is little union control over these huge funds, unless by collective agreement.

Pension funds have grown at a similar astonishing rate in Europe—but often under joint employer-trade union control from the outset through collective bargaining agreement. Most countries now have extensive schemes in place. It suffices to look at the developments in Sweden. Up to the 1950s, there was a modest government-paid flat-rate pension benefit. A new proposal set forth by the union peak council (LO) in the early 1950s called for dramatically increased, earnings-related benefits to be funded primarily by employer contributions, which could accumulate in Funds whose Boards would be composed of representatives of employers, unions and government. This mandatory pension system—called ATP—was endorsed by the ruling Social Democratic Party (SAP). It dominated politics until an election was called over the issue in 1958. The SAP won this election, and legislation creating the ATP was passed the next year. The funds began operating in 1960. There were restrictions on the scope of their investments; for example they were not allowed to own shares.

By 1970 the ATP funds provided fifty-five per cent of the net new financing of housing, and sixty-five per cent of the net new capital for the business sector.[33] While the ATP's three funds were thus becoming a major force in the Swedish economy, the LO started pressing for their resources to be used to provide venture capital for new, innovative enterprises. After an LO-led campaign, the SAP government passed legislation in 1973 establishing a Fourth ATP fund, to deal only in equities (rather than bonds and other liquid securities). This Fourth Fund was seen as a vehicle for providing unions with economic leverage via *owner-*

ship of firms. By 1980, the Fourth Fund owned 2.5 per cent of all Swedish stock, and accounted for a healthy proportion of the net new inflow of capital into the stockmarket. It was the largest single stockholder in a dozen companies, although it rarely takes the step of placing representatives on Boards of Directors; in these cases it shares its stock voting rights with local unions representing workers in the companies in which it has taken equity. These four national tripartite Funds clearly represent a more manageable proposition for Swedish unions than do the half million or so pension funds for the unions in the US. There is power in national consolidation.

No comparable country has taken union influence over pension funds as far as Sweden, but that country's example has sparked emulators elsewhere. In Australia, for example, in the 1980s the union movement launched a belated drive for superannuation (pension) funds modelled on the Swedish system, to be established industry by industry. The national union federation (ACTU) advanced in 1985 a well-argued proposal for a three per cent productivity based wage increase to be paid by employers into jointly-controlled superannuation funds. This plan was rejected by the employers and the Australian Conciliation and Arbitration Commission, and the issue has subsequently been fought out industry by industry. Union participation in the management of these funds is central to the campaign.[34]

In terms of the criteria identified above, pension and superannuation funds are collective funds in which:

- contributions are wage-related;
- holdings are liquid cash, which can be invested in stocks and securities (subject to restrictions, such as apply to the Swedish first, second and third ATP funds);
- the scope is national;
- ownership is strictly vested in the individual account holders, but is effectively collective;
- the funds generate income, which is used for retirement benefits;
- prudential considerations govern investment behaviour;
- control over funds is normally tripartite.

Useful as pension/superannuation funds have been in schooling unions and SD/L parties in the intricacies of finance, their design essentially limits them to the task for which they were established, namely to provide deferred income to their members. Attempts to push them too far in other directions, for example to play the role of investment source in new manufacturing enterprises, has led to disappointment.[35]

Employee share ownership schemes

Workers as shareholders in their enterprises is an idea with philanthropic roots in the nineteenth century. In Britain, for example, some Quaker capitalists like Rowntree turned their firms over to worker-controlled trusts, and this practice has been followed elsewhere on a small scale. Liberal doctrine has long advocated the distribution of *individual* shareholdings to workers in their firms, as a form of individualized economic democracy to complement political democracy.[36]

Share ownership schemes generally come in the form of:

- share option plans—where the firm offers employees, individually, options to acquire shares at a discount rate;
- share acquisition plans—where the firm offers employees shares directly, sometimes with restrictions on their disposability;
- unit trust plans—where the firm offers shares to employees indirectly, via a trust holding.

In all these variations, the shares are held or offered to workers as individuals, not as a group. The goal of such schemes is frequently to enhance employee loyalty to the firm, and to undermine support for the unions—although the schemes can take on a radically different character if they are negotiated by the unions themselves.[37]

In practice, systematic employee share ownership schemes have made most practical headway in France and in the US. Under the Gaullist government in France an ordinance on financial participation was passed in 1967, obliging companies employing more than one hundred workers to distribute a proportion of their profits to their workers. This was an umbrella ordinance, providing a framework in which joint agreements or contracts could be developed. By 1981, a total of 10 000 agreements had been concluded, covering five million workers.[38] In other European countries, such as the Netherlands and Denmark, tax incentives are held out to firms that are prepared to offer workers, individually, a share in profits in the form of equity. But the rate of take-up has been slow; sometimes such schemes are linked to related savings schemes established to mobilize investment resources. In Britain, the Finance Acts of 1978 and 1980 allow undertakings to issue shares to their workforce under a profit-sharing plan approved by the tax authorities, with a ceiling being put on such transfers (set at 1000 pounds in 1980). According to a survey conducted by the Industrial Participation Association, apparently very few firms have taken up this half-hearted option.[39] British Liberal Party policy calls for national legislation on the French model, offering tax concessions to firms providing individual shareholdings to their workers.

The greatest progress on this front has been made in the US, with a variety of savings plans, stock bonus plans, and *employee stock ownership plans* (ESOPs)—all of which are aimed at making employees joint owners of the company. By 1985, a total of 7000 companies had enrolled nearly ten million workers in ESOPs; and the number of new plans is increasing at ten per cent per year, due largely to tax incentives voted by Congress in 1984 under the Deficit Reduction Act.[40]

It is tax concessions, rather than any intrinsic social merit, that explain the phenomenal rise of ESOPs. That they may have little to do with worker control became clear in the 1985 takeover battle at Phillips Petroleum Corporation in the US, where management proposed an ESOP to its workforce primarily to entrench itself against takeover. Since then, according to respectable sources such as *Business Week*, a number of leveraging scandals have surfaced, further undermining the public image of ESOPs.

The essential point, for our purposes, is that all these worker shareholding schemes, particularly ESOPs, are aimed at workers as *individuals*, and not as members of a collectivity. While they may have some utility in giving workers and unions a more sophisticated understanding of financial matters, their capacity to promote collective capital formation is low (unless they are shaped directly by union-employer negotiations).

Unions, however, have developed their own proposals for financial participation by workers, and it is to these we shall now turn.

Employee investment funds

The idea of translating individual-oriented employee share-ownership schemes into collective funds under collective control (via trade unions), seems to have arisen first in Germany in the 1950s, in the form of the Gleitze plan.[41] Research continued to the point where a plan was adopted by the union peak council, the DGB, in 1968. This plan arose in the context of the intense debate that occurred in post-war Germany, over the distribution of wealth, culminating in the passage of the Capital Accumulation

Act of 1961, revised and supplemented in 1965 and again in 1970, aimed at stimulating savings by means of subsidies and channelling a portion of a worker's wages into investment. The specific proposal for an employee investment fund has not subsequently been pursued with much vigour by the trade unions in Germany; they have concentrated on other forms of co-determination (e.g. joint worker-director Boards of companies) and on trade union-owned enterprises.[42]

The idea of collective capital formation was next taken up in Austria, where the peak union body, the OGB, published a discussion paper in 1967.[43] Subsequently the OGB considered reports at its 7th and 8th Congresses, in 1971 and 1975. After reviewing various options, a proposal to form a *Central Capital Formation Fund for Workers* was adopted, financed out of existing reserve funds which companies were obliged to maintain to cover redundancy and end-of-contract payments to workers. The proposal then lapsed.

In the Netherlands, a proposal for profit-sharing, combining a comprehensive collective system and a company-based system, was advanced by the social democrat government in 1975. This was watered down by the non-socialist government in 1977, but revived again as the VAD scheme in 1980, providing for economic democracy for employees via the establishment of funds financed from companies' 'super-profits'. This idea was crushed by the non-socialist successor government in 1983.

In Denmark the debate on wage-earner funds goes back to the 1960s when proposals for economic democracy were being advanced. A report to the union federation (LO) conference in 1971 suggested the establishment of a wage-earner profit and investment fund, financed by wage-related employers' contributions and managed by unions. The workers would be entitled to individual shares, and they could dispose of these after a certain time. A Bill to implement the first stage of this 'employees' investment and divided fund' was introduced in the Danish parliament in 1973. This lapsed with the defeat of the government, and minority governments have not been strong enough since to revive it.

In Sweden the debate was taken up later than elsewhere, but with somewhat more determination.[44] The 1971 conference of the LO commissioned a report from a working group chaired by LO economist Rudolf Meidner. This was put to the 1976 LO conference, and adopted.[45] Two streams of development flowed into this exercise. One was the experience with jointly controlled pension funds, which emerged as the major political issue of the 1950s, but which had become established, as we saw above, as major investment sources in the 1970s. The other was the 'solidaristic' wages policy pursued by the unions through centralized negotiation with employers. This ensured that workers doing similar jobs received similar pay, no matter what may have been the 'capacity to pay' of the firm they worked for. The outcome in the years of rapid economic growth was that some successful firms received 'super profits', and the unions were anxious to see these ploughed back into productive rather than speculative investment. This was how it came about that at the 1971 union confederation (LO) conference, resolutions were adopted demanding that excess profits generated by the solidaristic wages policy be channelled to organs under the collective control of wage earners or the public, in order to increase the influence of wage earners in their firms.

Rejecting higher levels of company taxation as being inimical to economic growth, the 1976 Meidner report favoured the creation of a series of 'wage earners' funds' which would gradually secure to workers collective control over their firms. Shares were to be issued in proportion to a company's profits; and the funds could encompass a number of firms. The aim was not to create large executive agencies that would, after ten or twenty years, be able to run firms, but to increase the influence of wage earners over their working life. The idea was that as the funds acquired an increasing proportion of the equity in a firm, they would be able to nominate directors to the Board, subject to the consent of the unions representing workers in that firm or group of firms. (The voting rights were to be fifty per cent to local unions and fifty per cent to the funds.) The beauty of this scheme was that with one proposal, many of the labour movement's objectives were advanced; the funds would promote equality and industrial democracy; they would reduce the trend to capital accumulation in a few hands; they would redistribute wealth; and they would complement the solidaristic wages policy.

Meidner published a table showing how Swedish workers could take over their companies in twenty, twenty-five, thirty-five or seventy-five years depending on the levels at which the profits tax were set (twenty per cent down to five per cent). This table concentrated minds wonderfully.

The funds proposal developed considerable momentum in the labour movement, and came before the triennial congress of the SAP in 1978 where it was accepted in principle but with some modifications. By this time the SAP was in opposition, having lost the 1976 election (on the issue of nuclear power—the SAP supporting it—but some commentators say because of LO support for the funds). In the 1979 election the funds were a central issue, and the propaganda against the funds helped to defeat the SAP. This led to a major rethinking of the 1978 LO–SAP proposal—and to further modifications of Meidner's original design. Since then, there has been no further attempt to implement the Meidner plan in Sweden; it has been overtaken by the Edin plan for regional funds, which were established in 1984.[46]

While wage earner funds have not been established (to my knowledge) in their pure form, nevertheless they represent a model of socialization of capital which remains on the political agenda. In terms of the criteria identified above, they may be described as funds in which:

- contributions are profits-related;
- fund holdings are composed of equity created directly in groups of firms;
- ownership is collective, in the hands of the trade unions;
- income from the equity holdings can be spent on a variety of union-related activities (such as research);
- the funds do not themselves constitute a new source of investment.

The significance of the Meidner proposals was expressed by Korpi, writing in 1978:

> The LO proposal on wage earners' funds may mark a turning point in the strategy of the Swedish labour movement. This proposal indicated that the collective power resources and social consciousness of the workers had developed to a point where the dominance of capital in the sphere of production was no longer accepted.
>
> The great strength of the LO and TCO proposals for wage earners' funds is the idea that private firms, in proportion to their profits, emit shares to collectively controlled funds. This principle allows for a gradual transferring of economic power from private capital to democratically governed collectives in ways which will minimize disturbances in the economy. Legislation for this purpose implies that work as well as capital can give legitimate power in the economic sphere. Such a principle of justice will probably find widespread support among wage-earners.[47]

While this was no doubt true, the Swedish experience in the decade since then of successive attempts to implement the Meidner plan, has been disappointing. The initiative must probably now come from elsewhere.

Training and development funds

Funds under social control to facilitate investment and economic development are now a well-established phenomenon. Prior to unions and SD/L parties becoming interested in them, non-socialist governments have had frequent recourse to levies and establishment of funds, particularly to smooth out fluctuations in the trading of agricultural commodities. These are still a feature of agricultural support systems, notoriously so in the Common Agricultural Policy of the EEC.

Funds with similar sorts of purposes have been established in manufacturing industry. For example, the Labour Party in the UK was elected in 1974 with a platform commitment to establish a National Enterprise Board, with powers to invest in emerging areas of industrial and technological development. The NEB was duly established, but as we saw above its operations were considerably at variance from those envisaged by its architects. The principle has been carried forward in Britain by various local authorities, such as the Greater London Council, which established the Greater London Enterprise Board (GLEB) in the early 1980s. Although the GLC was abolished by the Thatcher government in 1985, the GLEB continues to exist. Development corporations on the NEB model now abound; suffice to mention the Australian Industries Development Corporation as a typical example.

All these public industrial investment funds share the characteristic that they are financed, in the first instance, out of public revenue, and not out of an industry levy. Once established, they can grow through their own investment activity, but there is no sense of profit-sharing or industry levy in their formation. Hence the scope of their intervention remains limited.

A new species of investment fund has been developed in Sweden, in the wake of the Meidner plan. While in opposition, the SAP, together with the LO, came out in 1981 in favour of a series of regionally based industry investment funds, financed by a combination of a payroll tax and a profits levy.

The build-up of these funds was to be quite slow—at the rate of around one per cent of the value of all quoted shares per year. It was envisaged that the funds would be controlled on a tripartite basis by regional boards that were initially to be appointed by the government, leaving open the option as to whether they should in the longer term be directly elected. The majority of board members were to be employee representatives.

At the time of the 1982 election, when polls taken indicated to the SAP that there was not enough understanding of the proposal, the SAP leader, Olof Palme, announced three further limitations on the proposed funds; they would only collect money to 1990; there would be a forty per cent ceiling on holdings in any one company for all five funds combined; and they would be expected to yield a real return (over inflation) of at least three per cent on their investments, to be paid into the ATP fund system.

On reassuming office, the SAP government commissioned three reports from technical experts to provide a foundation for the funds. These reports were published and a Bill was presented to Parliament in November 1983. Five regional funds were actually established at the beginning of 1984.

Each of the five funds is able to invest on the stock market, using money raised more or less equally from a payroll tax and from a special annual profit tax set to operate for the six years 1984 to 1990. Each of the five funds is managed by a board comprising nine members appointed by the government, of whom five represent employees' interests. The central employers federation (SAF), has refused to co-operate, and indeed actively opposes the scheme.

The SAP has avoided ideological debate over the funds, and emphasised instead their economic overtones—such as the contribution they can make to the country's investment programme, particularly in micro-electronics. Their eventual contribution to the socialization of capital is not likely to be great, but they have established the feasibility of forming collective funds under social control directly from a levy on profits. This is their key criterion, which is likely to be emulated elsewhere.

For example, in France, following the election of the Mitterand socialist government in 1981, proposals were advanced by the unions for such an investment fund. In March 1982, the Minister for Economics and Finance, Jacques Delors, issued a statement proposing the creation of employee funds via collective bargaining, to be financed either from employer or employee contributions, and to be managed for industrial investment purposes jointly by unions and employers. This led to a favourable reception by the socialist-oriented union confederation CFDT, in 1983. The communist-oriented CGT did not respond favourably, apparently because of the traditional union fear that involvement of unions in the management of such funds would suck them into the capitalist system. After 1984, the proposal was not proceeded with.

In Australia, following a visit to Sweden by a high-ranking union group in 1986, the peak council, the ACTU, proposed a National Development Fund to be financed mainly from superannuation funds, but also by a tax on imports, thus addressing itself to balance of payments problems (ACTU/TDC, 1987). This proposal was the subject of intense discussion in Australia in 1988.

A further departure in the practice of forming collective funds was registered in Sweden in 1985, with the establishment of *Renewal Funds*. These are financed from a profits levy imposed in 1985, to be used by companies for skills formation and R & D projects that are to be jointly agreed with the relevant unions. By October 1986, some 6000 companies had placed more than Skr 5 billion in renewal accounts into the Swedish Central Bank, and a year later the tripartite National Industrial Board had approved expenditure of Skr 1.3 billion on educational, research and various developmental activities.[49]

The renewal Funds in Sweden, and the proposed National Development Fund in Australia, represent a point of departure for the international labour movement. These are collective capital funds oriented explicitly towards intervention in industry, at the level of the enterprise. The capital is mobilized through a profits levy imposed by a government sympathetic to the unions, but justified by its use to further national economic and industrial objectives.

Social funds

Finally, we should consider funds which are targeted at specific sectors to achieve specific social goals.

For example, in Norway and Sweden, diversity of the press has been enhanced (as a basic democratic goal) through funds financed by a tax on advertising revenue.[50] In Sweden this fund is controlled by a tripartite Subsidies Council, which disburses assistance funds to newspaper operators to keep some titles alive, and to launch new ones. Since 1976, no fewer than seventeen newspapers have been launched with assistance in this way—with only one failure up to 1985.[51] This model has been translated into proposals for a Media Enterprise Board in the UK, and a Media Diversification Board in Australia.[52]

As another example, Sweden created the *Work Environment Fund,* under the Co-determination Act of 1977, financed by a payroll levy on Swedish industry. The Fund is managed by a tripartite Board, and supports research into the identification and control of work environment hazards.

Training levies which are channelled into a public fund to be used to support skills formation programmes for workers generally, are yet another form of generalized collective social fund.

These examples provide a further perspective on collective capital formation, emphasizing explicit social goals that can be realized through following such a strategy.

Where then are these initiatives taking the labour movement, and how should such financial participation programmes be systematized and theorized?

Approach to a theory of collective capital formation

What distinguishes all these funds, where they are financed out of some profit sharing principle, is that they constitute a form of socialization, not of the 'capital stock' as such (as in expropriation and nationalization) but of the 'flow of capital'. The strategy is to generate social capital in the future, by tapping the flow of funds released by economic activity, rather than to seek to appropriate capital accumulated in the past.[53] In this manner, prevailing property relations are not disturbed. As a strategic option, 'socialization of the flow' via collective investment funds, captures the spirit of gradualism: it is utterly transformative in the long term, yet feasible and politically moderate in the short term.

The design of collective funds should draw on the experience obtained to date, as well as theoretical analysis of the effects of choosing one option rather than another from among the eight criteria identified above. We can make a start on this process in this section, taking the criteria one by one.

1 Contributions to funds

All existing pension or superannuation schemes are financed by wage-related contributions, i.e. they are calculated as a proportion of the wage bill. The Meidner plan and the Renewal Funds, on the other hand, are explicitly couched in terms of contributions calculated as a proportion of *profits.* There are advantages and disadvantages associated with each approach.

Wage-related contributions are certainly simpler to administer, for there is little ambiguity about the total wages bill (apart from questions of direct and indirect costs). They make it difficult for employers to evade their responsibilities. However they have the disadvantage that they act in the same way as a payroll tax (in fact they are a form of payroll tax) and hence appear to employers to drive up the cost of labour *vis-à-vis* capital. This skews investment decisions away from the use of labour towards the use of machinery and equipment, and can even increase unemployment. A related effect is that wage-linked funds, if tied to the companies from which they derive their assets (see point 3), will become larger and more influential in labour-intensive rather than capital-intensive industries, i.e. in sunset rather than sunrise industries. This does not help unions secure influence over emerging high-technology areas of the economy.

Profit-related contributions are technically much more difficult to administer. Their operating rules are of necessity couched in the details of the company law, taking account of share issues, voting classes, share valuation, capital depreciation practices, calculation of profits by multinational companies, and other matters. The issues are dealt with admirably in Meidner's report to the 1976 Swedish LO congress, but need to be replicated country by country to take account of national company law and accounting procedures. Despite these difficulties, particularly the problem of multinational corporations reporting artificially low profits, the profits-related scheme has the *logical superiority* that it is designed to attack highly efficient firms whose surpluses have swelled as a result of centralized wage fixation, and where 'capacity to pay' is not taken into account in setting wage levels. A profits-related scheme also has clear advantages which outweigh the disadvantages of the wage-related approach; it skews investment decisions towards the use of labour, and offers the prospect of giving workers collective influence over the capital-intensive, high-growth, high-technology sector of the economy faster than in the older industrial sectors.

Social funds, on the other hand, are capitalized by targeting the flow of some specific economic category. For example, the press diversification funds socialize a portion of the flow of advertising expenditure. In the rural sector this is an old and well-recognized approach, as for example in the formation of 'price equalization' funds to smooth out the fluctuations in the prices of various commodities.

2 Fund holdings

All existing pension/superannuation funds are held in monetary form, and they have all the flexibility associated with money: they can be used to purchase equity shareholdings in a company, or government stock, or to make loans, or to provide venture capital. The advantage offered is flexibility—at the cost of worker identification with the fund. For in the eyes of workers, unless they have personal dealings with the fund controllers, such a monetary fund can appear to be just another chunk of capital as remote from them as a multinational bank.

Shareholding schemes, ESOPs, and the Meidner plan, on the other hand, all involve the formation of equity funds, built up through transfers of shares in a company, as a fixed proportion of its profits, into the funds. Despite their being marketable, the funds would not, in general, trade these shares (although they would become critical in any takeover situation). Equity funds represent a tangible level of ownership in the firm by its workforce. When held collectively, as in the Meidner plan, or in a Trust subject to trade union negotiation, they can be directly translated into management influence. A collective equity fund gives the workers a very real stake in the good management of the company (not for their own pecuniary interest, as in individual share ownership, but for their collective interest in future employment) and an extra incentive to insist on co-determination in all aspects of the firm's activities. It leads most directly to worker self-management.

3 Scope of the funds

All existing pension/superannuation funds are unlimited in their scope, (subject to the constraints of the Trust Deed) in the sense that they can purchase securities or shares in any firm or sector of the economy, both domestically or offshore. (Indeed, it is the speculative offshore activities of many such funds that is coming under close scrutiny.) Liberal shareholding schemes, on the other hand, provide equity for employees in one company only, namely the one in which they are employed.

The Meidner plan advocated a general scope for funds, recommending that they be set up on a sector or regional basis, with a national fund playing the role of a 'holding company'. Meidner expressly advised against single-company funds, on the grounds that they would undermine the aims of centralized wage fixation. They also suffer from the disadvantage that if the firm goes bankrupt, workers are liable not only to lose their jobs, but also their savings, in the form of collective capital assets.

An economy-wide fund is clearly very flexible. It can capture 'super' profits from individual firms, provided contributions are calculated on a proportional basis. Wherever it invests, it operates by leaving a new democratized ownership framework for worker participation. Its flexibility is offset by the advantages of worker identification with a sectoral or regional fund.

4 Ownership of funds

Although giving the appearance of being a collective fund, most pension/superannuation funds are in fact composed of their individual members' retirement benefits packages. It is the members of the fund who clearly own it (although what *control* this gives them is another matter altogether). Similarly, all liberal share distribution schemes, such as ESOPs, are based on individual worker shareholdings, with varying restrictions being placed on the ability of individuals to dispose of their shares on the open market.

The Meidner plan, by contrast, advocated a strictly *collective* form of ownership, with no individual being able to withdraw personal entitlements. Meidner insisted on this point as being fundamental, pointing out that if enough firms in the economy opted to operate profit-sharing schemes on an individual basis, then profit shares would in effect become wage and salary shares. The essence of the Meidner plan was that:

> that part of the growth in assets which accrues to the employees *remains as working capital within the enterprise.* We cannot stress this enough. The main objective would be frustrated if there were to be any withdrawals from the capital funds on a group or individual basis. To many this fundamental requirement of a system of employee investment funds may appear strange. It has sometimes been described in the debate as the expression of an authoritarian mentality which seeks to limit the free right of disposal on the part of the private individual in favour of a bureaucratically governed group. In reality, however, the choice is not between the individual's free right to dispose over a share of profits and collective power, but between illusory profit-sharing and real profit-sharing.[54]

The same considerations apply to any other monetary fund that is not designed exclusively to offer retirement benefits to individuals, such as the investment funds advocated in France by the CFDT, in Australia by the ACTU, and the Renewal Funds in Sweden.

5 Use of funds income

A well-designed pension or superannuation fund operates so that it can pay all its contractual retirement benefits to its members out of the *income* generated by its assets, rather than out of the capital of the fund itself. In this sense, a superannuation fund is a collective fund generating income to be used exclusively for retirement benefits.

But this is by no means the only sort of fund or usage of income that is available to the labour movement. All funds will generate income, whether in the form of interest payments on loans, cash deposits or debentures and securities; or in the form of dividends of equity holdings. This income can either be ploughed back into more equity or securities (a path of rapid growth) or it can be used for other purposes, such as to finance various trade union research, publishing, and leisure activities. It is in taking the latter course that the unions come to be an economic force to be reckoned with, for their activities can extend well beyond those supported out of wage and salary deducted contributions of the membership.[55] Meidner advocated this sort of expansion of union activity and he was right to do so. The significance of the Renewal Funds is that they represent a use of funds, that is under joint company-union control, for development and modernization purposes in the economy at large.

6 Investments by funds

The Meidner plan envisaged profit-shares being paid into funds by firms in the form of equity—and so the question of 'investment' of this equity does not arise. In monetary funds, on the other hand, the issue of how the funds are to be invested is critical. Many pension/superannuation funds are bound by tight regulations, or rules spelt out in their trust deed, requiring the Board to maximize returns by making 'sound' investments. This is termed 'prudential' behaviour, and it throws up very substantial policy issues for the fund members. How far should the fund go, for example, to maximize income? Presumably it would not be acceptable to invest in armaments manufacture, or in South African securities where these can be seen to uphold apartheid: but when it is a choice between speculative, high-yield investments such as in property development, versus longer term lower-yield investment in manufacturing industry, the issue for the fund managers is not so clear cut.

The key question is the margin of discretion allowed the fund managers in making investments, consistent with prudential behaviour. It is clearly not acceptable to invest the funds in some social cause and thereby jeopardize the fund income, and through it the retirement benefits of members. But some form of discretionary margin is essential if the funds are to fulfil their social potential.

Unions in the US are beginning to exploit these aspects of their pension funds, both in a negative fashion (in boycotts and union recognition battles) and in positive, interventionist fashion (such as directing funds to construction of low-cost housing, alternative energy sources, and other matters).[56] As noted above, the proposals for national development funds, and the Renewal Funds, take this process a step further in that they are explicitly targeted towards innovation and industry restructuring.

It is in this manner that collective funds offer workers a means of influencing industry policy, not just via indirect pressure (e.g. exercised through tripartite advisory committees) but *directly*, via the control of investments generated by a large fund. Such a development takes the unions down a radically new path, the implications (and dangers) of which are central to the future of unions.

7 Control of funds

The struggle for control of pension funds in the US has been going on now for over one hundred years, and is far from being resolved. In other countries, the question has been settled by direct negotiation when funds are established; it may be agreed that the funds will be controlled jointly by employer and unions, or on a tripartite basis, with representatives of government or the public being included; or even, in rare cases, by the unions alone.

The Meidner plan envisaged wage earner's funds, as funds exclusively under the control of the union. This was to counterbalance existing shareholders' control. This aspect of the proposal has its critics in the social democratic party in Sweden. Korpi for example argues that a true democratization of investment and capital would require the setting up of *citizens' funds* rather than *wage-earners' funds*. He stated, in 1978:

> According to the LO and TCO proposals, only part of the citizens, the wage-earners, are entitled to participate in the governing of the collective funds. The proposals further leave control over the governing of the funds to the internal processes within the unions. It can, however, be

argued that the "franchise" in the governing of the funds should be extended to all citizens. The specific interests of the employees, derived from their work in the production organizations, can be satisfied through rules, and legislation assuring their influence within the firm. Such a change would be a transformation of the wage-earners' funds into "citizens" funds.[57]

There is no question that a broadening of the control over collective funds makes them politically much more acceptable. It can be argued that it was insistence on *union control* of wage earner funds that led to the abandonment of the Meidner plan and its replacement by the Edin plan for regional funds in Sweden.

In practice, tripartite control is in my view quite adequate for unions to be able to exercise general influence over the economy, for example through an industry development fund. Where the object of the fund is to directly enhance collective worker influence over a firm's Board, which is the object of the Meidner plan, then full union control becomes more difficult to trade away.

8 Collective funds in capital and securities markets

Collective funds are a source of capital, which is traded on securities markets. Now, capital is conceived in current financial terms as a combination of debt and equity, with their quite different social and institutional origins and 'cultures'. Debt derives from the financial system, mainly the banks, which in turn acquire their funds from people's savings; it carries no connotations of 'control' over the business other than the sanction of foreclosure if the repayments fail. Debt attracts a return in the form of fixed 'interest' payments.

Equity on the other hand derives from the wider industrial system. It represents an explicit 'share' of the capital, carrying control to an extent laid down in the Articles of Association of the company. It attracts a return in the form of variable 'dividends' paid at the discretion of the company's Board of Directors.

In considering the role of collective funds, we must start by recognizing that the world of finance capital is rapidly changing. Already debt is international to an extent undreamt of twenty years ago. Country after country, whether under a conservative or SD/L government, has abolished exchange rate control and allowed finance to come into and go out of the country as the markets provide for. This financial 'deregulation' is a trend that probably has some way to go before it runs up against the wall of all 'free' market operations, namely bankruptcies and recession.

But the associated development, and one which has not yet received attention, is the trend to blur the difference between debt and equity, i.e. to offer 'securities' which are a hybrid between the two, and which, moreover, are international as well. The trading of shares, in other words, is bursting its current bounds where stock in 'listed' companies is bought and sold on stock exchanges via brokers. The international financial community, with its all-electronic networks, is on the threshold of creating a truly international equity market in the same way that it has already created an international market in debt. People in Australia will be able to buy shares in GM, denominated in US dollars, via a Japanese merchant bank. Financial institutions will offer securities that promise a mixed return—half fixed interest, half dependent on profits. They are already approaching this with 'variable interest deposits'. Companies seeking new capital for expansion will raise it by offering the international financial community 'securities' that give a combination of traditional rights of 'lending' and 'ownership'. This trend is called in the jargon, 'securitization'.[58]

The internationalization of debt and equity, and the blurring of the distinction between these two, presents the theory of collective capital formation with a wholly new and unexpected problem. On the one hand, it offers collective funds new possibilities on an international level. For example, a Swedish fund would be able to invest in an Australian fund, which in turn could invest in a UK fund, and so a chain of labour movement investments would be created, making these organizations potentially a dominant influence in international markets, and very difficult for a national conservative government to unravel.

On the other hand, these developments make the design and application of funds that much harder, for there are more loopholes which smart accountants and lawyers will find to avoid the legal requirements spelt out by legislation establishing the funds. The fundamental distinction maintained by Meidner between an equity and a securities fund, has come to be blurred.[59]

The politics of collective capital funds

Given this brief theoretical excursion through collective funds, how is the labour movement to formulate policies to democratize capital, and what are the likely forms of opposition?

There is in my view no single perfect form of collective capital fund. Proposals will have to be developed for specific purposes. There is much merit, for example, in the sort of National Development Funds (NDFs), financed from superannuation sources and new taxes on imports, that have been advocated by the ACTU in Australia and the CFDT in France. How could such a fund work in practice?

Legislation establishing the Fund would ensure that it be under secure democratic control, probably of a tripartite nature. The Fund would have to operate under broad guidelines laid down by the legislation; these should stipulate that a certain proportion of the Fund's holdings be channelled into socially useful but not necessarily highly profitable enterprises (although the Fund should not be required to subsidize public services which are more appropriately supported directly out of public revenue).

As the National Development Fund (NDF) accumulates assets, it would rapidly become one of the largest investors in any national economy, and as such could exert enormously powerful leverage over national investment strategy. Where the Labour movement sees a failure on the part of private capital to invest, for example in manufacturing industry, it could use its position on the Board of the NDF to channel funds into manufacturing enterprises. In each case the NDF could insist on industrial democracy and a planning agreement as the price of its assistance. These would be the prime functions and roles of the NDF from the point of view of democratizing the economy, and in this role it would complement the strategic intervention of unions at enterprise level seeking to transform work.

However the NDF would also have other desirable side effects. For example, it would play the role of a 'buffer stock' in the share market, helping to even out fluctuations in prices (in the same way that a commodity marketing board, e.g. for wheat, or milk or eggs, evens out prices in the commodity market). It would also play a role similar to that exercised in Italy by the State Holding Company, which moves in when firms are in trouble, sometimes suspending trading and keeping workers on pay, until the management problems are sorted out. All these operations could be conducted on the basis of strong industrial democracy principles, again under the influence of the labour movement representatives on the Board of the NDF.

An adequately financed NDF under democratic control would constitute an important step towards collective or social control of capital formation; it would form a key element in a labour movement paradigm of economic democracy. It could only be established by a Labour or Social Democratic government propelled by trade unions which have acquired considerable financial expertise and sophistication, through the control of superannuation funds. But if such a government were to fall from office, the NDF would pose its conservative successors with a real dilemma. They would be ideologically opposed to the Fund, and would wish to dismantle it, but this would be very difficult to do, particularly if the Fund had acquired substantial holdings in a wide variety of productive enterprises. Even if the profits tax were suspended, the Fund itself would still exist and it would continue to generate income from its investments. (The Thatcher government faced just this sort of dilemma when it proceeded to dismantle the Greater London Council—but the *Greater London Enterprise Board* established by the GLC as a local development fund continues to operate as it was set up to do, providing investment and employment in the London region.)

There is also much merit in Meidner-style sector and region-based equity funds generated by a fixed proportion of firms' profits. As Meidner argued so convincingly in his 1976 report, such a fund would operate as a very effective counterpart to more conventional employee participation/co-determination schemes—for it offers unions direct influence over companies as trustees of workers-as-shareholders.

Superannuation funds too will continue to be an important means by which unions can acquire financial sophistication, and as they grow they will become major components of the national economy, as they have in Sweden.

These sorts of developments would not only be of fundamental importance in themselves, but they have 'multiplier' effects in that they offer a totally new perspective on traditional labour movement issues. Just by way of illustration consider the issue of concentration of economic power that is of such concern now as a result of the takeover activity in recent years. There are two types of 'control' that society can place on these developments. One is an *external* control, of limiting holdings to a certain percentage, as in anti-trust legislation in the US, and anti-monopoly legislation elsewhere. This is certainly effective up to a point, although it can be eroded by a variety of strategies involving creation of new companies. In any case, it has nothing remotely 'socialist' about it.

The other form of control is an *internal*, dynamic and democratic control: to ensure, legislatively, as companies grow through takeover, that the influence of the workforce in the expanded company grows too. Through this mechanism, there will be created an equilibrium size for firms beyond which the greater resources will have to be balanced against the greater dilution of control. This is the form of control that is achieved by providing for workers to acquire *collective equity* in their own firms.

What can the objections be to the path of democratization outlined here?

From the Right, the major issue is likely to be the *collective* nature of profit-financed funds. The battle will be fought over the issue of *individual* holdings (e.g. ESOPs) versus *collective* control, with collective control exercised through trade unions being painted as anti-democratic. A clear commitment to economic democracy on the part of the SD/L parties and unions, provides a ready means of responding to these arguments. Such a commitment provides for an *extension* of democratic principles of association (via parties and unions) from the political domain proper, to the domain of the economy and industry. It represents an alternative to 'democratization' by the market.

From the Left, for some Marxian socialists it seems that the very idea of a gradualist 'socialization of the flow' is a diversion away from what they see as fundamental social change via class struggle. Thus Boris Frankel, in his otherwise remarkable book *Beyond the State*, pours cold water on the Meidner plan. In the course of a long discussion concerned with what he sees as the non-feasibility of 'alternative economic policies', he claims, specifically in relation to wage earner funds, that they are unlikely to be successful because 'private capitalists will bitterly resist the certain destruction of their power'; and the programme will only work 'as long as particular national bourgeois classes are politically weak'.[60] These are the only substantive arguments he offers. Of course all that these points do is confirm that the programme of socialization/democratization (not 'nationalization' as he calls it) of capital will be a politically fraught and bitter affair—and it will depend crucially on the attaining of political power by the democratic labour parties and the launch of a programme of economic democratization from this position of relative dominance.

Again, it is the paradigm of Associative Democracy that stresses the role that collective funds can play in providing workers' and citizens' associations with a direct involvement in shaping the economy. To secure the diversification of the press, for example, the orthodox SD/L approach would be to establish a Regulatory Commission financed out of general revenue (and hence subject to all the fiscal constraints that this implies). The alternative sketched here is to link diversification of the press with the current flows of revenue generated within the publishing and advertising industries, by tapping into these flows and creating a social fund whose outlays will then be recycled *within the same industry*. Such a fund can then be justified on quasi-'ecological' grounds, as maintaining a supply of young, independent publications which can be expected to secure the long-term health of the industry (in the same way that young trees need constantly to be planted to maintain a forest in a healthy state). The aim of maintaining a pluralist political culture, and in particular creating and re-creating a space for the expression of views by the social and labour movements, need not provide the sole political justification for such an approach.

Further, the creation of capital funds under social control provides the material basis on which alliances may be struck between the labour movement proper (i.e. SD/L parties and trade unions) and the various social movements. As we noted above, for example, a stand-off between environmentalists fighting to save native forests from logging, and trade unions fighting to save loggers' jobs, could be averted by the Board of a collective fund agreeing to invest in alternative commercial activities in logging areas (such as in 'value-adding' downstream processing of timber into wooden products and materials). This would provide the basis for a negotiated political settlement between the two movements, creating the conditions for a political alliance—with the proviso that the investments need to be made wisely with all due fiduciary precautions and subject to overall parliamentary oversight. The worst outcome for the funds would be to allow them to become sources of political patronage and pork barrelling.

It is in opening up these sorts of possibilities that the political potential of collective capital funds becomes manifest. They are an essential component of the *constructive discourse* of a renovated social democracy. Frankel's aside, in the discussion cited above, that such funds 'would hardly constitute a socialist economy' misses the point that the funds are advocated as a means of initiating a process of transformation which engages with the real, present structures of an advanced economy—not as a final form of socialism, whatever that may look like.

This brings us back to the 'socialization' yearnings of the

founders of the labour movement in the nineteenth century. They hoped to achieve a means of effecting public regulation over the economy, but they thought, in those simpler times, that the economy was transparent and could be run from a single control point. Hence 'state ownership' seemed to be unproblematic and a logical step forward. We know better now. We should keep in mind the *ends* they hoped to achieve, but modernise the *means* needed to achieve those ends.

3.3 DEMOCRATIZATION OF SOCIAL PROGRAMMES

One of the principal achievements of the SD/L movement in the twentieth century has been the consolidation of a system of provision of social services and security, financed out of taxation. This can be theorized as a process of 'decommodification' of labour, taking essential matters like education, health and welfare, and income support in general, out of the market domain, and protecting them within a universally-financed public sector available to all.[61] The bad old days of workers and their families facing starvation if they are unemployed or on strike for a lengthy period, have been put behind us by these determined efforts.

This achievement is built squarely on that earlier breakthrough, the democratization of political life through the universal franchise, which makes the activities of labour's SD/L parties possible, and the building up of a framework of citizenship based on this.[62]

Throughout the Western world, the welfare state now finds itself on the defensive. There is great pressure on the public health and education sectors, with private systems making steady encroachments financed partly out of public revenues. The provision of pensions, social security and other monetary benefits, including unemployment allowances, is under great pressure. Growth of public expenditure on such benefits has increased rapidly, accounting for around twenty per cent of GDP in OECD countries in the 1970s, and nearly thirty per cent in the mid 1980s, but this growth is being checked by 'fiscal crisis', or 'tax revolt'. The political arena is awash with calls to 'trim' the public welfare sector, and to privatize many of its functions.[63]

Meanwhile the problem of poverty has not been solved; indeed it grows worse. There is now a 'new poverty', due to rising levels of unemployment, growing numbers of one-parent families, and others who are excluded from the labour market. Finally, the welfare state itself has in many ways grown sclerotic, hierarchical, and unresponsive. It has been under attack not only from the New Right, but from 'claimants' unions' on the Left, organizing beneficiaries to more effectively demand their rights.

In the face of these difficulties, traditional SD/L parties and governments find themselves floundering. Lacking a strategic framework, they find themselves drawn into a debate over efficiency of service delivery, 'crowding out' concerns, and questions of 'relative eligibility' of recipients. Pressures to 'target' welfare and community services are stripping the system of its universality, which gave it its legitimacy and political cohesiveness in the first place; these pressures are creating the conditions for one social group to compete with another for services, denigrating each others' claims in the process. This can only lead to a further shrinking of the public provision of services to the point where it is directed solely at outright poverty alleviation, buttressed by images of the workhouse revived from the nineteenth century.

How can the paradigm of Associative Democracy assist in formulating a strategic response to these dilemmas? There *is* an alternative formulation of the need for a healthy public welfare sector—but to identify it we must first look at the origins of the current system.

Rationale of the welfare state

The origins of the welfare state are diverse. One strand goes back to the initiatives taken by neo-absolutist regimes in central Europe in the late nineteenth and early twentieth centuries, such as the introduction of social insurance in Germany by Otto von Bismarck and in the Habsburg Empire by Eduard von Taafe. These initiatives were aimed explicitly at undercutting the appeal of the nascent Socialist labour movement; they constituted the 'carrot' while the 'stick' was the outlawing of early SD parties, particularly the German. This strand contrasts with liberal initiatives taken in Anglo-Saxon and Scandinavian countries, embodying schemes of corporate or contractual insurance, modelled on previous legal approaches; such schemes absorbed early worker co-operative schemes (the 'mutual societies') established in the nineteenth century.[64]

These pre-war schemes were initiated 'from above', taking the emergent working class as their object. It was only in the post-war period that the SD/L movement formulated a systematic approach of its own, utilizing its industrial and political strength, and becoming, as it were, the subject of its own history. The essential characteristics of this approach were, firstly, an attempt to maintain employment levels through Keynesian macro-economic management, and secondly, a bid to remove the market element from the provision of essential services such as housing, education and health care. Typically, the first target was to reform traditionally punitive systems of poor relief, and to replace them with comprehensive social insurance schemes. This was, in Marshall's terms, the claiming of social rights of citizenship.

The objective of such a strategy was to blunt the wage earner's dependence on market forces—in the labour market, and in the market for household goods and services. At the outset, the strategy involved the labour movement in making some difficult choices. Public services would have to be provided on a universal or national basis if they were to acquire legitimacy, but this would cut across the centrality of wages as source of income, and with this the power base of the trade unions. The universality of the welfare system was never completely grafted on to the particularity or specificity of the labour-market system of income generation, and this remains a critical point of weakness today. This lack of congruence has been exacerbated in countries such as Australia and New Zealand, where the unions secured a measure of 'wage-earner' welfare at the turn of the century, in the form of compulsory arbitration of industrial disputes. This emphasis at an early stage on the centrality of the breadwinner's wage retarded the development of a system of universal services.[65]

It can also be argued that a second basic assumption in the laying of the foundations of the post-war welfare state was its projected *marginality*: it was expected that economic growth and full employment would provide the key income support, and social security and unemployment benefits would play the role of smoothing out the wrinkles in the growth process.[66] Massive unemployment in the 1970s and 1980s has exposed the weakness of this assumption, and the vulnerability of a tax-financed system based on it.

It is in Scandinavia that the most sophisticated social policy strategy has been pursued. In place of allowing social welfare programmes to be established quite separately from economic programmes (introducing a divide that has dogged the welfare state ever since in Anglo-Saxon countries), the SD/L movement in Scandinavia succeeded in integrating these two strategic prongs, at least to a first order level. The bridge between them was the 'active labour market policy', embodying centralized wage fixation and facilitation of industrial restructuring via training schemes and employment programmes—feeding into macro-economic management programmes, on one hand, and keeping the lid on social security programmes, on the other. Provision of monetary unemployment benefits has been seen as the last and least desirable option in Scandinavia where it is regarded as very much a 'passive' labour market policy. Hence social policy came increasingly to be seen as the complement of economic and industry policy, both being integrated by labour market policy.

Income support

It is in the area of income support that the welfare state has found itself in most difficulty. Most industrial countries have legislated for some form of minimum income scheme to provide a social safety net for individuals or, more usually, families.[67] These are financed out of general tax revenue, or, in the form of national insurance schemes, from joint employer and employee contributions. Such schemes are naturally subject to means tests, and are paid as supplements to bring people's income up to a socially acceptable level.

These income support schemes are commonly regarded as having severe limitations. The level of benefits is generally too low to maintain self-respect; it is calculated, if based on any rational footing, on consumption patterns that are biased by moralizing and paternalistic assumptions; and it is linked with 'poverty traps' that keep people at the level of subsistence, rather than act as a springboard for them to take their place as productive members of society. Too frequently, people are humiliated in exercising their rights to claim a benefit, rather than being encouraged to do so. Most importantly, income support schemes are rarely linked to any training or skills formation schemes that would have the effect of reintegrating beneficiaries in the wider economy. Finally, most income support schemes have been built up by piecemeal social engineering, and are grafted on to pre-existing welfare and insurance institutions and agencies, making the administration of such schemes extremely complex, and bewildering for the recipients.

It is in this context that New Right attacks have had some real impact. Based on notions of the 'tax burden' and the 'burden of public expenditure', and reinforced by sensationalized images of 'scroungers', 'bludgers' and women 'living in sin' at the expense of the community, there has been irresistible pressure to trim income support schemes, to *target* them more efficiently at those 'most in need', and to re-introduce notions of the 'deserving poor' inherited from the early Poor Law system in Britain (for example, through 'work for the dole' schemes introduced to stop the unemployed from being idle). These attacks can all be understood theoretically as reinforcing a dependence on wages as a source of income, and hence at *recommodifying* labour.

It has been learnt in the Anglo Saxon countries that defence of the *status quo* is not the way to meet these attacks. In Thatcher's Britain and Reagan's US, the New Right scored significant political victories in squeezing the income support component of the welfare state, and in privatizing many of the sources provided publicly; while in other countries where SD/L parties hold government, this New Right influence has prevented any further expansion in levels of public expenditure from taking place, and indeed has forced cuts in many social programmes.

The way forward, it seems to me, is to learn from the Scandinavian experience, and seek to move social policy and income support out of its political and economic isolation, to become integrated much more effectively with economic and industry policy.

The key development which impinges on this issue, as it did on the question of industrial democratization, is the restructuring that is occurring in industry under the impact of computerization, new forms of work organization, and the disintegration of the global Fordist apparatus of economic regulation. These upheavals create a radically new, post-Fordist context within which social policy needs to be framed; a social security framework can now be convincingly characterized as providing the essential social infrastructure needed to facilitate restructuring. Income maintenance, restraining provisions ('life-time education'), relocation assistance—these measures all take on a new meaning when seen as underpinning processes of economic and industrial adjustment. From such a perspective, SD/L parties can mount a rather more effective defence of public expenditure in the face of New Right calls to roll it back; the argument is moved away from questions of defence of social rights, 'relative eligibility', and care for the under-privileged, to issues of facilitation of long-term economic survival through establishing appropriate social frameworks within which industrial restructuring may take place.

Employing the AD paradigm, we are led to ask how such a social programme can be seen as a means of democratization, utilizing associations of citizens and workers.

What sort of democratized social support structure is a feasible and practical goal? The context is that a lifetime in employment is no longer a realistic expectation for the majority of the population. Hence new ways of structuring the traditional tight links between income and work, need to be formulated. Trade unions are starting to show signs that they are adjusting their attitude to the concept of 'job for life', and are promoting a shorter working week, more flexible working hours and part-time employment—but this process is complicated by the eagerness of many employers to combine such changes with sub-contracting employment relationships that they hope will bypass unions altogether. This is a neo-Fordist option. A wider social framework for these negotiations is clearly needed.

From another perspective, it is clear that if the political notion of democracy is ever to mean more than merely the aggregation of a mass of individualized interests, then there must be instituted mechanisms of social cohesion. The question of income lies at the heart of this issue. While income is tied exclusively to employment, via wages and salaries, with other sources being seen essentially as supplementary, then there can be little progress in establishing rational, universal systems of income maintenance which embody notions of equity and equality, but are also geared to a rapidly changing productive economy. Strong as the case may be for targeted programmes of support for workers and families displaced by technological change (the compensation 'safety net' principle), the procedural and administrative problems involved in identifying recipients and running such programmes are overwhelming.

The alternative is to come to grips, once and for all, with the concept of a *Guaranteed Minimum Income,* for individuals and families, as the cornerstone of a structure upholding the democratic rights of individuals in a socially cohesive, responsible and flexible fashion.

Guaranteed Minimum Income schemes

There is widespread support, from opposite ends of the political spectrum, for moves to establish GMI schemes. In terms of general principle, the idea of breaking the necessary nexus between income and work, is broadly attractive. From the Left, the German neo-Marxist theorist, Claus Offe, argues that steps towards a GMI are justified, not so much by 'invoking old socialist ideals', as by reference to the fact that the chances of earning a wage in the market have dwindled greatly, and that the collectivity of employed persons will not be able much longer to support the income needs of the population through employment-related taxes. He argues that those who oppose a GMI would have to be able to show that there is really some hope of reducing unemployment levels via traditional economic management, or that the 'realist' option is not simply a disguised 'dualization' of society into the 'haves' (employed) and the 'have nots'. He sees it, in other words, as a social means of overcoming divisions.[68] The French theorist, Andre Gorz, argues similarly for a GMI scheme, linked to a notion of a 'lifetime of work' spread out at the convenience of a worker/citizen, on grounds that economic and industrial restructuring render past conceptions of 'full employment' illusory.[69]

From the Right, the notion of a GMI has long liberal roots, going back to the 'social credit' ideas of Major Douglas, and to the notion of a 'national dividend', as well as to the famed 'negative income tax' of Milton Friedman, introduced as a concept in 1962.[70] This neo-liberal position was expressed well by Robert Theobald, writing in 1963. In his *Free Men and Free Markets,* he rejected an 'extreme, Adam Smith version of the free-market mechanism', and focused instead on problems of structural unemployment in a dynamic economy, and the hardship this caused. People have basic entitlements: 'All western societies', he said, 'should ensure that each individual obtains sufficient resources to allow him (*sic*) freedom in his choice of actions. . . the initial step on the way to eliminate poverty is to supply money rather than moral uplift, cultural refinements, extended education, retraining programmes, or makework jobs.'[71]

Liberal schemes fall into two camps, depending on whether they embody the notion of a 'universal allowance' or 'national dividend', or are linked solely to the income tax system.

A recent proposal for a National Dividend Scheme has been developed in the UK, again in the context of automation, by Roberts. His scheme involves a basic subsistence income called the National Dividend (ND) being paid to all citizens irrespective of any other income. Citizens are then free to receive additional earned and unearned income, subject to income tax, with the tax unit being the individual rather than the family (ensuring that women receive an independent income). Taking the UK as the example, about half the national income would be distributed as ND, and half as wages, salaries and profits. The ND would be financed by a combination of Value Added Tax (VAT) and a smoothly progressive income tax. It would replace most social security payments, including unemployment allowances, old-age pensions, family income supplement, child benefits, student grants, and personal tax allowances. Receipts from VAT would finance the ND, while a progressive income tax would finance the collective 'social wage' services sector. Roberts claims that although there would be a large circulating flow of money through the government system, relative prices and incomes would remain unchanged, and the average family would pay no extra tax because of the negative-tax effect of the ND. The ND would require *less* administration than the current combined taxation and social security systems.[72]

Friedman favoured a cash minimum income as a way of encouraging free markets and discouraging bureaucratic government excesses. His plan would be run by the tax authorities, and would utilize balancing cash credits after tax liabilities had been determined. Friedman's proposal has been widely discussed in the US and UK.[73]

In Australia, GMI schemes were popularized by the Henderson Commission of Inquiry into poverty in 1975, and the Australian Council of Social Services Task Group on GMI which also reported in 1975, the final year of the Whitman Labour government. The Henderson Commission recommended an income tax linked GMI, with every income unit (e.g. family) being credited with a minimum income, and all subsequent income being taxed at a single proportional rate.[74]

Because these schemes can end up with very high marginal tax rates at high income levels, bringing with them great resistance on the part of citizens to pay taxes, more recent versions of the GMI have suggested financing it with a quite separate consumption tax or mix of taxes.[75]

All these approaches to the GMI, whether they involve a 'universal allowance' or a 'negative income tax' are characterized by certain common principles. They envisage, firstly, the replacement of various existing welfare benefits by a single cash benefit which does away with the distinction between contributions and payments. In their pure form, such schemes propose an integration of the taxation and social security systems.

Secondly, both approaches adopt a purely monetary approach to social welfare. This was made explicit in the quotation from Theobald given above, and in the common thread linking Friedman to Roberts and many others. Social wage programmes advocated by the SD/L movement have no place in such a scheme.

Thirdly, both approaches envisage a GMI operating as a complement to a radically deregulated labour market. Unions would have less relevance, and the price of labour would tend to fall below a subsistence level, with the shortfall being made up by the GMI payment. Work that could not have been done profitably before could now be performed, particularly in the services area.

It is this latter characteristic of GMI schemes that has made SD/L parties and unions wary of them, despite their obvious positive features (such as simplification of administration, encouragement of greater gender equality, encouragement of job mobility and retraining programmes).

Universal allowance schemes as advocated by neo-liberals have major inherent problems. Three of these are worth noting. Firstly, the level of the allowance is constrained by the capacity of the taxation system. There would be constant pressure to reduce the level of benefits, from taxpayers who are fortunate enough to be in full-time employment. Thus the *cohesive* character of the GMI will be whittled away. Secondly, the simple universal allowance schemes allow inequities to develop, particularly in the case of people covered already by major contingency benefits (accident payments, supporting parent benefits). Thirdly, there is an excessive reliance on monetary means of combating poverty, and little incentive to link the GMI scheme directly with an economic strategy, nor to supplement it with social wage services.[76]

Thus, while GMI schemes as proposed represent radical departures from current practice, and go a long way towards divorcing income from work, nevertheless they have problems that for the SD/L movement must be seen as very serious. Is it feasible to incorporate a GMI scheme into our notion of economic democracy in a way that circumvents these problems?

GMI and economic democracy

An alternative approach to GMI schemes, and one which derives directly from the paradigm of associative democracy, is to link GMI with the democratization of capital, via profits taxes.

Fiscal schemes on their own will be inadequate as financing tools for a genuine GMI and associated social wage services; a broader class of funding sources will need to be tapped. I am convinced that genuine democratization of social policy as an adequate complement to post-Fordist economic and industrial restructuring, will occur only if the GMI component draws on industry funds in some way. This principle has already been established by trade unions negotiating superannuation schemes (i.e. retirement benefits) financed out of industry revenues; and it has been greatly extended in the 'wage earner funds' proposals discussed above. While such funds have been discussed solely in terms of their socialization of the ownership of capital, there is no reason in principle why they cannot be extended to provide a means of *recycling* some funds from industry profits towards maintaining the social fabric that allows those profits to be generated in the first place. In this sense, the profits taxes could be seen as a 'structural adjustment levy'. Such an extension is clearly beyond the capacity of trade unions to negotiate directly with employers; it could only be introduced by an SD/L government as part of a comprehensive industry development/training/technology promotion package negotiated as virtually a 'social contract' with industry.

It is now clear why I maintain that a radical rethinking of the bases of the 'Keynesian Welfare State' is needed, and why genuine democratization of social policy needs to be placed on a completely different footing. The objections of the New Right would be swept away in such a process.

What would be the likely labour market effects of adopting such an income support scheme? The GMI would not be a substitute for paid employment, but a complement to it. Employment would continue to be the major source of income, and unions would still be involved in negotiations with employers over award rates of pay and conditions. Although a GMI scheme would create a large flow of money through the government system, relative prices would not be disturbed after the initial inflationary effect of a consumption tax had worked its way through. Relative incomes would certainly be changed, with significant redistribution from the better off to the poorer.

The key question would concern the overall disposable income of workers' families where the main earner (usually the male) is on average weekly earnings, and the partner is doing perhaps part-time work. Under these circumstances each individual would receive the GMI separately (resulting in considerable economic emancipation for a housewife not in paid employment), but their overall income would depend on the combined outgoings of income and consumption taxes employed to help finance the GMI. Detailed dynamic models of the economy are needed to simulate this and other situations, to *tune* the GMI scheme so that workers' households on average weekly earnings come out ahead.

Unions would continue their present functions; they would be involved, as now, in collective bargaining over wage levels. However, the members of these unions would be able to influence not only the level of their wages, but also their GMI through their representation on company Boards and collective investment funds. Thus the sectionalism of unions, which has been such a problem for them in the past, undermining collective political action, would tend to be blunted. The flexibility of the labour market, which is so dear to the New Right theorists, could be enhanced, but not at the cost of a decline in union influence. The character of unionism would also change. Unions would become more concerned with the quality of the work experience, and not just with the quantity of remuneration. This would be a desirable direction for the unions to move in.

The impact on profits will clearly depend on the financing arrangements that are settled on. But whether these are confined to fiscal measures (e.g. income and consumption taxes) or extend to profits recycling, the effect of a GMI scheme would clearly be to expand the scale of the social component of a nation's gross domestic product. This is the essence of the proposal, and there is no point in trying to obscure this fact. I maintain that this sort of expansion is acceptable to a broad coalition of political interests if it is introduced in a responsible way as part of a general industry development package.

There are other features of such a GMI scheme that commend themselves to the SD/L movement.

For example, the payment of a GMI to individuals, would provide a minimum level of financial independence that many women in a domestic situation have never experienced. This would encourage greater equality between the sexes. It would give women who are trapped in a violent marriage a means of escape. (This is why it is better to pay the income to individuals rather than to family units.) The only 'relationship' recognized by the GMI scheme would be that of parent and child (for purposes of paying child benefit) and so all the current humiliating investigations of the sexual life of single mothers on social security would be dispensed with. Of course the GMI on its own is not going to emancipate women, or undo the damage of centuries of patriarchal institutions, but it would be a step which *favours* this emancipation, rather than hinders it.

Under a GMI scheme, people would be enabled to decide to seek work for a variety of social reasons (self-fulfilment, socialization, challenge) in addition to the usual desire for a substantial income. But the whip that has driven people to work in the past—destitution or the degradation of unemployment benefit—would cease to operate, and more people would be able to seek occupations outside full-time paid employment. And those in such employment would be less afraid of standing up for their rights to humane and dignified working conditions and would swing their unions behind these issues more so than in the past. Provided the GMI/industry development package contained adequate provision for training, workers would be encouraged to keep their skills up to date by taking sabbaticals. This could be linked with their union-employer agreements on technological change and restructuring, which are tending to incorporate paid training leave as one of their essential features.

Will people who receive GMI want paid employment at all? Critics of GMI focus on the potential for an enhancement of personal freedom, and picture a consequent collapse of the work ethic. For example, in Australia the Asprey Committee on taxation reform (1975) offered the comment that a GMI scheme would have 'consequences for incentives to work and save which make it impossible to consider such a scheme seriously'.[77] Such observations betray a sad misunderstanding of the social motivation to work, and are more in tune with mid-Victorian workhouse attitudes than those appropriate for a society at a point where distribution of paid work is coming to be seen as a real problem. A GMI scheme would encourage a positive attitude to work, because the whip would be removed, and likewise a positive attitude towards productivity enhancement and technological change, for the costs of adjustment would no longer be borne directly by the displaced worker.

The French radical theorist, Andre Gorz, proposed a 'social income for life' in his text *Paths to Paradise,* financed by a tax on automated industry. He argues that since automation of industry is destroying jobs, and with them the basis of paid work, the *taxing of automated production* should finance a GMI. While this appears to have superficial resemblance to my own proposal, and while it certainly has the virtue of linking GMI with economic restructuring, Gorz in fact embeds his proposal in a comprehensive notion of political pricing that would be quite intractable.[78]

It is essential that the GMI be conceived as part of a comprehensively democratized system of social services, and *not* as a substitute for public health, education or community services. For one thing, there are elements in the social welfare/community services system that cannot be reduced to a monetary income—and one of the hidden reasons for New Right advocacy of GMI is precisely to eliminate such services and discretionary payments. They would include services provided in the home (e.g. nursing, meals-on-wheels). There will always be categories of recipients who need more than a flat-rate payment, such as the severely disabled, victims of occupational injuries, and so on. And there will be cases requiring special payment, subject to administrative discretion.

Lipietz goes further, and argues that a GMI scheme should be complemented by a 'third sector' of voluntary community work, performed by recipients of the guaranteed income. This proposal is designed to combat the 'something for nothing' perception of the GMI, and it offers an avenue for the democratization of local provision of community services.[79]

Above all, to return to the point made by Claus Offe, a GMI scheme offers about the only feasible means of preventing industrial societies sliding, over the course of the next decade, into a 'dual nation' status of employed and unemployed, with the unemployed becoming a 'sub-nation' of marginalised and demeaned people who are ripe for recruitment not only by the punk entertainment industry but by quasi-fascist political organizations as well. It is this possibility that must be taken seriously by SD/L parties in seeking ways of approaching social policy, and which could well act as the spur to adopting the admittedly ambitious and far-reaching democratization proposals advocated here. More generally, such a democratization will be an embodiment of a 'social contract', and a tangible sign that a society can be built on a sense of co-operation rather than on rampant and competitive individualism. The GMI scheme would therefore encourage a climate in which other holistic social practices and arrangements could be expected to take root and flourish—such as workers co-operatives, community co-operatives, and democratic citizen initiatives. All these stand little chance of being realized in a climate dominated by the selfish vales of the New Right.

3.4 DEMOCRATIZATION OF TECHNOLOGY

So far we have been concerned with ideas of democracy, freedom, markets—the traditional concepts of political theory. But surely one is entitled to ask: Isn't it all too late? We go on talking in terms of these political *forms*, while in the real world technology is radically changing their *content*.

The constraints on our polity today are evidently not simply the nineteenth-century constraints of income and power inequalities, important though they may still be. The real constraints would appear to be technical, and these are seemingly beyond any sort of 'social' or 'democratic' control. Our choices appear to be narrowing, as our lives come to be dominated more and more by vast technological systems—in transport, in the work place, in health care, even in the home. Computerized systems are appropriating the knowledge once held by people. We talk about industrial democracy for workers—but what relevance does it have to a worker who is required to push a button on a numerically-controlled machine to produce a part, when the programme running the machine might be produced on a CAD/CAM system in an adjacent office, or in Detroit or Yokohama?

Is political 'democracy' itself, i.e. the electoral process, to be reduced to little more than a charade of pressing buttons to choose between the options which have been carefully screened and selected for us by the experts?

A paradigm of associative democracy would indeed be an impoverished social goal if it were to be constrained in this way by some 'logic of technology' that narrowed the range of the 'social' and 'political' to a mere residuum in the name of technical efficiency and progress. To make sense of this situation, and to find a way out of these seemingly overwhelming difficulties, is one of the great challenges of our time. I suggest in this text that there is a way out, but to find it we need to discard some deeply held convictions and ideas about the nature of technology and its social dimensions, and we need to be creative enough to invent some new principles of political intervention in complex socio-technical systems.

Technological determinism

Where do we start in this new and puzzling terrain?

We have to start by opposing an idea—a powerful and conservative idea. It is the idea that technological choices are dictated by 'objective' criteria of efficiency, and that the technological forms we use determine social organization. In the workplace, for example, is the organization of work dictated by the technology employed? Are hierarchies of authority that are built into moving assembly lines, an essential precondition for productivity in industry? Until recently, the conventional answer to this question was yes: it was seen as 'Luddite' to question the technological imperatives of mass production systems. Elsewhere, in the community, the same dogmas hold sway. Energy systems, we are told, have to move to the use of nuclear fuels if they are to remain efficient; epic battles have been fought by community groups with electricity generating authorities to force an admission that there is in fact an element of social choice involved. In transport systems, there have been similar claims that a particular technology, for example, gas turbine engines in aircraft, dictated a series of social and technical choices, such as the decision to proceed with supersonic transport, and the building of airports to accommodate such developments.

This idea, that there is a logic to technological development that determines the social form of work and social systems, is possibly the single biggest obstacle to the achievement of a just and equitable society. The idea is known as 'technological determinism', or it masquerades as a notion of 'autonomous technology'.[80] It is as widely subscribed to on the left as it is on the right; indeed in 'vulgar marxist' terms the 'forces of production' are held to be the determining influence on all social development.

The theoretical position that underlies a democratizing strategy of intervention in the process of technological change, is one that understands technology as the aggregate of a series of social choices made in the past. Technologies carry the scars of past struggles and compromises.

Technology, then, is a social construct; it is shaped by social forces and choices; and it changes through a process whereby some options are taken rather than others. Always these options represent *social* interests. The choice of one option rather than another furthers one social interest or group at the expense of another (in money, power or other terms).[81]

The US author Langdon Winner has developed this theme in two influential recent texts.[82] Winner, too, is concerned to bring out the political character of choices which are made within what appears to be a purely technical setting. For him, the most intractable obstacle to bringing technology under democratic control is not some purported 'ruling class' but the widely held myth that technology is autonomous, above politics and value-neutral.[83]

We have gained a perspective then on technology that demythologizes its apparent 'rational objectivity' and reveals it as a social entity whose process of change is amenable to choice. It is inherently 'democratizable'. But the paradigm of associative democracy goes further and offers us the *means* of democratizing technologies, through the activities of trade unions and associations of citizens working in tandem with the resources of the State made available by an SD/L government. This is the key to social control of technology, which ultimately makes the associative democratic approach so compelling, Furthermore, this perspective sheds further light on some old political problems. For example, it is clear that the State can play only an orchestrating role in the process; all 'Statist' illusions of socialism as something that can be 'legislated' into place are revealed as being fantasies. The process of democratization of technology clearly cannot be directed from a single point, from the vantage point of a central planning ministry or any other agency.

On the other hand, the complexity and scale of the process of democratization, as revealed by some of the examples to be given below, show that the resources involved will be beyond those of any autonomous association of citizens or workers. The State will need to be involved in the process as provider of resources and as the means of securing and enforcing the complex agreements and contracts that will be necessary along the way.

To democratize technologies we must first develop a theoretical framework within which social and political criteria can be brought to bear. To start with, how do we define technologies?

Technologies—more than mere artifacts

Technologies are basically human-made means for getting certain prescribed things done. They operate according to rules or procedures which may be spelt out in symbolic form (as in programmes, recipes, and algorithms) or in the physical form of electrical, mechanical, hydraulic or pneumatic systems. All technologies, whether they be in the form of software or hardware, share the twin features that:

- they are designed, in accordance with certain principles, to meet specified criteria of performance;

• they embody constraints on the behaviour of a defined system.

For example, a pump may be designed to deliver a certain volume of water at a certain level with a certain energy input; it will then operate by forcing water to flow into certain channels conditional on certain trip mechanisms being activated (such as valves being opened or closed). A pump is a set of constraints designed to operate on the behaviour of water. 'Science' provides the raw material for the design of technologies in that it specifies the possibilities and the limitations of the matter being processed. Within these constraints, the design process is free to find the best means of satisfying the performance criteria spelt out.

Technologies as hardware—machines, bridges, cars, computers—are utterly familiar, even if their design process is still largely a mystery. Technologies as software—programs, algorithms—are becoming more familiar, particularly as computers are more widely used. The modern approach which views all 'designed, constraining' systems as technologies is still unfamiliar, but it is fundamental to understanding what is meant by 'democratization' of technology.

For example, technologies may be compared with bodies of law (legislation) which *prescribe,* rather than describe, the behaviour of persons and of associations of persons.[84] Conversely, one can characterize 'the law' as a major, complex, and ancient technology, a complex set of rules or algorithms designed to allow the conduct of business and politics without recourse to violence. The analogy between a complex computer program, with its loops, subprograms and logical structure, and a piece of legislation, with its clauses and sub-clauses, is an exact one; indeed, they are susceptible to identical formal analysis.

Unlike fluids, which flow through pumps according to certain regularities which can be described using concepts like viscosity, pressure and volume and the relations between them—unlike such fluids, people do not adjust their behaviour automatically to the requirements of a given legal system. These are transcendent questions, such as whether the laws are 'valid', and whether one 'ought' to comply with them; these may be termed 'meta questions'. Even so, from this perspective we have some insight into what is meant by democratization of technology.

Consider the long struggle that has ensued to 'democratize' the law. Quite apart from the revolutions that occurred over this issue in the ancient world, in the modern era we can look to the English civil war, with the Commons demanding that they have a say in the promulgation of the laws, particularly those regarding taxes; to the American Revolution with its emphasis again on 'no taxation without representation'; to the end of the nineteenth century and the struggle to extend the franchise to allow all citizens, through their representatives, to participate in the framing of the laws. This long social and political travail, whose fruits we enjoy today, and which cost so many people their lives, saw so many revolutions and rebellions launched and so many crushed, and occasioned so much passionate intellectual debate—all this can be comprehended as a process to democratize 'the law'. And the law can now be seen as but one facet of the multitude of 'soft technologies' that are currently employed to order our social and economic lives.[85]

Generalizing from this experience, we can appreciate how long and difficult will be the process of democratizing the other technologies which constrain us in rational and irrational ways, such as the complex transport, health care, energy supply and other systems that we depend on today.

We have a rich tradition to draw on in this process. We do not have to invent anew the goals of democracy itself, but we do have to give new content to terms like *equity, justice, authority* and *control*, to extend the domain of their meaning from their traditional interpretation (normally, referring to the social distribution of income and of rights) to a new technological context. Put another way, we have a rich variety of social concepts we can draw on in *evaluating* technological choices; we have to learn to characterize technologies as more or less *authoritarian*, more or less *interactive*, more or less participative, more or less amenable to external control or surveillance, and so on. This is clearly an abrupt departure from an engineering tradition which evaluates technologies purely in terms of efficiency, cost, or labour demands.

Now time-honoured political categories like justice and equity have frequently had their essentially social nature obscured so that discussion of them gets side-tracked by notions of individuality. But this cannot happen in the case of technologies. For it is obvious that a jet aircraft or air traffic control system is not designed by one person, and it will not be utilized by people on their own. Technology is essentially a social construct in a double sense—in the sense that is shaped by social forces, and in the sense that it is designed and used in a social setting.[86] This makes the task of formulating a politics of democratization of technology a little easier, and it underscores the fact that choices will have to be made, not individually, but by citizens in associations—in their trade unions, professional societies, community groups and public campaigns. This brings us back to the relevance of our paradigm of *associative democracy*.

Case studies of democratization

It is time for some examples. What in concrete terms would a democratized technology that embodied notions of equity and self-fulfilment look like?

Metal working tools

Let us start in the workplace, with productive technologies, or tools. In particular, let us look at lathes—tools for cutting and shaping other products out of metal. Hand-operated lathes that were under the control of a skilled metal working craftsman are everywhere giving way to Computer Numerical Control (CNC) machines that embody microprocessors to control the cuts. Given that this has the potential to enormously enhance the productivity of a metal-working firm, let us assume that it is a favourable development to be supported.

But *what sort* of CNC? Here the options present themselves. The key to CNC machining is the program: this is what gives the technology its flexibility. The same machine can cut different patterns simply by slotting in a new program, on a floppy disk, or magnetic card, or whatever. The program has to be written, that is designed, by software engineers. What criteria will they use in designing their programs? Will they build in options and flexibility to give maximum scope for the machine operator to use his/her acquired skill (for example, by being framed in terms of a basic series of cuts to be assembled in a particular pattern by the operator)? Or will it be a program in which absolutely every motion of the machine for a particular pattern is embodied in the instructions, giving no role for the operator other than that of pressing the button to start the machine, and cleaning away the metal scrap? This is a *real* choice—and it has enormous implication for the level of pride and satisfaction that the operator will take in the job, and through this for the likely level of productivity and overall worker-management relations in the factory producing the patterned parts. Hence the choice carries both individual and social implications.

The choice cannot be made in the abstract, by some quality

circle, or 'participative committee' or by a Parliamentary committee on science and technology. The choice has to be made in the process of design of the software, a labour process which is under the control of the management of a firm of CNC machine producers, but one which is dependent on the skill and expertise and values of the software engineers. It is, in other words, a social process. What pressures and forces can be brought to bear on this process?

It is clear that an initial step is for workers themselves, through their unions, to impose certain criteria via collective pressure, on the design process. This must involve, at the outset, the unions representing both the machinists and the programmers, coming together and agreeing on a set of desirable features of the programmes (such as building in scope for skill and choice, career enhancement, possibilities for taking group decisions). These unions could seek to have these features accepted by the management of the firm producing the CNC machines. A series of negotiations therefore is involved—between workers themselves, between workers and management, and then between the CNC firm and other firms as they seek to market the new and 'alternative' technology to metal parts firms, who will have an established workforce and technology.

This is just at the level of collective negotiation and criteria. There are still many stages that must be gone through beyond this level. We can envisage state-funded skill and design centres that promulgate the new 'humanist' designs of software and support them with commissioned research that demonstrates their superior efficiency and productivity over more 'authoritarian' programs. We can envisage unions themselves calling on public funds to work with technical consultants to elaborate more sophisticated criteria which will then provide the parameters guiding the design process. We can envisage SD/L governments formulating a 'technology policy' in terms that bind them to purchasing or specifying only CNC machines that embody the 'humanist' rather than the 'authoritarian' programs in public enterprises and in those firms fulfilling government contracts. Finally we can envisage the laying down of certain standards of design in, initially, self-regulatory standards authorities, and ultimately by statutory regulation. All these are steps towards a genuine democratization of the design of programs for CNC machine tools, bringing the social process of design under progressively wider and wider public influence.[87]

Microprocessor-based systems

CNC machine tools are but one of a host of new programmed tools embodying microprocessors. Others include:

- computerized typesetting machines, replacing manual typography;
- automatic bank tellers;
- word processors, replacing typewriters and their operators;
- computerized travel booking systems;
- computerized telecommunications directory assistance systems;
- computerized railway track signalling systems, replacing manual signal operators;
- 'smart' diagnostic systems replacing medical general practitioners.

The same process of democratization will have to be gone through in each of these cases, in the same way as described for CNC tools.

Since most of these are tools to be used in the workplace, the brunt of the task of democratizing will fall inevitably on the trade unions. They are having to learn to *extend* the skills and techniques learnt in 150 years of negotiating wage-fixing systems, i.e. democratizing income, to a much broader and technically demanding complex of issues. Just as unions discovered in the twentieth century that they could conduct their struggle with greater effectiveness at the level of the State, negotiating the provision of public 'social wage' resources to underpin monetary wages, so unions are coming to understand that this process of democratization of tools can also be conducted at several levels, and that public resources can be called upon, such as public research centres and publicly funded innovation programmes to assist in the process. If unions fail to accept these challenges, then workers will be condemned to operate in the totally alienated, authoritarian, aseptic environment that IBM has in store for them—in a quiet hum of white machinery undisturbed by human intervention, backed by marginal service armies of data processing operators hidden away in twenty-four hour operations bunkers in suburban centres. This will be the price paid for failing to provide a democratic alternative to the 'hard business' agenda in the area of high technology.

One example where trade unions have grasped this challenge and have sought to impose humanist criteria on the design of new computerized technology, is in the area of typesetting. This was done through the UTOPIA project, where a group of Scandinavian printworkers' unions combined their resources, and with the help of technical advisers, brought a new concept to the point where it was licensed as a product. This example shows not only that collective intervention in the process of technological change is possible—but how complex and demanding such intervention is.[88]

The significance of the UTOPIA project for our purposes is that it illustrates how workers may intervene collectively in the design process of a new technology by imposing alternative, more human-centred, criteria. *This is associative democratization* in practice. It does not involve a parliament, or a political party, but an association of workers seeking to have their say, equipped with technical advice, and a framework within which they may intervene. The project also shows how large are the resources required for successful intervention—in just one facet of one industry at a time. Clearly the project of democratization of all new workplace technologies is quite beyond the resources of the trade unions on their own; this merely underlines the necessity for the process of democratization to be accomplished utilizing *alliances,* in this case between technical engineers and skilled workers, as well as with the support of public resources.

Programmed learning systems

Now let us move right outside the workplace, and consider the case of programmed learning systems, to be used at school, college or in the home, from the point of view of the user. These systems involve, at the simplest level, a computer and printer and a program that dictates questions which are offered sequentially as each one is answered 'correctly'. Other media can be added—screens, video material and audio material (e.g. Texas Instruments' *Speak'n Spell*). At a more sophisticated level, the systems become more interactive and optional, mimicking the role of a real human teacher as they probe the student's understanding of a concept or subject, and utilizing the insights gained from the field of Artificial Intelligence.

There are many criteria available to guide the design of these programmed machines, and each set has radically different social implications. An authoritarian conception of education—'giving the facts'—can be embodied in the machines. Cultural attributes (use of words, pronunciations, assumptions concerning etiquette and behaviour) can be built into them. But choices are available: there exists a whole spectrum of alternative conceptions of learning based on the student's own skills and couched in terms of problem-solving procedures rather than rote learning.

How are these consumer technologies to be brought under some form of democratic control, so that there will be a variety of learning theories embodied in the software of these machines? A New Rightist might reply: Leave it to the market. But this is to side-step the problem. The market provides choices, but within a framework laid down by standards authorities, public pressures, and ultimately, the law. So the market is not an adequate solution in itself.

In this case it would be up to professional societies to intervene at one level, and consumer action and community groups at another, to influence the direction in which such technologies evolve. The consequences of certain options being taken rather than others, not just for teachers and their work, but for levels of literacy, numeracy and even the foundations of national cultures, are profound. A government may be making ringing declarations in favour of disarmament at the United Nations, but allowing into schools imported learning systems which teach physics exclusively through war-oriented ballistics, missile and rocket examples.

Again it is unrealistic to expect associations of citizens to democratize such learning systems on their own. Public resources and public institutions will be needed. At the strictest regulatory level, new designs could be licensed, and vetted beforehand by some public agency whose deliberations and decisions would be available on the public record. At a slightly less stringent level, an Office of Technology Assessment could consider various classes of technologies, evaluating their social potential and implications, and make recommendations over design criteria that are published. These could then be taken up by citizen and consumer action groups for example, to extend collective pressure on suppliers.

It is not my intention here to exhaust the means of democratizing technology. I wish only to illustrate what an involved, complex and all-important process it is going to be, and how narrow is any conception of democracy that remains tied to seventeenth and eighteenth-century political institutions such as parliaments.

The politics of technological change

I maintain that there is a defensible theoretical position underlying the paradigm of associative democracy, namely *that the hard and soft technologies which shape our lives and our social interaction are all designed, whether openly or not, implicitly or explicitly; and that the criteria guiding this process can be arrived at, and imposed, in a democratic and associative manner.*

This is a fruitful point of view, not only for explaining technology, but for understanding the wider society as well. If criteria can be *arrived at* in a democratic and associative manner, it means that they can reflect an integrated set of technical, economic and social goals. These goals inform the process of specification of the design criteria as we saw in our example of CNC machine tools, where the programming design criteria can reflect narrow Taylorist goals of authoritarian management, or broader 'humanist' goals of skill enhancement and interactive management. The two approaches can best be described as *competing paradigms*—and, indeed, this is the terminology that is coming to be used in the literature on the sociology of technology.[89]

The clash between competing paradigms is not a purely intellectual or academic clash; it is not resolved in the learned journals. Our terms are chosen to reflect a clash that is actually taking place in the market-place. Products and services are being produced according to different paradigms, and they are fighting against each other for their commercial survival. This is the significance of the decline in the dominance of the mass production paradigm, and the rise of a series of 'post-Fordist' production systems: it is a battle, or transition, that is fought out clearly in the global market-place. Mass produced goods are finding it increasingly difficult to survive in markets where the emphasis is on quality, reliability, and flexibility. The new computerized production systems, equipped with new 'post-Fordist' work organization and management philosophies, are responding to the new market opportunities with greater success than their competitors who are still tied to mass production systems and philosophies.[90]

To revert to my claim above, the criteria that characterize an alternative paradigm can be *arrived at,* and *imposed,* in a democratic and associative manner. This claim opens up a vast project for a *politics* of technological choice. It means that unions and political parties must become involved in the battles between competing paradigms—as they already are (but still only tentatively and cautiously, feeling their way in this strange territory of technical argument). While the clash between competing paradigms will ultimately be resolved in the market-place, there is space for associations of workers and citizens to become involved in the specification of the criteria that make up the paradigms. Indeed I would go further, and claim that this will become one of the principal areas of activity for unions, parties and governments, as they move on from seeking to resolve questions of *distribution* (shares of income and all the associated issues such as taxation) to pay more attention to questions of *production* and *consumption* and the values that inform them.

And so we close the circle. The clash of paradigms opens up a politics of technological choice, which will increasingly become the substance of mainstream social and political negotiation. The paradigm of associative democracy integrates the two concerns—the broader social issues as well as the technical. It is the perspective of democratization of technology that provides the strongest argument in favour of the utility of such a paradigm.

The project of democratization of technology as expounded here constitutes a radical departure from previous attempts to 'popularize' technical decision-making. It is not a question of answering the same questions (e.g. which technology has greater technical efficiency, lower costs, less social adjustment needed) with an expanded and more 'participative' means of taking technical decisions, e.g. through Parliamentary committees. It is a question of *posing fundamentally new questions over the choice of technology*. This is what is achieved by bringing together separate streams of thought, the one from the political theory of democracy, and the other from the critique of technological determinism: we pose a fundamentally new problematic of democratization.

This becomes clear if we step back a little and ask: What does it mean for people to enter into social relations? In traditional political theory this question is normally analyzed in terms of power relations, which are held to derive from property relations, and from these flow the notions of equity and justice with which we are familiar. I am suggesting that we now need to take cognizance of the fact that property relations are not the only or even the most important forces which shape or structure our social relations; the primary influence is the structuring by technology. Furthermore, while technology has social effects, it is also shaped by specific social interests, and the process of democratization needs to start with the analysis of these interests in the concrete setting of a specific technology. There is, in other words, no such thing as a single 'technically correct' solution to a problem, but a range of solutions offering different levels of influence or control to different social groups. Hence the barrenness of any approach to technology which sees it as 'neutral', and ready to be activated in a simplistic Marxian view, in the cause of the proletariat as soon as its capitalist masters are expropriated; or equally bad, an approach which sees the technology as imbued with a transcendental capitalist logic that makes it immune to any 'economist' trade union or popular democratic attack.

The traditional approach to politics, then, has been all too narrow. I would submit that it is more fruitful to ask what is just or equitable, not only about a system of property relations, but about a complex technological system, giving these tested human concepts of justice and equity new life in a new context.[91] It is this that I would like to think goes back to the spirit of the finest work of Marx. He saw through the degradation and suffering of the early years of the industrial revolution to the possibility of a new social order beyond capitalism. Some way further on we can now see through the oppression of vast authoritarian technical systems to the possibility of a liberated social order, in which our technical systems are the servants of sophisticated human and social choice and not their purported masters.

3.5 A DEMOCRATIC ECONOMY

So far we have looked at reforms aimed at democratizing economic and social life, based on the citizenship rights won in the democratic political domain. But our discussion is not complete until we look at how such a democratized economic order would work in practice. Would it collapse in anarchy? Are there co-ordination mechanisms available that will make the democratic economy function more efficiently than its hierarchical/authoritarian capitalist predecessor? In any *real* economy, the following sorts of issues need to be resolved:

- the nature of productive enterprises—their ownership, control and management;
- wages, prices and profits;
- allocation of investment and production decisions—the role of markets and of planning;
- regulation of international trade.

There has been a renaissance of investigative work on these issues in recent years. What I am calling a 'democratic economy' is called, in another context, 'feasible socialism' (Nove) or 'democratic socialism' (Brus, Selucky) or 'market socialism'.[92] A theoretical gulf separates these sophisticated constructions from the previous simple-minded notions of socialism as a 'free association of free producers'.

For reasons explained above, I am avoiding use of the term 'socialism', in that while it stands for a set of values (which large numbers of people, including myself, share) it is not precise enough to generate a particular economic programme. Nove's 'feasible socialism' is, in fact, nothing other than a democratization of capitalism, and in many ways (as we shall see below) not as radical as the paradigm of associative democracy expounded in this text. If democratization is what we are aiming for, then it seems sensible to me to say so—hence my preference for the term 'democratic economy'.[93]

How then can we expect the 'real' issues identified above to be resolved in a democratic economy? To close this exposition, we need to look at each of them, albeit briefly.

Nature of enterprises

In a democratic economy, there need be no rigid restriction to any single form of enterprise, public or private. Firms' social desirability would be measured, not just in terms of their productivity and efficiency, but also in terms of their accountability and accessibility to public influence.

Selucky model

The Czech exile Radoslav Selucky put forward in 1979 an interesting model of a democratic economy which can form the starting point of our discussion. Selucky set out his scheme in the form of a number of assumptions, or principles, which included the following:

- The means of production are owned socially and managed by those who make use of them.
- Social ownership of the means of production is separated from the State.
- Producing and trading enterprises are autonomous *vis-à-vis* the State and independent of each other. They operate within the framework of the market, which is regulated by a central indicative plan.

- The institutions that provide health, education, and welfare services are wholly exempt from the market.
- The right to participate in direct management of the work units operating in the market is derived from labour.
- The right to participate in direct management of the work units exempt wholly or partly from the market is derived proportionally from labour, ownership, and consumption of the provided services and utilities.
- The right to participate in indirect political control over, and regulation of, the socially owned means of production is derived from one's position as a citizen.
- Health and education services and social benefits for the disabled are distributed according to one's needs.
- The principle of self-management is limited to micro-economic units only.[94]

In this model, there are firms competing with each other in the market place, driven by consumer choice, but owned and managed by their workers. In other words, it is a radical version of economic democracy. There would be no government-owned firms; if the government is involved in taking over a firm, it would only be on a temporary basis until it could be placed under workers' control.

There is a large 'public sector' of firms or organizations providing health, education and welfare services, i.e. schools, hospitals, universities, or psychiatric institutions. These are managed by boards that draw their membership from the workforce, owners, and from the wider community that makes use of their services. These services are provided without monetary charge, but according to need.

There is an indicative planning mechanism that operates in conjunction with the central democratic political structure (legislature and executive) to ensure that the economy functions within certain guidelines that are decided through the political process, i.e. by elections.

The model presupposes a mix of organizations operating at each level, to ensure participation in associations of workers (trade unions), of consumers, and of professional groups, as well as political parties.

Nove model

A widely discussed alternative to Selucky's model was put forward in 1983 by Alec Nove, a Scottish specialist in Soviet economic affairs. Nove's model of 'feasible socialism' is similar to Selucky's with the important exception that he is not so rigid in the form that producing and trading enterprises may take. As he says:

'[Selucky] appears to envisage an evolution toward one type of producing unit. In my view it is possible and desirable to have several . . . It is essential to recall the assumptions of political democracy. The citizens can choose, for example, what sorts of private initiative to encourage or to tolerate, the desirable forms of co-operatives, the extent of workers' participation in management, and much else besides. They can experiment, learn from experience, commit and correct errors . . . Suppose that we have a legal structure which permits the following species:

1 State enterprises, centrally controlled and administered, hereinafter [called] *centralized state corporations;*
2 State-owned (or socially owned) enterprises with full autonomy and a management responsible to the workforce, hereinafter [called] *socialized enterprises.*
3 *Cooperative enterprises.*
4 *Small-scale private enterprise,* subject to clearly defined limits.
5 *Individuals* (for instance, freelance journalists, plumbers, artists).'[95]

Nove's description of this group of five types of enterprise makes it clear that his 'feasible socialism' is really a democratized version of our present social system.

In the first group, Nove includes banks and other credit institutions, and large utilities like electricity or telecommunications networks. These have to be centralized to ensure the integrity of the whole network; it would clearly be defeating the aims of democracy to give managers and workers in one power station such rights that they could over-ride decisions taken elsewhere. Where these centralized state corporations operate in monopoly fashion, they would need broad tripartite management structures (workers, State, consumers) as recommended by both Nove and Selucky. Criteria of efficiency would reflect social purpose. The internal planning of the enterprise would be connected to the indicative planning of the government.

Other firms, called 'socialized enterprises' by Nove, perform the thousands of operations required by consumers and by the larger centralized firms. They operate in a competitive environment, responding to consumer choice, and provide a major role in their management for their own workforce. They form a democratized 'small business' sector; bringing them into our discussion represents a long overdue consideration of the role of small business by the SD/L tradition.

Nove discusses at length why competition is essential; it seems unnecessary to insist on this other than to a socialist dogmatist. In an advanced economic democracy of the sort envisaged, the level of social concern and understanding would be such as to permit social restrictions on undesirable competitive and promotional practices (e.g. promotion of unhealthy products using sexist images). The major difference between Nove's socialized enterprises and co-operatives, derives from their different property relations. In the socialized enterprise the means of production do not belong to the workers, but to the community, and the government would have some role in ensuring their proper use, and in winding them up.

Private enterprise would act as an important consumer valve, particularly at the local level. There would be no restriction on the setting up of a small business run by an individual, even with a few employees. Nove suggests that there might be a limit set to the size of such businesses, either in terms of people or capital employed; when they reached that limit, a choice would be made as to whether to convert to a co-operative or to a socialized enterprise, with due compensation being paid to the entrepreneur. Such people are working in and organizing the business. Nove contrasts the income earned by them with unearned income arising from absentee ownership of capital or land in our present economic system.

I find little to quarrel with so far in Nove's formulation. My differences with him are more concerned with the environment in which enterprises operate; these are taken up below. Let us use Nove's five types of enterprise as the basis for a description of the workings of a democratic economy.

Wages, prices and profits

Subject to centrally negotiated guidelines, wage scales will continue to be influenced by the supply of, and demand for, specific kinds of labour. The level of wages will be determined by the controlling boards of economic enterprises, on which workers will form a majority. Hence, in effect, workers decide on their own wage levels, subject to competitive pressures on costs, and medium term investment plans.[96]

There would need to be a politically-determined limit to wage and salary differentials, and this, combined with central wage fixation within an appropriate forum, would constitute an associative democratic incomes policy. Those in the private enterprise sector who made greater returns would be pegged back (but not completely, because of the personal risks they run) by progressive income taxation.

The role of the trade unions would continue to be the protection of the overall economic interest of employees; the right to strike (e.g. against an authoritarian management) would be upheld. However, I believe unions would play a much more sophisticated and interventionist role than they do now.

On prices, as Nove states, 'Soviet and other experience proves conclusively that comprehensive price control is impossible to administer'. Some prices, particularly those charged by large, centralized monopolies, would have to be politically determined, because they could contain hidden subsidies of various kinds, as they do now. (For example, most public sector telecommunication utilities charge similar tariffs for urban and rural telephone use, even though the cost of supplying services in rural areas is much greater than in urban areas.) But in the competitive, socialized, co-operative and free enterprise sectors, prices would be set via bargaining between suppliers and customers, and through normal market mechanisms. Again, the consumer and intermediate goods markets will have to be carefully regulated to ensure that they operate in the public interest.

Profits in this system, at the level of the firm, will provide a measure of efficiency in 'adding value', and will not in any sense indicate 'exploitation'. Perhaps they should be called 'operating surplus' or 'net income' to avoid these verbal associations. Profits at the level of the economy as a whole constitute a very different issue. There, at the macro-economic level, the balance between profits and wages, savings, investment and consumer demand, needs to be determined according to technical procedures and political criteria, and not by reference to any sort of simple rule of 'profit maximization'.

Questions relating to the proportion of surplus to be invested in the form of new capital, and the distribution of the balance through collective social and human services, will be key democratic issues to be settled largely at a political level. The difference from the present system will lie, not just in the democratic control of firms themselves, but in the public availability of data to make meaningful macro-economic decisions, and in the availability of forums in which these issues could be discussed seriously. This brings us to the key issue of the social control of production and investment decisions.

Social control of production: markets versus planning

Debate over the notion of socialism this century has revolved largely around the question of planning versus markets. Socialism has come to be identified with planning, with the exception of the group of theoreticians advocating 'market socialism'. The very basis of the socialist enterprise arose out of repugnance with the effects of uncontrolled market forces, and the undeniable inequalities in wealth and power they generate. Marx talked of markets taking social decisions behind people's backs, and of socialism beginning an era of history when decisions could be made consciously. Meanwhile, 'planning' has acquired nasty connotations due to its associations with central planning and the command economy in the USSR and Eastern Europe. 'Planning' also has top-down elitist connotations, which any democratization proposal has to overcome.

Along the way, the debate has been complicated by illusions, both on the part of proponents of planning, who thought that vast volumes of information flow were unproblematic, and on the part of opponents, who advanced the view that information flow considerations would make any form of planning impossible. The USSR is held up as an example that central, command planning does not work; Yugoslavia, with its high unemployment, high inflation rates and regional imbalances, is held up as an example that market socialism cannot work.

At the outset, it needs to be stated that much of this argument is formally at cross-purposes, and in practical terms it leaves a lot out of the picture.

Formally, there is little difference between properly functioning markets and planning. Any feasible planning procedure needs to be iterative if it is to overcome impossible information constraints; in other words, a central bureau needs to send out repeated draft plans and receive corrections before a *balance* can be struck between overall supply and demand. These drafts can be based either on target *outputs* (with production and service units responding in terms of the inputs they would require to meet these targets) or on *shadow prices* (with production and service units calculating their optimal input requirements and outputs according to a given rule, e.g. production maximization, cost minimization with respect to a given output, or profit/surplus maximization).[97] This iterative procedure is formally identical to the clearing action of a market under the control of a 'fictitious' auctioneer, who calls prices until demand balances supply.

Practically, for all the talk by the New Right of the virtue of markets, capitalist businesses loathe the market, have always done so, and will go to extreme lengths to avoid it. The last 150 years of business history are packed with examples such as rings and cartels; cornering, hedging and insider-trading; and vertical integration by firms to avoid the 'uncertainties' of supply and demand. As firms get larger, so they devote more and more effort to planning in order to minimize the shock of changes in the market; for their internal transactions (e.g. between subsidiaries of a multinational) they operate a pure planned economy, never a market. In spite of this, all of these firms vigorously and loudly protest against any form of planning in the public domain, as an interference in the free enterprise system.

Let us penetrate behind this rhetoric and establish some points unambiguously. A democratic economy is inconceivable without a measure of centralized and decentralized planning, particularly for major capital or producer goods (e.g. energy, production machinery) and for the allocation of labour and the development of skills. On the other hand, it is inconceivable that the thousands of consumer goods could be allocated by any mechanism more efficient and less bureaucratic than a series of markets, provided they are under democratic and forceful regulation.

So we have a triad of social control:

- democratic planning of major sectors (e,g. labour, producer goods);
- competitive market allocation of most goods and services in the consumer sector;
- free or subsidized provision of 'social wage' goods and services.

This is a perfectly acceptable and practicable triad, that marries democratic choice with efficiency and social equity.

Market co-ordination

I would argue that it is time the SD/L movement dispensed with its futile hostility to markets, and concentrated on making them work for the public interest. By opposing markets in principle, we foreclose any possibility of using them to expand the domain of individual liberty in a complex and regulated society.

By embracing markets in principle (already done in practice by trade unions, in the labour market)—but on democratic terms, and in opposition to monopolists and cartelists—SD/L parties can undercut the appeal of the New Right, and take the initiative on issues of social co-ordination.

This approach is endorsed by two UK commentators, Miller and Estrin, who state in a recent Fabian pamphlet on 'market socialism':

> Markets are an efficient way of producing and distributing a very large number of mundane items, from tomatoes to transistor radios ... Markets give their participants a certain kind of freedom. They tend to expand the range of choices that may be made, and they give each person a variety of partners with whom to deal ... Markets tend to dissolve personal power. Although they certainly place constraints on people's behaviour ("market forces"), they free people from dependence on particular individuals such as petty bureaucrats.[98]

Yet there is much fundamentalist opposition to markets in the SD/L movement. Marx's strictures have been echoed down the years. There are claims that markets fail to provide the level of 'conscious' social decision-making that could be reached; that markets inevitably emphasize inequalities; and that markets essentially represent an obstacle to the achievement of socialist values.'[99]

The fundamentalist assertion that markets are 'blind' and need to be abolished, is in my view a counter-productive reaction to *unregulated* market behaviour. What we should emphasize, instead, is that markets that are left to themselves rapidly degenerate. They tend to concentrate power into monopolies, and they provide a happy hunting ground for speculators. The general public can be fleeced by fraudulent conspiracies, price-fixing cartels, insider trading, and a host of other tricks invented by human ingenuity and greed. But these are *pathologies,* not examples of a healthy social mechanism.

Despite the rhetoric of the New Right, there is no such thing as a 'free market'. Markets are not 'natural'; they have to be carefully established and nurtured, like plants. But, like an untended garden they can grow wild and then they have anti-social effects. Conversely, markets can become fossilized, and can benefit from a dose of 'deregulation' to boost competition which may in fact make an economy more egalitarian. In general, markets are good servants, but bad masters.

Planning

What sort of planning would be done in the democratic economy? I would envisage a national planning bureau being an important arm of government (eventually subsuming Treasury, as well as Departments of Industry and Trade) with a Minister controlling it and a standing Committee of Parliament constantly interrogating its work. It would be required to maintain a suite of models of the national economy (focusing on different aspects, e.g. input and output characteristics, or price, wage and income macroeconomic characteristics) and its social, demographic and environmental setting. It would be empowered by Parliament to collect relevant data to feed into (technically: 'identify') these models; and it would simulate different investment, output, and distribution policies on these models, making appropriate recommendations at designated time intervals to Cabinet, Parliament and tripartite bodies.[100]

This process would generate targets that are optimal with respect to the criteria deployed by the government of the day. Planning criteria (e.g. maximization of incomes for the rich versus equality of incomes for all) would become distinguishing characteristics of political parties, and elections would provide a political means of choosing which criteria to use in producing the optimal targets within the planning bureau. The targets chosen would then be conveyed to the relevant enterprises. Most of the key national targets (e.g. energy self-sufficiency, power generation) would apply to State-owned national monopolies, and it would 'simply' be a matter of good management to ensure that they be achieved (but there is a world of detailed work subsumed by that word 'simply'). Other targets would be contained in planning agreements that the government might conclude with socially owned enterprises and co-operatives, in return for public equity or assistance.[101]

International trade—the future of multinational enterprises

It is well known that world trade is now dominated by the Fortune 500 multinational corporations (MNCs) and that these are the companies that tend to dominate the overseas transactions of any individual nation. It is also well known that efforts by nationalist reforming governments to exercise some influence over MNCs operating in their territory have been met by political opposition, obstruction, and even resort to armed force to overthrow them. (Numerous examples can be cited: the overthrow of Mossadeqh in Iran in 1951 followed by the installation of the young Shah, after BP oil assets were threatened; to the activities of ITT and other MNCs in Chile under the Allende regime, in 1970 to 1973.)

MNCs represent a particular cause for concern for a democratic reforming government, in that the seat of power lies beyond the direct reach of government, and the headquarters can call up heavy sanctions, such as boycotts, freezing of loans, and lock-outs from markets. These sanctions can lead to the fall of the government.

In a democratic economy, MNCs will, in my view, be allowed to continue operations, but subject to a 'good citizen' code of behaviour. The difficulty of enforcing such a code is acknowledged, but there is no alternative if the foreign policy of the democratic government is not to be dictated by MNCs. Implementation of such a code was attempted in a rather half-hearted way by the Liberal Canadian government over a ten-year period, from 1974 to 1984. But the results were meagre. It can be concluded that a code needs to be backed by adequate sanctions for misbehaviour (defined, for example, as excessive repatriation of profits and tax avoidance; plant closure without adequate consultation or warning; inadequate local processing or research and development; restrictions on export activity by subsidiaries, and so on)—and the most effective sanction of all is outright nationalization. A host democratic government must be prepared to take this ultimate step—but only after exhausting all available avenues for bringing the MNC to heel.

I do not know whether globally-operating MNCs will remain in perpetuity. I am sceptical as to whether they will ever come under adequate regulation by some supranational authority (or if such an authority were to be established, it would represent a considerable restraint on the part of a national democracy).[102] And so the only feasible path forward seems to be to bring their operations in each country under control within that country, with all the inevitable difficulties this will entail. The liberal and social democratic governments which have allowed the MNCs to grow to their present size, have left the democratic world with a terrible burden and obstacle to overcome, given the global reach and power of these organizations, and their capacity to play off one government against another. However, they are not insuperable, and are likely to be tamed by a combination of national enforcement of 'good behaviour', combined with some international initiatives. In world trade, for example, leverage can be exercised by nations clubbing together when they have similar products to sell (e.g. in OPEC-type producer cartels)—and this should be pursued by a democratic government if it enhances its international bargaining power, particularly *vis-à-vis* US or European MNCs.

Finally, it is worth mentioning that it is open to democratic nations to combine together, through United Nations auspices or in some other way, to establish genuine international public enterprises. An example of this was the proposed International Seabed Authority (ISA) that was almost established in the 1970s out of the Law of the Sea treaty. Such an ISA would have been publicly run and capitalized, and would have operated commercially as the monopoly harvester of seabed minerals in international waters. It would potentially have had huge revenues, with which it could have compensated producer nations hard hit when their traditional mineral exports declined as a result of ISA activities. The ISA provides a model for other cases of international public enterprise.[103]

3.6 POST-FORDISM AND THE ASSOCIATIVE DEMOCRATIC ECONOMY

It will be by blending the insights from the post-Fordist perspective with the strategies of direct intervention favoured by associative democracy, that the SD/L movement stands to make its greatest contributions in the 1990s and beyond. The post-Fordist perspective focuses on the need for flexibility and a capacity for innovation in an economy geared to dynamic structural adjustment. It is distinguished from competing neo-Fordist perspectives in its insistence that flexibility and productivity are most efficiently based on the skilled input of workers taking increasing levels of responsibility for the design of their jobs, their workplaces, their products and ultimately the management of their enterprises. This approach is accommodated and facilitated by the democratization of company structures, by the development of social investment funds, by planning agreements, and the host of other innovative measures available to a movement which is convinced of their relevance and practicability, and is prepared to use its strength in the political arena to bring about such structural transformations.

The danger in all this is the threat of dualization, of the development of a social gulf between a skilled, employed elite and a mass of under-skilled, under-employed and politically alienated majority. This is where an over-arching political paradigm of solidarity makes its critical contribution. This is why a GMI-based welfare state, integrated with economic and industrial strategy, is such an essential component of an SD/L vision of the political future. But solidarity is underpinned at every level by associative democracy, by a mix of intervention at the local level and at higher levels which transcend the local, through national organizations such as unions and social movements. It is underpinned by the insistence that productive enterprises need to accommodate the interests, not just of their workers, but of other stakeholders such as customers, suppliers and the host community. This process will generate a dynamic which will bring the question of ownership of social productive resources—a question postponed for the best part of a century by the SD/L movement—right to the top of the political agenda. This question must be tackled, if only to ensure the survival of our species on the planet. For the biases towards destruction and spoliation built into the present ownership structures, and the divorce of the monetary and financial system from productive activities, will surely lead to planetary extinction unless some drastic changes are instituted. It is survival which will ultimately justify the democratization of technologies, of enterprises, of capital, and of the economy itself—and it is only the SD/L movement which can see such a process through to a successful conclusion.

FOUR

THE POLITICS OF ASSOCIATIVE DEMOCRACY

The 'provisional utopia' we have sketched, with its proposals for democratization of economic, industrial and social life, is presented as a coherent, practicable and feasible paradigm to guide the interventions of social movements, unions and political SD/L parties in what we may anticipate will be the turbulent 1990s. It is no more, and no less, than a set of ideas. But we know from our study of history, and from reflection on our own experience, that to formulate a good and exciting idea is not the same as to see it put into effect. How realistic, then, is this 'provisional utopia'? Could a political party espouse such a programme of radical democratization, and survive as an electoral force? Could a trade union leadership sell it to their membership? Assuming that the answer to these questions is yes, what are the obstacles and sources of resistance that such a programme will encounter in the real world of industry and the economy, and how may they be overcome? These are issues that must be faced up to.

In seeking to respond to these problems, I aim to show in this chapter that the Associative Democratic paradigm generates a momemtum that can be expected to sustain an SD/L party in government, while mobilizing people through social and industrial organizations to achieve their own goals, and providing the basis for a dominant political coalition to be constructed and maintained.

A serious strategy of democratization must look first to the immediate obstacles confronting it: misrepresentation in the press and wider media; opposition and sabotage on the part of vested interests who see their influence waning; and outright political or military subversion. I shall argue that the best means of meeting these anticipated sources of opposition is through further democratization: the best defence against media manipulation lies in a democratized and diverse press; the best defence against economic sabotage is enhanced worker influence in companies; and the best defence against military subversion is democratization of the armed forces. We tease out these points below.

The strategy of democratization of economic, industrial and social life is conceived as an extension of political democracy; hence it is predicated on SD/L parties gaining and maintaining power in the various components of the politico-judicial-administrative machine we call the State. How is State power to be theorized in the AD paradigm, and how does this depart from previous and extant SD/L theorizations? What are the prospects for further democratizing the State machinery? What do we have to say about privatization and deregulation, the catchwords of the New Right?

Of equal significance, the paradigm of Associative Democracy ascribes the major transformative role, not to SD/L parties, but to autonomous organizations or associations of citizens and workers, coalescing as major social and industrial movements for democratization. How are these associations—the various social movements and the trade unions—to be theorized, and what strategies and programmes ought they to be pursuing?

Finally, we look to the ideological and theoretical issues that need to be tackled as the SD/L movement transforms itself from embodying a *culture of opposition* to a *culture of the responsible exercise of power* within a democratized system. This cultural shift will perhaps be the most difficult transition of all in the complex process of 'becoming' of the AD paradigm.

4.1 OBSTACLES TO DEMOCRATIZATION

What obstacles will a reformist SD/L government meet, both internally, within the institutions of the State, and externally, within the wider economy and society, as it seeks to accommodate and promote the democratization measures that we have been discussing. To what real extent, then, do the 'State' and associated institutions of social co-ordination represent obstacles to change, and to what extent are these obstacles themselves susceptible to democratization? This is the issue we cannot evade. We shall consider as examples the respective roles of: the media; the economic apparatus; and constitutional issues and the armed forces.

The media: manipulation and democratization

It is now commonplace to observe that the media—press, radio and television—play a dominant role in the political life of a democracy. Not only is information the currency of power, but the media have themselves spawned new styles of demonstration and direct action pitched at the TV cameras, and a series of 'think tanks' and research agencies that seek to influence public opinion directly through the media.

Behind the success of the New Right in shaping the public political agenda stands a massive media exercise, whose dimensions are still not widely understood. Alex Carey has studied the campaign that lay behind the Reagan phenomenon in the US. He concluded, writing in 1986:

> Beginning in 1975 a massive campaign of persuasion was launched by American business. Its purpose was to overcome the scepticism about American institutions (including business and the economic system) which had been engendered by Vietnam and Watergate. The campaign combined patriotism and celebration of the American economic system. It embraced two levels: the popular and the intellectual. The popular level included the use of all media to carry free enterprise faith and "economic education" to the masses—but also corporation-run competitions about the virtues of the free enterprise system which involved tens of thousands of kindergarten children and their teachers. The intellectual level of the campaign comprised a large number of lavishly funded think-tanks but also forty "Chairs of Free Enterprise" funded by business, at universities and colleges.[1]

In 1978 a Congressional inquiry revealed that American business was spending $1000 million per annum on its popular proselytizing campaign which, in the words of the *New York Times*, constituted 'a study in gigantism, saturating the media and reaching practically everybody'. In the same year Dr Edwin Feulner, President of one of the largest 'think-tanks' (The Heritage foundation) happily summarized the think-tanks' intellectual achievements. 'The American public policy arena is awash with in-depth academic studies', he reported, which lead 'to the inescapable conclusion that the free market operates more efficiently, more humanely and less expensively than any statist or socialist alternative'. In an address to businessmen in Sydney, Feulner pressed home the point that what he (and Neo-Conservatives generally) is on about is *propaganda* on a massive scale. Feulner concluded: 'Proctor and Gamble does not sell Crest toothpaste by taking out one newspaper ad or running one television commercial. They sell it and re-sell it every day by keeping the product fresh in the consumer's mind. The institutes I have mentioned sell ideas in much the same manner'.

Alex Carey was rightly worried by these developments. He concluded that historians are likely to see:

> our century as distinguished by three developments of great political importance: the growth of democracy; the growth of corporate power; and the growth of propaganda as a means of protecting corporate power against democracy.[2]

The selling of the hard business political agenda is but one aspect of media subversion of the SD/L project. Another, less subtle aspect, is outright misrepresentation of labour and social movements, or their trivialization. This is practised daily by the popular tabloids and their imitators in radio and television.[3]

In these various ways, the media have come to be dominant influences in shaping the political agenda, and in defining *the range of the possible.* Without voices of their own in the media, and means to check excesses in propaganda and misrepresentation of their programmes, the SD/L movements will wither and die.

This is becoming an issue critical to their survival.

The defence of a democratic press that will not cave in to massive New Right campaigns and outright subversion (e.g. via 'misinformation' tactics) lies in active democratization and specific measures to promote press and media diversity. Initiatives are needed to address: limitations on ownership concentration; economic assistance to media alternatives, in the interests of press balance; right of reply to aggrieved parties; reform of the law of libel and contempt; measures to protect journalists who pursue unpopular stories; and complementary measures to flush out journalists who are covert agents of the CIA or other agencies, (e.g. by requiring a public statement of affiliations or sources of income, in the manner of declarations required by members of Parliament.) Unions of journalist should, in the interests of the profession as a whole, establish standards of professional conduct and insist on their being complied with.

Thus the further democratization of the media, going beyond

the simple catchword of 'freedom of the press' but without any overtones of 'controlling' the media, is not only desirable in itself, but is a component part of a strategy of democratization in other areas of social life. We shall come across this principle elsewhere in our exploration of political strategy: let us call the principle the 'democratization of democracy' as a defence against the subversion of democracy.

Strategies of diversification

As Tom Baistow says in *Fourth-Rate Estate* (1985):

> Formidable though the dual task of democratizing the press and making it financially viable may be, there has never been any shortage of proposals: government subsidies for the weaker papers and launch-capital grants for new ones, funded by an advertising tax on the Swedish model; a levy system that would redistribute profits from the more successful groups among the struggling titles; loan funds to finance modernization and the rationalized sharing of plant, as in Holland; a national press corporation that would provide printing facilities at favourable rates to encourage new publications...[4]

In Baistow's view, some of these are more practical than others, but none have been implemented in Anglo-Saxon countries because of their politically 'sensitive' nature.

Three approaches to democratization have been found to work in practice. Negative controls on press concentration have been applied successfully in Italy and West Germany. Legislation passed in Italy in 1981 stipulated that no owner would be allowed to control more than twenty per cent of the market, and also limited the amount of the market that could be held by advertising companies. In 1982 Germany's anti-monopoly federal cartel office quashed a deal through which the Springer group would have merged with another to control more than fifty per cent of the national newspaper and magazine market. On the other hand, bold legislation enacted by the socialist Mitterand government in France in 1984 limiting any proprietor's holding to fifteen per cent—aimed at the Hersant empire headed by its three right-wing Paris dailies, *Le Figaro*, *L'Aurore* and *France-Soir*—came to nothing, and the high-powered Pluralism Commission was disbanded.

Subsidies are now widely applied to keep alive press diversity that would otherwise shrink in the face of advertising pressures. These have been introduced on a large scale in Scandinavia by the social democrats in Sweden and in Norway. For example, in

Norway in 1966 a committee representing various press organizations and government considered the financial situation of the daily press and made a number of recommendations, which were adopted by parliament. These included direct subsidies, the insertion of official announcements in all daily papers, and various indirect measures including exemption from value-added tax. A government information document in 1983 estimated that these support measures add up to between fifteen and twenty per cent of newspaper turnover, and that there would be far fewer papers in Norway without these measures. It is significant that these measures appear to have bipartisan support.

Thirdly, new publications have been assisted with public grants of various kinds. In Sweden a Press Subsidies Council is funded by a tax on advertising revenue.[5]

We discussed these Scandinavian subsidization ventures above, in the section on democratization of capital, since they were funded by a levy imposed on the media industry itself (and collected at the point of advertising). Democratization of capital for a particular social purpose, in this case press diversification, therefore performs a dual role in supporting the overall dynamic of democratization. It is a case of one part of the AD paradigm meshing with another, the two reinforcing each other.

Thus it is clear that diversity in the press can be promoted by governments, by restricting ownership, by subsidies and indirect assistance, and by providing seed capital for new ventures—provided there is political will to intervene in this way.[6] The Norwegian experience indicates that the industry can come to welcome such intervention, and that it poses no threat to the 'freedom of the press'. In this way, an SD/L government can diminish the harm inflicted on it by a hostile press, and promote its own cause by assisting the labour and social movements to publicly debate their policies in their own press.

Economic institutions and public power

There is no doubt that if and when a programme of economic democracy starts to take effect, there will be countermoves from elements amongst the employers that go beyond mere misrepresentation in the press. There will be active economic destabilization.

This has traditionally been seen in somewhat black-and-white terms, with the left talking of 'economic sabotage' or 'capital strike' when business refuses to invest, or when there is an outflow of capital from a nation in the throes of economic restructuring. Whatever may be the opinions of individual ideologically-opposed businessmen (and they can sometimes be very vocal opponents of SD/L governments), it is mistaken to imagine that the business sector *as a whole* will voluntarily deny itself profits in favour of 'mere' political opposition to a government. If there is shortage of investment, it is more than likely provoked by a hostile financial environment (e.g. high interest rates) or by a climate of uncertainty.

The answer to this uncertainty is a programme of *conditional* commitments, and a strategy of co-operative accommodation. It should include not just positive proposals, but sanctions for non-co-operation, such as state takeover of a firm which is actively opposing a programme of reform that has majority support (e.g. refusing to pay taxes, or ostentatiously siphoning off profits).

Again, the best defence against the subversion of economic democracy, is democratization. Where Boards of Directors are plotting against a government, the best defence is to open up the Board to worker and public representatives. If the strategy is to oppose existing economic power with a process of democratization, and this meets with the resistance to be expected, then the tactics need to be couched in terms of isolating the pockets of resistance as far as possible. The movement—SD/L government, unions, social groups—needs to project an attitude of firmness but reasonableness, of doing things by the book, through the processes of the law, so that opposition is, and is seen to be, *unreasonable*.

The pace of change is all-important. Any attempt to push the pace too fast will inevitably perish in a determined counter-attack, and it will take years for the movement to recover from such a setback. On the other hand, if the pace is too slow, so that change becomes imperceptible, then the momentum is lost, and popular activity wanes.

This is not an insuperable dilemma. It requires a reasonably astute leadership of both political and industrial wings, and a framework of agreement on the pace of change, as laid down in a social contract with conditional clauses.

What the history of the movement in the twentieth century shows is that retreats, evasions, and excessive compromises are all too often the response of SD/L governments to business counter-attacks, and that these invariably lead in the end to loss of a political base and electoral defeat. Once a programme of change is initiated, there is no going back on it: there must be a strategically determined line of advance, qualified where appropriate by tactical retreats and feints.

The lack of such a strategy was the undoing of the Callaghan Labour government in the UK, 1973–79. It was elected to office on a wave of enthusiasm following the defeat of the Heath government by the miners' strike. It came with a radical programme containing strong measures on industry policy, planning agreements, and other measures (all expounded by Holland in the *Socialist Challenge*)—but with the balance of payments crisis of 1974, and demands from the IMF to hold sterling, its nerve collapsed and it abandoned its programme. It then limped from crisis to crisis, seeking to impose statutory wage controls on trade unions, culminating in the famed 'Winter of Discontent' in 1978. The Thatcher government was the inevitable result in 1979, and the UK labour movement still has not recovered. All this can be ascribed, not only to inept leadership, of which there was plenty, but also to the prevalence of many of the illusions discussed above, particularly the inflexibility of the programme in the face of economic deterioration.

It is a strategic perspective, a sense of where the movement is headed in the medium term, that can see an SD/L government through an economic crisis without capitulation to capital, international finance or the IMF. This is one of the key functions of the AD paradigm—to provide just such a strategic perspective.

Constitutional issues and the armed forces

In the last resort, of course, the turmoil unleashed by a transformative strategy of economic and social change might result in a 'suspension of democracy', and the advent of a neo-fascist government of one kind or another. There is, of course, no shortage of instances of this sort of development in the twentieth century, and it would be foolish, if not irresponsible, to discount it in countries where the democratic roots are deepest.

Even in Britain, with its constitutional balance of powers dating back to the settlement of 1688, the commitment to democracy cannot be taken for granted. Sir Ian Gilmour, Conservative member of the UK Parliament, wrote in 1977:

> Conservatives do not worship democracy. For them, majority rule is a device . . . democracy is a means to an end and not . . . an end in itself . . . And if it is leading to an end that is undesirable or is inconsistent with itself, then there is a theoretical case for ending it.[7]

Such statements are rarely made so explicitly; Gilmour even suggests openly that military action may be justified against a democratically elected Left-wing government that is attempting to implement a radical transformative program. Such a view is shocking because it is rarely stated so openly, in the West; while elsewhere, as in Pinochet's Chile, where the dirty 'war against Marxism' was stepped up again in 1986, it appears to be the norm. Yet the view that democracy may be overthrown from the Right is, we must admit, merely the complement of the view oft repeated on the Left that an unjust system ought to be overthrown. It is, in a sense, a case of the Left's chickens coming home to roost.

The fact is, of course, that democracy is a very precious and fragile social entity that needs to be constantly nurtured and protected. This is sometimes hard for the party of Labour to persevere with, in the face of the swaggering arrogance of conservative party members, both in Parliament and without. But there can be no fudging on the issue: democracy is the greatest weapon in the hands of the labour movement, and its defence must be accorded the highest priority. There are risks involved, but this is always the case in any real-world undertaking.

On the one hand, there are no guarantees in any democracy that 'the rules of the game' will be respected. Within the limits of parliamentary democracy, there are social gains that can be formulated and must be fought for in order to defend the whole system from becoming an irrelevance in a world dominated by big capital and international finance, with all the limitations that playing by the rules imposes, and without any certainty that in the end any thorough transformation will be effected. On the other hand, there can be no doubt what would happen if the pace were to be forced and groups on the Left went underground to engage in armed struggle as a 'complement' to legal democratic activity. Such a move would trigger, at the very least, an increase in State military surveillance, and loss of civil liberties, as in West Germany and Italy in response to the Red Army faction and the Red Brigades. At worst, it would provoke an unleashing of counter-terror on the civilian population, as has happened with appalling consequences in Uruguay and Argentina where death squads roamed the streets in the 1970s and 1980s. Such an outcome is to be avoided at all costs: it must be recognized as the logical result of the 'revolutionary option' showing signs of success.

In my view, the SD/L movement needs to take a cold, hard look at its prospects, and take certain precautionary steps against any 'suspension' of democracy some way down the path of transformation. A straight military coup is unlikely in an advanced democracy. What is more likely is a manipulation of the Constitution, with an artificially generated 'political crisis' being resolved by suspension of an elected government. This is what happened in Australia where the Whitlam government was 'dismissed' in 1975 by the Governor-General as a result of the political crisis provoked by the Opposition deferring supply in the Senate. This remains a threat wherever constitutions allow Upper Houses to retain residual powers over Lower Houses (as in virtually all Australian states and federally); the obvious remedy for SD/L parties is to implement strong measures of constitutional reform when they are in government.

If there is a political stalemate, then resort to a government of 'national unity' backed by expressions of confidence from the armed forces could be triggered—or the armed forces themselves could become highly politicized, as has happened recently in the Philippines. For democrats, the best defence against reactionary and secret political meddling by right-wing officers, and certainly against a coup itself, is the open democratization of the armed forces, making them transparently a part of civilian life, with uniformed men and women enjoying the same liberties as any other citizen, including the basic right to form their own trade union.

The task of defence itself should be democratized, via the formation of a citizens' militia. Examples abound, such as the UK Home Guard, which gave excellent service during the Second World War and would have given better but for the jealousy of professional officers; or the Swiss or Swedish Militias. At the same time, secrecy in the armed forces should be fought against, for while ostensibly hiding defence moves from 'the enemy', it in fact acts as a cover for officers to keep their plans and stratagems from the civilian population.

Similarly, the active but covert opposition of security organizations, such as MI5 and MI6 in Britain, or ASIO and ASIS in Australia, can be anticipated when SD/L governments take office. The best cover for their subversion (which has been documented in numerous instances) is to allow them to remain secret. Subjecting their operations to public scrutiny, with due allowance for matters of genuine 'national security', is an essential component of any democratization strategy.

Hence the best defence of democracy is, again, more democracy. It is a stabilizing force in itself. For the more secure our political democracy (e.g. curtailed powers of Upper Houses to over-rule a government formed in a lower House; restriction of gerrymanders; fair voting systems) the less room there is for anti-democratic forces to organize. The more secure our economic democracy, the less scope there is for a clique of wealthy business people to use their companies for purposes of organizing political opposition to a reforming government.

So far, we have been considering 'external' obstacles to the success of an SD/L democratization strategy. But equally serious obstacles are generated internally, from within the labour and social movements themselves.

Pragmatic evasion within SD/L parties

Once the labour movement became an electoral force, it was prone to a brake on its further development, generated not from enemies outside (e.g. media misrepresentation, or economic subversion) but from within the ranks of party or union membership. There is always a tension, of course, in electoral organizations like SD/L parties, between those who formulate 'provisional utopias' for the movement to strive towards, and those who simply use these parties for their personal advancement, and view all talk of 'alternative futures' as a threat to the security of their parliamentary seat or other party-nominated position. They seek to quash such talk by claims that the party (either in government or opposition) must be prudent and responsible; it must avoid 'adventurism' and above all must be seen not to be 'wasting' public funds.

Now these are, of course, quite legitimate claims. It is true that a party seeking office must be prudent and responsible; but this does *not* mean that it has to be unimaginative and tailist (i.e. simply tailing public opinion, rather than helping to shape it).

Take as an example the issue of workers' cooperatives. There may be a debate in the SD/L party, and a policy adopted that such co-operatives be encouraged, on the grounds that they provide an alternative to hierarchical management systems where workers have no say because they have no ownership. This may be linked, as it is in this text, with a programme for drastic industry development based on a new climate for co-operation and co-determination between employers and unions. The party fights an election on this platform, and wins.

Once the party is in power, the 'realists' can take over and argue that the party's immediate task is to create jobs; co-operatives are only going to provide at best a marginal improvement in employment overall and therefore the government cannot be seen to be throwing too much money at workers' co-operatives, if any at all. In this way, the realists can subvert the intentions of the programme by their appeals to the supposed immediate needs of the movement.

In my view, this will always be a mechanism for defeating the long-term aims of democrats who elect to work within the open structures of an SD/L party—and therefore it needs to be faced up to. Let us call it the option of *pragmatic evasion.* Those who use it may not do so to consciously subvert the long-term aims of the movement; they may be, and indeed are, more than likely to be genuinely concerned about the short-term electoral damage that will be inflicted by embarking on a programme that offers long-term transformative results. Hence there is no point in resorting to psychological explanations, or calling such people traitors.

Electoral tailism, or pragmatic evasion, does not have a coherent paradigm or vision of its own, but a hostility to the paradigms of others. It is a lowest common denominator form of politics.

There are both theoretical and practical means of countering pragmatic evasion. Historically, the 'solution' to this problem has been sought in the party's election manifesto being viewed as a binding document, with the party putting pressure on its government to implement the terms of the manifesto in full—even if some of these actions attract a great deal of publicly orchestrated opposition. It is in seeking to resolve this tension between the party and government, between the commitments of the manifesto and the unexpected pressures encountered in government, between the perceived mandate for change and the structural opposition to change as soon as it is attempted—it is in these activities that the Labour parties in the UK, Australia and New Zealand, for example, have spent a lot of their time and energy in the past ten years, looking for solutions in terms of 'control' over the government by party committees. The trouble with this 'solution' is that it is always trying to fix issues after the event, and it always gives the public the impression of a government in hock to groups of 'faceless' men and women. Furthermore, such a 'solution' assumes that all the wisdom is to be found in the party, and leaves to one side all the resources of public administration that can be drawn on when in government. It is therefore a 'solution' that is bound to fail.

I would suggest that we need to cast the problem in a different light. In cybernetic terms, a 'once for all' party political programme is a form of open-loop control—a very brittle strategy, and one that is tailor-made for the 'realists', or 'pragmatic evaders' to argue that the 'time is not suitable' and the 'conditions are adverse'. Much more flexible, of course, is feedback control. In political terms, feedback control implies being able to react quickly to events to keep an overall strategy on course. It means putting people into positions of responsibility, and then allowing them to exercise that responsibility—but within strict overall guidelines that are laid down as 'policy'.

The SD/L tradition illustrates the dangers of expecting a party or a movement to remain accountable to its constituents on the basis of a fixed programme, irrespective of changing circumstances. One way to avoid this illusion is obvious enough; it is to make commitments *conditional* or *contingent* on certain conditions in the real world coming to pass. Obvious or not, this solution is taking a long time to be accepted as part of the culture of the labour movement. An interesting example of it is indexation, e.g. of state pensions, or of state securities, or, more radically, of basic wage rates as part of a comprehensive social contract.

Conditional commitments are widely accepted outside the political domain. In finance, for example, the purchase of options is a neat example of a conditional commitment, while on the stock markets many takeover offers are made conditional on there being fifty-one per cent acceptances (the implication being that the offer will lapse if not enough people take it up). And the principle is universal in the world of engineering, both in hardware terms ('trip' mechanisms, etc) and in software terms ('if this' . . . 'then' programming statements, or conditional diamonds in flow charts). It has just taken a long time for such an obvious principle to be articulated clearly in the political domain, as a democratic stratagem.

Domenico Mario Nuti has recently elaborated on this idea, taking as his starting point the difficulties facing planning, and in particular the centralized command planning prevalent in Eastern Europe and the USSR. Nuti advocates the use of *conditional commitments*—commitments which are conditional on certain events occurring, and which are called up if, and only if, these events occur.[8]

Such 'conditional commitments' are feasible only in comprehensive social contracts struck on the one hand between the SD/L party and the unions (e.g. the ACTU–ALP Accord in Australia) or on the other hand between employer organizations and unions (and perhaps other social movements) as in Sweden and Austria. This is yet a further reason why social contracts, and the 'political trade unionism' that they imply, are in my view an essential prerequisite for any meaningful advance to greater economic or social democracy.

4.2 THE ROLE OF THE STATE

In most texts that discuss the transformation of the social and economic order, the question of the role of the State, and the process of winning and holding State power, would be the dominant theme. But the paradigm of associative democracy departs from this 'statist' obsession, and instead sees the major impetus for the democratization of social and economic life as coming from the organized citizenry and workforce itself. The role of the State is seen as being to assist this process, but not to displace it.

The strategy formulated here can be encapsulated in a simple proposition, namely that the democratization of the State is a necessary but not sufficient condition for the transformation of the social and economic order. It is *necessary* because, without it, all efforts to democratize capital, industry and economic processes would be blocked by hostile laws, a hostile government, and a hostile press. But it is not *sufficient* because the real democratization must occur within the structures and processes located in the economy and society.

We tease out this proposition in this section. We shall look first at how the State has been theorized in the literature of the labour and social movements, and whether this helps us much. We shall then look at the role that an SD/L government can play.

Theorization of the State—false trails

As we have seen, the paradigm of associative democracy does not view the State as an entity floating over and above the rest of society, with its own idealized 'interests' to protect (e.g. the 'surveillance State'). Within the AD paradigm, the State is viewed as an arena of social competition for resources, and as a means for imposing order (regulating) where disorder creates loss of amenity for ordinary citizens and workers. State structures (e.g. for planning) are needed if the democratic economy is to function, while law enforcement will always be a community responsibility under any social regime; on the other hand, the AD paradigm rejects bureaucratic notions of social democracy as an amalgam of 'nationalized industries' and the 'welfare state'. The paradigm thus adopts a 'pragmatic' approach to the State. But this has not been the dominant view on the Left. In their zeal to see the 'logic of capital' reproduced in every layer of society (hence: 'capitalist State', 'capitalist production', 'capitalist society'), theoreticians who have contributed to the revival of the Left since the 1960s have failed to give an account of the State that is adequate in the face of the challenge from the New Right. The old 'mechanical Marxist' formulation of the State as guarantor of the prerogatives of capital, gave away in the 1960s and 1970s to a more sophisticated but no less erroneous series of perspectives on the role of the State as basically being that of upholding or underwriting the process of private capitalist accumulation. Such an approach effectively foreclosed any meaningful debate on the notion of the State being an arena of social struggle, and, as a major employer, a dynamic system in its own right.

The notion of the State as a unified, homogeneous actor underlies conceptions of it playing the role of an 'ideal collective capitalist' who appears to have omnipotent abilities to outmanoeuvre or trap the working class. Beyond this, many theorizations attempt to explain the nature of state institutions by reference to the logic of capital accumulation, and thereby remove all possibility of developing an adequate account of State intervention to regulate key aspects of the economy, particularly at its margins (e.g. where it intersects with ecological or human health questions).[9]

The theorization of the State as epitome of repression draws from an unsophisticated conception of the State's repressive apparatuses, for example the police, keeping the proletariat in check. Such a view derives, obviously enough, from the view of the police or the army that one obtains from a picket line or demonstration; it reflects the experience that 'restoration of public order' is more frequently directed against workers than against others, as for example racist provocative demonstrations by quasi-fascist organizations. It is also a view that finds ready historical continuity with the brutal and sadistic repression—what can only be called state terror—of the nineteenth century and earlier: the floggings, torture, hangings, imprisonment, and transportation. But for all this, such a view offers no perspective on any *alternative* use of the administrative apparatus of the State.

Political theory in the past two decades, following the work of Marcuse and more recently Foucault, has also identified a network of structures of social regulation outside the 'State' proper, but in the areas of education, psychiatric services and social welfare.[10] This situation is contrasted with that of the nineteenth century, when the life of a worker and family was dominated by the despotism of the workplace; the state played a role mainly as coercer, through brutalization, fear and exemplary punishment, while ordinary people seldom came into contact with the professions. Whole areas of modern life—social services, universal education, health care—were unknown or in a rudimentary state. Consequently the production process and employment relations had been the dominant focus of socialist theory. It is true that our modern, complex democracies are very different. People's lives are impinged on continuously by social groups and forces that lie outside the employment relation and the State (narrowly defined). In health care, our options are defined for us by professionals—doctors, nurses, psychiatrists; in education similarly, as also in housing, community services, building and planning. In the world of trade and industry, again the options seem to be fashioned by professionals—accountants, lawyers, operations researchers and modellers, engineers. And at the points of social discipline—the judiciary, the prisons—again much of human interaction is with professionals rather than with brute force.

But in place of viewing these professional services as sites for further democratization by the SD/L movement, a prominent theoretical school associated with Althusser has characterized them as merely a functional collection of 'Ideological State Apparatuses' (ISAs), 'corrupting' proletarian consciousness through education, welfare, the prison, and hospitals.[11] Such a view comes up against its limits quickly enough when the poor and the unemployed organize to prevent cutbacks in the State services that Marxian theoreticians loftily dismiss as 'therapeutic paternalism'. The left critique failed to identify the core of 'social wage' services that were part of Marshall's notion of 'citizenship' and to differentiate it from its bureaucratic overlays; it also fails to provide any basis for demands to make the activities of the professions more accountable, particularly where they are seen to be overstepping their authority (as in the current debate over child protection responsibilities).

These 'false trails' have all in their different ways acted as a deadweight on the Labour and social movements, discouraging them from any form of intervention to contest control of the machinery of State power. By contrast, the essential perspective expounded here is not to see the State as a bloc, with its own or anyone else's interests paramount, but as a social arena for deciding issues, a set of social resources to be allocated by those decisions, and a means of enforcing those decisions. The labour and social movements have democratized some parts of this huge slice of the social and economic order better than others, but the movement cannot hope to preserve the gains it makes in economic and social life unless it extends the basis of popular participation and control in *all* the areas and institutions of the realm we call 'the State'. I would suggest that the most fruitful theoretical approach is to see the State and its constitution as the ultimate 'soft technology', and therefore subject to design, with each design carrying a different conception or set of principles of politics and ethics.

Harnessing of the State

Given that this machine we call 'the State' can be influenced, in its operation and design, by SD/L parties winning majorities in parliament and promoting their supporters to key public service positions, what should be the strategy of the labour and social movements to these pre-eminently 'political' issues? I concur with the Italian democratic theorist Norberto Bobbio: defence of the democratic 'rules of the game' is the path of least resistance and greatest influence. Even with all the frustrations this involves, adherence to constitutional legality provides the best framework for determined advance in the wider spheres of the economy, industry and community.

This is not to say that the political machinery of democratic States is perfect—far from it. The strategy of democratization of the economic, industrial and social domains needs to be complemented by determined moves to *further democratize the political domain*—but through due process, and through upholding constitutional conventions even when there are short-term party political disadvantages flowing from this (for example, in electoral redistributions, or in allocating chairing positions to parliamentary committees). Such an approach needs to tackle the constitutional, parliamentary, governmental and judicial components of the State machine, to fashion a democratic polity adequate for the governance of a democratic economy.[12]

Constitutional reform

The *constitution* is the basic soft technology that allocates functions to the arms of government, prescribes the rules governing them, and the procedures to be employed in the case of deadlock.

Every advance by the SD/L movement in the political domain has been wrung from an unyielding constitution but conversely, every such advance consolidates the constitutional position of the SD/L movement and provides it with a platform for further transformation. This is the double-edged character of constitutions.

Where constitutions offer impossible obstacles to any reforming government, there is no option but to use all remedies available to change them. Such obstacles include:

- excessive veto powers in an Upper house;
- open-ended dismissal procedures vested in Governors;
- impossibly stringent conditions governing amendments to the constitution;
- gerrymandered electoral distribution;
- insensitive voting systems (e.g. 'first past the post');
- inadequate regulation of elections;
- excessive restrictions on the power of parliament *vis-à-vis* other state agencies;
- excessive restrictions on the power of federal parliaments with respect to states' powers.

These obstacles are all susceptible to reform through referendum or some other aspect of the political process—particularly at times of crisis when constitutional obstacles are seen as being manifestly unfair.

On the other hand, there are constitutional guarantees that the labour and social movements have won and exploited, which must be safeguarded. The most important of these is observance of legality, for this is ultimately what an SD/L government depends on when enacting reforms. If it expects others to comply with its decrees, then it must itself observe and defend legality. This means, for example, not only handing over executive authority to opponents when elections are fought and lost, but in less dramatic ways, upholding the status of public officials even when their actions or judgments lead to short-term party political set backs. It is the status of officials such as electoral commissioners, auditors-general and ombudsmen that can shield SD/L parties from outrageous acts by their own members who seek to abuse office or otherwise act at variance with SD/L party norms.

The democratic economy, while giving greater scope to workers and consumers to have a direct say in what they produce or consume, will require democratic central planning and policy development facilities that will need oversight by a popular assembly. I do not wish to enter into a technical discussion as to how such an assembly should be designed, nor as to the respective merits of Westminster-style systems or presidential-style systems. The point is that certain functions will have to be carried out by an assembly, and certain functions by a duly-appointed executive authority (government); previous socialist fantasies concerning the 'withering away of the State' can be dismissed as nonsense. There has been too much blood shed in the twentieth century in political upheavals for anyone to suppose that a rational citizenry would elect to power *any* group of people without adequate machinery to ensure that they behave as they promise to do, and, if not, that they may be ejected with due dispatch.

Parliamentary reform

A democratic polity will consist of a pluralist system where major differences are expressed through legally-formed parties. Legislative forums will be needed to debate the major issues, and to serve as a means of exposing and checking the exercise of power. Parties themselves will need to be regulated, to ensure that there are no unfair advantages (for example, in election expenditure) and to ensure that the choosing of candidates fulfils the requirements of natural justice.

Parliaments are basically public forums through which control of public resources is allocated and overseen. Well-run assemblies, like the US congress, function essentially as institutions laying down in general terms how things ought to be ordered, and conducting investigations to see whether their prescriptions are being complied with. To do this they need flexible standing orders; a well-developed committee system; facilities and resources; and powers to discipline themselves and those they are questioning. While in opposition, SD/L parties can make use of these features of a parliament to expose a conservative government. In power, however, SD/L governments frequently see parliament as a nuisance and seek to evade it; this in my view is a short-sighted policy which merely devalues the institution as a legitimate repository of popular power. The strength of parliament lies not in its simple majority belonging to one side or the other, but in its committee system, and in its ability to command information and disclosure, forcing matters on to the public record. This feature can be used to advantage by an SD/L party holding government, just as much as when it is in opposition. To take an obvious example, when controversial legislation is passed, granting or extending economic or social rights, the SD/L majority party should institute parliamentary hearings to determine the extent of compliance with the new laws.

We have long outgrown Marx's disparaging remarks about parliaments as being mere 'talking shops' in his eulogy of the Paris Commune. In a social order where information is the currency of power, we should interpret parliaments today, with their ancient liberties and procedures, as machines for effecting public disclosure of information that private persons or firms wish to keep private for their illegitimate advantage. This is a power not to be given up lightly.

Political parties

Political parties in a democratic polity will form around general ideologies or paradigms as well as around particular issues. I see no reason to doubt that SD/L parties, and other major conservative opponents, will exist for a long time to come. Parties themselves need to be organized along internal democratic lines; this means dispensing once and for all with Fordist right-wing notions of keeping 'the membership' in line, and equally fruitless 'revolutionary' notions of organizing parties like guerrilla units, with tight internal discipline and a crushing standard of dedication. Modern parties are social organisms where a number of interests intersect, and where electoral activities ought to be balanced by membership-training, intellectual debate within a party press, the support of serious social and economic research, and an openness to broad social movements and campaigns. Parties that become mere electoral machines will quickly wither and die.

The outstanding example of a party that draws on tremendous popular resources, and offers a total social involvement to these members (youth groups, special interest groups, party press) is the Swedish SD party. But it is probably unrealistic to expect all SD/L parties to achieve this standard. The outstanding examples of parties that train their members in political theory and the importance of ideology, are the Communist Parties. The SD/L parties neglect this aspect of their operation to their peril.

Because parties fulfil public functions, it is perfectly legitimate to demand that they receive funding, in proportion to their size or electoral activity, and that there be a ceiling on expenditure by parties to ensure that there is generally fair competition between them. (With the sums now spent on television advertising, this is becoming a critical issue.) The argument for public funding of parties in the 1980s is identical with that advanced in the 1880s for public payment of members of parliament—and in each case it is the party representing the labour and social movements which gains from the arrangement, since it cannot expect to depend on wealthy backers.

Judiciary

In a democratic polity, disputes between social groups or individuals will occur, and can be expected to be settled largely through the political process and the columns of the press. Nevertheless, courts and a judiciary will be needed to deal with disputes that cannot be settled through such debate, and to enforce standards of inter-personal behaviour which are set by the parliament or are part of a common heritage. It is the judiciary which today remains most resistant to democratization, and hence most in need of sustained attention by reformist SD/L parties. Issues needing reform include:

- questions of access (legal aid, legal machinery);
- questions of accountability (appointment and responsibility of judges, resourcing of popular institutions such as juries);
- questions of diligence (protection of civil liberties, adequate resourcing of criminal investigation);
- questions of procedure (democratization of the solicitor/barrister dichotomy, introduction of class and public interest actions).

A democratic polity, like any other society, will need places of confinement in which to isolate anti-social elements, but these must not and should not be places of punishment. The degree to which the civil rights of prisoners are recognized is a very good index of the sophistication of a democratic polity.

Government administration

It is the public administration or executive arm of government, that has grown most spectacularly in recent decades, and which is attracting most of the attention of the New Right. An efficient administration is needed by any SD/L government with transformative intentions; above all such a government needs active and intelligent chief executives and staffs within government departments and statutory authorities—and I agree with Hugh Stretton that it should not shrink from dismissing those with opposed views, and appointing its own people, provided due process is respected.[13] Efficiency of administration and open dealing ('freedom of information') are synonymous, and discredited notions of 'security' must be rigorously opposed by SD/L governments. In a democratic economy, where workers have access to management information, it is unrealistic to expect citizens not to demand, and obtain, similar access to cabinet and top-level administrative decisions. Openness is also supported by ensuring that senior officials be accountable to parliament as well as to the government.

These then are the constitutional and administrative issues which need to be confronted by any SD/L party that is following a democratic, transformative strategy. Its rationale for securing positions of public power is partly to offer positive support and resources to the agents of change in the community, and partly (perhaps more importantly) to hold at bay the instruments which could be used to frustrate the agents of change. This is again to underscore the need to uphold legality and democratic proprieties at all costs, and to wage a campaign of political democratization as the best defence of democracy in other spheres.

4.3 THE FUTURE OF THE PUBLIC SECTOR

In very broad terms, one may say that the major export of Thatcherism in Britain has been privatization, while of Reaganism in the US, it has been deregulation. These processes have become the firm articles of faith of the New Right around the world; in realistic terms, they have set the political agenda governing the future of the public sector that SD/L parties, in and out of government, will have to live with. These parties and movements are learning, in the late 1980s, that dogmatic opposition to the whole of the privatization and deregulation case is not politically feasible.

I maintain that the paradigm of Associative Democracy provides the SD/L movement with a framework within which the pressures for privatization and deregulation can be accommodated, thus taking the sting out of New Right attacks, without abandoning the Labour and social movements' historic commitments to a strong public sector. This is a somewhat ambitious claim which I hope to substantiate in this section.

Privatization

In the British experience of privatization there was no green paper, no white paper, no definite piece of legislation, no second reading speech, and the concept was not even contained in the Conservative Party manifesto for the 1979 election when the Tories came to office. It was not really an issue in the 1983 election. Even today there is no distinct policy document from either the British government or the Conservative Party defining privatization, justifying it, outlining its objectives or spelling out its future applications.[14]

This is the way in which the most significant conservative political initiative in the post-war era has been launched—as described in a conservative commentary!

Poorly focused and articulated as it may have been, the Thatcher privatization effort has had a dramatic effect on the British public sector. More than eighteen major enterprises (and over three-quarters of a million houses) have been sold; share ownership has doubled; projected government revenue from the programme stands at some twenty billion pounds in 1988-89; and instances of contracting out of central and local government level now run to thousands of cases. Up to the end of 1987, there had been forty-two separate episodes of sale of public sector enterprises in Britain, which in itself has created a mini-industry of financial advisers and brokers.[15]

Yet the programme got off to a very hesitant start. While in opposition, in 1978, the Conservative Party under its new leader, Margaret Thatcher, developed proposals for dealing with the nationalized industries and the unions, and particularly the trade unions in the nationalized industries. The fate of the previous Conservative Heath government at the hands of the National Union of Miners was uppermost in their minds. Proposals were formulated for ending statutory monopolies in the public sector and for increasing the competitive environment in which the nationalized industries would operate; this was seen as politically more feasible than actual sales, or 'denationalization'.[16]

The early years of the Thatcher government saw these competition enhancing measures enacted, such as through the *Electricity Act,* which removed the statutory monopoly of the Central Electricity Generating Board, and the *Transport Act,* which allowed free entry into express coach services. This was followed by liberalization of British Telecom in 1981. It was only after these measures were in place that outright denationalization was considered feasible, and given an acceptable name in the term 'privatization'.

The use of the word has now been expanded to cover many other activities apart from sale of major nationalized industries. It is now deemed to cover such matters as:

- increased resort to 'user pays' principles;
- contracting out of government services;
- sale of State-owned assets;
- facilitation of competition between private and public sector institutions.[17]

While it is ideological fervour that has driven the privatization programme in the UK, the movement has now spread internationally, acquiring more pragmatic overtones as experience is acquired. France has gone further than any other country except Britain, denationalizing many of the industries previously nationalized by the first Mitterand government, but reconstructing them and injecting them with private capital prior to sale. The French have perfected techniques of valuation of public assets. After starting badly with the glass maker St Gobain, whose shares rose twenty per cent above their offer price when trading opened, they did much better with the electricity monopoly CGE, and further honed their skills in the divestment of banks and insurance firms. In Italy the pragmatic element has been to the fore: privatization has taken the form mainly of sale of minority participation in subsidiaries of the two great public holding groups IRI (industry and banking) and ENI (hydrocarbons—oil and gas) rather than outright sale; public sector efficiency and access to capital have been the guiding issues. Similarly, in West Germany, there have been disposals of state holdings in Volkswagen, and attempts are being made on the giant Bundespost monopoly, but ideological fervour has been tempered by a sense of political advantage which public sector assets yield for elements of the governing conservative coalition.

In Canada, the conservative Mulroney government embarked on a wholesale privatization plan after their victory in 1984. A dozen crown corporations had been sold off by 1987, while plans for dealing with the two largest public enterprises, Air Canada and Petro-Canada, became embroiled in political fights.[18]

Socialist governments have initiated privatization moves in Spain and New Zealand, while the topic has dominated the agenda of the Hawke Labor government in Australia since 1987. In Spain, the State-owned SEAT car works have been sold to Volkswagen, and there is a programme of sales under way affecting the vehicle, tourism, textile and computer industries. In New Zealand, the Lange Labour government initiated privatization moves in 1986 with partial sales and equity in the Bank of New Zealand and Petroleum Corporation of NZ. One year later, more than 50 000 investors had applied for thirteen per cent of Petrocorp. It was then announced that equity would be sold in Air New Zealand and Development Finance Corporation of NZ, while the government would sell its controlling interest in Petrocorp. These moves have been accompanied by 'corporatization' of State-owned enterprises that were previously run by government departments: forestry, property services etc. In 1987 it was announced that two of these new corporations would also be issuing equity bonds to the general public. In the budget of 1988 the Labour government declared it would go all the way and sell its entire stake in the Bank of New Zealand.

In Australia, plans to partially divest public corporations were being discussed all through 1987, with the government losing a debate with the ALP for lack of specific proposals and adequate rationale. However, the capital injections needed by large operations such as the airline Qantas, and the need for greater public sector efficiency, mean that this issue will remain on the political agenda in Australia.

How can the SD/L movement formulate a strategy for dealing with this question of the relations between the public and private sectors? In the first case, it must be acknowledged that defence of the public sector as it stands, without constructive proposals for its reform, is a recipe for disaster; not only does it give the political initiative to the New Right in calling for total privatization, but it can only lock the public sector into a financial and economic ghetto in which it will ultimately perish. However, it must also be acknowledged that public sector enterprises (as distinct from education, health and welfare services, which are a different matter) represent substantial public assets, sources of government revenue, and instruments for government policy (for example, for purposes of equity pricing, allowing rural consumers to pay the same price for postal and telephone services as urban customers). Where is the balance to be struck in this matter?

Along with many other sympathetic observers, I would advocate a non-dogmatic approach. Partial, and even complete, privatization can be in the public interest. It is the efficiency, equity and organization of the entity that should concern the SD/L movement, not the simple criterion 'public or private'. The paradigm of associative democracy helps to place this debate over private sector-public sector interaction in a fresh political context. By making democratization the goal of strategic interventions, in both the public and private sectors, rather than 'nationalization'; and by focusing on democratization as the key to expanding popular influence and control, rather than relying solely on public ownership, the paradigm offers some criteria for evaluation of proposals that have strategic significance.

When offering the private sector some form of participation in the public sector, governments are in a uniquely strong position to set the terms of this involvement within a political framework. Offers of participation can be used openly, not just for technical reasons of raising capital, but to achieve social goals.

For example, run-down enterprises can be restructured and offered to private consortia, on condition that industrial and economic democracy guidelines be complied with (subject to sanctions for non-compliance). In this way, partial or even complete privatization can be used to establish 'lighthouse' projects demonstrating the virtues and practicability of employee participation, while incompetent public sector managements are disposed of.

Government contracting arrangements can be utilized in the same way. When calling for tenders, it is open to governments to use their position as defenders of the public interest to insist on certain minimal conditions and standards being met by candidate contractors. The US federal government has exploited this approach most effectively, in insisting that all federal contractors pursue equal employment opportunity policies. The ripple effect through the rest of the economy can be considerable, for contractors cannot assume one employment policy with regard to the government and a different one for other clients. Moreover, through this approach the government is not *imposing* its values on a reluctant business community through legislation; competition ensures that those firms which find the government's conditions and standards to be repugnant, simply do not bid for government contracts.

The approach advocated is not limited to transfers from public to private sector (as envisaged by the loaded term 'privatization'). In the other direction, governments are actively acquiring public assets particularly in the high technology sector where innovative ventures depend on public equity to help them get off the ground. In these cases too, when government is invited to become a joint venturer in a private consortium, the opportunity can and should be taken to impose certain social conditions on such involvement. In relation to technological innovation, these could include reference to such criteria as: social utility of the innovation, local R & D content, technology transfer from multinational joint venturers, and employee participation.

Moreover, governments are forming new enterprises which can be wholly government-owned, or joint ventures with private sector partners, to perform specific social functions. Such enterprises in the past have been largely confined to energy utilities, but SD/L governments with a sense of future trajectories can establish a public presence in the knowledge and information industries by launching new ventures. For example, the Cain Labor government in Victoria has formed publicly-owned companies in this sector, such as Knowledge Victoria Ltd and the Victorian Education Foundation, which seek opportunities to enhance the State's education and training resources. This sort of activity is a long way from the ideological concerns of New Right 'privateers', but it is a logical activity for an SD/L government operating within an innovative model of *private–public sector interaction*, informed by the AD paradigm.

Within such a framework, it is logical for governments to divest themselves of assets which are not being used efficiently or effectively, or to acquire new assets where there is a strategic call for them.[19] It is not the place of governments to actually *operate* these enterprises; that is the role of managers who are accountable to a Board which can be appointed by government. From this perspective, the New Zealand 'corporatization' programme, in which State enterprises operated by departments were restructured as 'corporations', makes eminent sense. Yet it was opposed vigorously by the NZ Labour Party, which was wedded to a notion of 'socialization' through government ownership and government operation of all enterprises.

The New Zealand experience is instructive for another reason. The privatization and corporatization programmes there have been forced through by a determined government, against the vocal opposition of the party membership. The opportunity to use this programme as a means of mobilizing support for democratization, and to actually enhance economic democracy, has been thrown away. The government has 'won' its battles with the party, at the cost of widespread disillusion and demobilization. This is not the way forward for the SD/L movement. It is not the way things would happen were the party to embrace the paradigm of associative democracy, and set its government the task of restructuring the public sector in such a way as to raise the level of democratic participation in efficiently run enterprises.

Deregulation

Deregulation became the Reagan administration's watchword, formulated in primitive ideological terms as 'getting government off business' back'. Fuelled by New Right economic rhetoric, 'market forces' were given a renewed lease of life in one industry after another, sometimes with beneficial effects (where artificial monopolies have been broken up) and more frequently with disastrous results (in telecommunications, where charges have risen and standards have fallen; and in air transport, where public safety has been seriously threatened). The scope of federal agencies, such as the Environmental Protection Agency (EPA) and Occupational Safety and Health Administration (OSHA), set up during the 1970s, was drastically cut back, through political appointments, budget cutbacks, and legislative paring back of powers.

The New Right case for deregulation was that industry was unable to compete or adjust to new conditions under the 'regulatory burden' that federal agencies and regulations imposed.

By simply responding with 'knee-jerk' defence of regulatory structures, the SD/L parties cede vast tracts of political territory to the Right. The fact is that regulations should always be kept under review, to check whether they are necessary, and if so, whether they are achieving the desired effect. (Again, parliaments can play a critical role in performing this 'regulation review' function.) The fact is that regulation can lead to over-regulation and over-bureaucratization—a tendency that must be actively checked. Proposals for regulation of some social or economic problem, when examined in depth, may simply be a cover for inadequate analysis, or substitute rules and procedures where structural reform would be more appropriate.

By focusing on democratization and the role of social organizations in achieving social outcomes, the AD paradigm has much in common with the deregulationist trends—but is without the 'pro-business, anti-State' ideological overtones brought to the issue by the New Right. Within the AD paradigm, it is perfectly consistent for SD/L parties to identify social functions that are best carried out by non-government agencies (in the public or the private sectors). The French socialist theoretician Michel Crozier has coined the phrase 'the modest state' to capture this point.[20]

By adopting this perspective, it becomes possible for an SD/L government to mount a strong case for regulation where it is really necessary, as in controls on certain consumer goods.

Such a perspective also encourages the involvement of community groups and civil agencies in the delivery of services in the public sector, in place of bureaucracies which can become sclerotic and unresponsive. Good examples can be found in community-run public housing developments in The Netherlands and in Victoria;[21] or in the delivery of social services programmes by community groups in Sweden.[22]

In this model, the government underwrites the funding of services such as childcare, health clinics and even schools, but their management is in the hands of properly constituted and managed community organizations.

This is not to argue for a 'weak state'. On the contrary, a State that is not seeking to do everything itself, but actively sets the rules and framework within which other organizations perform public functions, has to command and enforce its authority. Schmitter and Streeck make this point in their interesting discussion of an 'associative model of social co-ordination': they insist that a 'strong state' is needed to guarantee arrangements entered into by associations negotiating with each other.[23] Hence there is no question of the SD/L movement abandoning its commitment to a strong state and a strong public sector.

Defence of the public sector

The grounds for regulation and public enterprise as well as public provision of 'social wage' goods and services, can best be defended by being stated openly. The Labour and social movements have everything to gain by themselves developing criteria of public sector accountability, and proceeding to deregulate or privatize, through SD/L governments, elements which do not satisfy these criteria. Defence of the public sector, and its impact on governments' budgets, motivated solely by pressure to save public sector jobs, will in the end prove to be politically suicidal.

In my view, SD/L advocacy of a strong public sector should rest squarely on its contribution to the maintenance and stability of a democratic order. The public sector is the very embodiment of a notion of an over-riding 'public interest' that transcends private interests. It is the basis on which social solidarity can be constructed and maintained. It is the domain in which principles of universal eligibility and entitlement—principles which are of fundamental importance in imparting a sense of social cohesion—are upheld. It is the domain in which democratic public enterprise can monitor and discipline wayward elements in the private sector. It is above all the greatest asset possessed by the SD/L movement in its historic quest to curb the atomising and authoritarian tendencies being promoted by the New Right. Hence the necessity, in my view, of developing sensible approaches to privatization and deregulation, in order to free energies for an adequate and effective promotion of the essential role to be played by a strong public sector in any future social order.

4.4 THE FUTURE FOR SOCIAL MOVEMENTS

We have formulated an approach to democratization that places the major transformative initiative in the hands of associations of citizens and workers, rather than with more formalized state agencies. Such a strategy is critically dependent on the social movements surviving and acting as a renewing source of social innovation and energy, and subject to a leadership which can formulate political programmes with SD/L parties. Just how realistic is this theorization, and how feasible is the strategy that flows from it?

Scope of social movements

The evidence supports the proposition that social movements are becoming *more* important as agents of change, throughout the world. Where some idealism and a sense of (in)justice used to be channelled into membership and activity within a political party, guided by a mission to conquer state power, it is increasingly the case that citizens address issues through *ad hoc* campaigns and movements, which then make their appeals simultaneously on several fronts, the political being merely one of these.

By 'social movements' we mean any of the groups listed in chapter 2. The term encompasses environment and conservation groups; peace and disarmament groups; consumer rights organizations; social justice and civil rights campaigns; movements of indigenous peoples; ethnic and gender groups, such as women's organizations, gay rights campaigns, and ethnic cultural organizations—local and national groups, groups concerned with defining their own autonomy and those seeking openly to affect the political process, groups open to anyone and those that define and restrict their membership. 'Social movement politics' is alive and well not just in the West, but in the East and South as well.[24]

One might argue that the existence of campaigning groups of one sort or another is an index of the health of democracy, in that they show that issues are being aired, and addressed, if not remedied. The groups themselves provide an important learning experience for their members in the political realities and democratic processes of the social order, in a way that no educational system could. They also bring citizens face to face with questions of political and economic power, and force them to analyze the power structures of the social order in a way that they might not have done without such stimulus.

Radicalization within social movements

Let us use a particular example to trace how this occurs. Consider the case where a local group forms to protest against the dumping of chemical wastes in their vicinity. They voice their anger, and no doubt expect the mere articulation of concern to lead 'those in charge' to 'do something about it'. They soon find, however, that no one listens to them. So they discover the need to prepare their case and make their campaign as broadly-based as possible. But even when they have won a sympathetic press, and a sympathetic local council and other political support, they soon find themselves confronting the organized lobbying power of an industry. They uncover a hidden underside to 'respectable' capitalist business. They are then forced to seek alliances with other community organizations and with the trade unions representing the workers in that industry. This in turn forces them to generalize their protest, and to generate positive proposals for dealing with the problem they formed to protest against.

This takes them into new fields such as the analysis of industrial processes to see how wastes arise in the first place; they are led to analyze the underlying causes of the phenomenon they are protesting about. They identify a very narrow view of their obligations espoused by the chemical firms, and find that the market does not allow for the costs of disposal to be included in the price of the products. They are led, in short, to discover for themselves the phenomenon of economic 'externalities' (i.e. matters lying external to the balance sheet, and not taken into account within the costings carried out by the firms). This may lead the group to formulate proposals for incorporating these 'externalities' within firms' accounting procedures, for example by advocating a 'clean up' tax to be imposed on the industry as a whole for as long as a chemical wastes problem remains. Already the group has moved from a particular issue to the development of proposals that would have quite fundamental economic implications. As they seek in this way to broaden and deepen their campaign, they come up against the protective layers of the business status quo, and are forced to contemplate action through the political system to achieve the *general* changes that will solve the *particular* problem they started out protesting against. And this brings them back to SD/L party organization, policy-making conferences, and the electoral process. For it becomes clear that the small local group can identify a problem readily enough, but its solution can take them deep into the political and social order before they get their hands on the levers of change. This is the process called politicization, and it remains the best description of the life cycle of any social protest movement.

Theory of social movements

The activities of the social movements have thrown the theoreticians of socialism into turmoil. Some of the more traditional labour movement thinkers simply place the social movements outside the socialist pantheon, because they do not fit the schemata of a 'politics of class'. On the other hand, some of the theoreticians within the social movements are equally blinkered, and either deny the need for any alliance with the trade unions and the labour movement, or see it as too outmoded and concerned only with 'structures of power' (like Rudolph Bahro). Other socialist theoreticians like Andre Gorz espouse some aspects of the social movements but reject others. (Gorz appears to support local community employment initiatives and ecology groups, but opposes the anti-nuclear peace movement, supporting, like many French socialists, an Atlantic defence posture.)

Each social movement has thrown up an arresting and challenging theoretical problematic of its own. The women's movement has posed a whole series of questions that probe the connections between age-old patriarchal and male supremacist attitudes and the structures thrown up by capitalism, by the labour movement, and most recently by other social movements themselves; all are having to confront the fact that some of their assumptions must be described as sexist. At the same time a new perspective on the traditions of the socialist and SD/L movements themselves has emerged, showing how relatively narrow has been the social basis of their concern (largely: those of male, skilled, white breadwinners). In this way, problems have been opened up which will take women and men, collectively and individually, on a long journey of political discovery in search of a solution.[25]

Similarly the ecology, conservation and environmental movement has forced a painful realization on the labour movement that much of its socialist creed was imbued with nineteenth-century notions of dominance over nature and endless exploitation of resources that are now quite inappropriate, and indeed part of the problem rather than of the solution.[26]

How then are these insights to be fused into a common programme or strategy of social transformation? Some recent writers have explicitly acknowledged the contribution that social movements can make, and must make, to the project of forging a post-capitalist social order. Boris Frankel, for example, in his latest work, *The Post-Industrial Utopians,* argues that the socialist future must embody 'eco-feminist' values or it will not come into being at all.[27] Useful as this is, to my mind it remains a rhetorical gesture; it does not generate a means of translating these values into practicable and pragmatic elements, nor does it provide any means for discriminating between policies that might bring the ecological and feminist movements closer to the labour movement, and those which might drive them future apart. Another approach is exemplified in the work of the American theoreticians Albert and Hahnel, in their *Socialism Today and Tomorrow.*[28] They formulate a notion of 'totalist socialism' which incorporates four spheres—the economic, political, kinship and community. These reflect the elements of any alliance or set of alliances that must be forged as part of a transformative project. They provide, as it were, a checklist of values—anti-capitalist, anti-authoritarian, anti-patriarchal and anti-centralist—that a movement for change needs to embody. Leaving to one side questions of the adequacy or pertinence of these values, the problem with this approach is that it fails to tackle the practical issue of developing a constructive and transformative strategy that can provide the basis for the essential bridge that must be constructed between the trade unions and the social movements. We wish to move from rhetorical gesture to strategic perspectives.

We are led to ask, then, whether the AD paradigm offers a way forward. I would argue that the paradigm outlined in this text does not hinder, and may even help, the process of forging a cross-class and cross-movement alliance for change. In its concreteness, the 'provisional utopia' outlined allows us to demonstrate how, if at all, it may advance or defend the values espoused by the social movements, and offer a means of resolving the issues they raise. Let us look at two of the movements to see how this process may work out: in the peace movement, and the conservation/environment movement. Other examples could be given, such as public housing co-operatives, or alternative energy groupings.

Peace movement and the AD paradigm

The peace movement is a case of associative democracy in action: people joining together around a common concern to work through the democratic process to achieve changes which will reduce the risks of war, particularly nuclear war. Most people are motivated to join the peace movement out of a generalized sense both of the futility of the arms race and of the dangers of nuclear war no matter who emerges as 'victor'. Some join to oppose further militarization of the oceans or of space. For many, their involvement begins and ends in the mass mobilizations, in the lobbying activities, and in the direct actions like the famous women's picket at Greenham Common. But for others, it becomes clear that while these activities expose the issues, they do not in themselves pose solutions. A more sophisticated current within the peace movement inevitably moves on to consider such issues as:

- the strategic role of a posture of neutrality in international affairs;
- the stages through which public opinion can be brought to support, and demand, disarmament negotiations between the power blocs;
- the issues of 'armed neutrality', or defensive postures to be adopted by a nation state;
- the future of the armaments industry;
- the future of US and Warsaw Pact bases in third countries.

This current, then, shifts the focus of the movement away from a generalized desire for peace, and concentrates it on issues of security, survival and the arms trade. In the process, they may lose the support of those who belong to the movement for emotional reasons only; such people are shocked by talk of the peace movement supporting a domestic armaments industry in order to pose a genuine defence posture as an alternative to membership of a nuclear bloc. Such are the contradictions in any social movement.

It is when the peace movement can formulate precise proposals, not just on disarmament, but on conventional defence postures and the future role of the armaments industry, that it is in a position to effect alliances with other groups. But how does it go about this process? On armaments, for example, it might formulate a policy of no jobs in weapons production, and seek support for this from the trade unions. This is, in effect, a moral appeal to the movement, asking workers to forego jobs and thereby make economic sacrifices for the benefit of the community as a whole. Such appeals can generally command wide support, except, understandably, from the workers and unions singled out to make the sacrifice. A more sophisticated approach, and one which would have more chance of success, would be that which contains specific proposals regarding such matters as: the level of armaments production needed for domestic defence purposes; a clear policy on arms exports; and, above all, specific proposals for conversion of surplus armaments capacity to other ends, i.e. to 'socially useful' production, that will not jeopardize the jobs of the workers in the industry.

This is where the AD paradigm with its proposed extension of democracy into the economy and industry, and the willingness to intervene directly in economic issues, comes into its own. For it is obviously unrealistic to expect a delegation from the peace movement to sit down with a delegation from the trade unions, in order to hammer out a programme for conversion of the arms industry. The complexities of the issues would far outrun the powers of such a group. But it is possible for a *collective investment fund* that is exercising some real social control over investment, to channel investments in the armaments industry in a certain direction, at the direct request of workers in the firms involved, and in response to macro-level negotiations and discussions between the unions and the peace movement. New jobs can thereby be created as armaments jobs are phased out.

The same considerations apply to the related industries of nuclear power generation, and uranium mining. In each case, the peace movement gets to the point of formulating a social case for the abandonment of these activities but is stymied by the task of formulating proposals that go beyond merely asking workers for voluntary economic sacrifice. And in each case, the paradigm of economic democracy offers a way out of the dilemma, *for both sides*: for the unions, to meet the genuine concerns raised by the peace movement, and for the peace movement, to formulate proposals for redirection of jobs and industry development that can be effected by a collective investment fund.

In this way, both the labour and peace movements help to lead each other beyond their formative culture of protest, to a culture framed around the exercise of power and direct intervention in the economy.

Conservation movement and the AD paradigm

A similar line of argument can be applied to the conservation movement. People are drawn into the movement through their realisation that endless growth, and a rapacious attitude to natural resources, combined with a cavalier disregard for the effects of generating and dumping wastes, will lead in the end to ecological catastrophe. They are drawn by the challenge of saving forests, or saving fisheries (particularly whales), or saving the urban and rural landscape, from blind and greedy spoliation. Some currents in the movement wish to keep their protests permanently linked to these symptoms; they advocate direct actions and confrontations of various kinds, and oppose the seeking of consensus. Others, whom I would characterize as being more sophisticated, look to the underlying causes for these trends, and locate them in the defective economic system that fails to account for externalities. (For example, it allows firms such as mining companies to account only for costs of extraction in the prices charged for minerals, and not for the costs of rehabilitation.) The protesters are then led to demand more stringent regulation of the mining industry, calling for government intervention to insist that the firms bear the costs of clean-up themselves, rather than passing these on to the community. Such demands then call up the inevitable industry reaction; lobbies are formed; international cost competitiveness considerations are drawn into the argument; and the New Right can weigh in, claiming that industry is already 'over-regulated'.

The way out of this familiar impasse is again provided by the paradigm of economic democracy. Take the case of forestry. After the spectacular battles between 'greenies' and forestry workers have dominated the TV news bulletins and front pages, the serious business of finding a means of regulating the logging of natural forest, and of generating an alternative source of hard and soft wood, has eventually to be addressed. Some common ground has to be established: the 'greenies' come to understand that they cannot advance their cause by showing more concern for trees and furry creatures than for the social plight of unemployed loggers and their families; while the unions come to understand that a tree in a forest represents more than its cash value as hardwood, and that the maintenance of jobs can be achieved only within an overall, ecologically sustainable industry plan. Even the more progressive logging firms can join this coalition, if they are capable of understanding where their long-term interests lie.

But again the sticking point in the negotiations to achieve such a common position, will be the unspoken assumption that voluntary sacrifice is required by workers who are to give up logging jobs. An approach that is likely to be more successful, is one that involves the social control of investment and industry planning, to phase in a new approach to the harvesting of timber. Such an approach might be the funding of new plantations and mixed timber–pastoral agriculture, which would provide controlled yields and reduce dependence on natural forestry reserves. The formulation of such specific economic proposals clearly takes the conservation movement well beyond its formative culture of protest; but, again, I would argue that such is the only route for the movement to follow if it is to achieve its legitimate aims, in collaboration with the labour movement.

Problems facing the social movements

While the social movements seem to be as healthy as ever, they face a number of intrinsic difficulties. Some of these are contingent on the nature of public participation in any open society; some are linked to the special issues around which the movements are organized.

Organization

Some social movements have a necessarily short life cycle; they arise in response to some issue of the moment, and when that issue is dealt with they disband. Their appearance and dis-

appearance
the democr
are formed
proach. Ob
groups, glol
izations, so
rights grou
these mover
dictions or
disappear c
organizatior

Of course
great deal
women's mc
internal org
hierarchies
this way, th
importance
movement,

There are
there is the
formed by the Left, it is open to the New Right to form a counter-group, which will probably be better financed and better organized and more skilled in getting its message across. This is evident particularly in the moral quagmire of sexual politics, where the efforts of gays and other campaigners for self-determination in sexual preference, and for an end to discrimination based on gender preference, are frustrated by the counter-campaigns of Moral Majority groups who find a ready outlet for their conservative views in the press and media.

A related problem is that of the transient nature of many groups and campaigns, which depend for their success on the efforts of certain key individuals, whose departure often spells the end of the group altogether. This problem can be alleviated to some extent by public funding of groups, but while this solves some problems, it only creates others (dependence, and accountability to public authorities, for a group whose essential rationale may be protest).

Legitimacy

Where a number of groups have been formed around a particular issue, and are competing for the attention of the media,

ifficult for a 'genuine'
difficulty faces an SD/L
fy its actions within a
g. chemical dumping control
community response which the
eaction to its proposals, then a bias
better organizing resources of middle
to have the wastes removed from their
ommunity response, and reaching a deci-
plant is to be sited, it is necessary to make
poorer organizing resources of a working class

e, in short, the difficulties involved in seeking to
te or mobilize public opinion in a democracy. They are
oblems which are going to be 'solved' by the social
ements, but they need to be part of the social organizing
rategy of the SD/L parties.

Alliances

Of a different character are the problems involved in forging the political alliances needed to actually *solve* the problems whose symptoms provide the stimulus for the formation of a group or campaign. As we have noted, social movements arise in an act of protest. They may be protesting against senseless arms races and exterminism; against patriarchy and male-supremacist procedures that lock the social order into 'dominant' and 'submissive' modes; against wanton destruction of our common environment, a theme captured so well in the phrase 'only one earth'; against ignorant racism and other manifestations of intolerance. *Dissent; rebellion; 'protest and survive'*; this is the culture of the social movements. But the fact is that a movement cannot survive indefinitely on protest. To mature and take its place in the social order, it must formulate positive and constructive proposals, as well as criticize the actions of others. Yet while coming to exercise a degree of 'responsibility', the movement must attempt to retain its mass base and keep it in a state of mobilization. This is the supreme problem for the social movements and it must be resolved if they are to shape the social order of tomorrow.

The unions similarly have had to learn how to adapt and modify their culture—one that grew out of violent dissent and rebellion—to enable them to exercise a degree of authority, both in the workplace and in the wider economy and polity.

The way forward, as I see it, is this. The social movements will inevitably become more organized, and develop the constructive counterpart to their protest activities at two levels—at the level of the leadership, and at that of the mass base. At the membership level, a new form of protest is going to have to be forged, so that the group espouses aims wider than those it started with. For example, as we noted above, environmental groups protesting against indiscriminate logging of native forest areas will start by expressing their outrage at the wanton destruction of an environment fashioned over thousands of years. But although the protest might win media attention, and could have some considerable political clout, it will run up against the entrenched economic interests of the logging firms and of the workers whose jobs are threatened. Eventually, with goodwill on both sides, a *modus vivendi* may be worked out, provided an appropriate consensus is reached by the leaders. At this leadership level, what is involved, as we have seen, is the seeking of common ground, and the reaching of a series of agreed stages to the phasing out of some practices, such as clear felling of native trees, and its replacement by alternative timber resource harvesting practices.

The framework for such an agreement is necessarily political. This means that the social movements will have to organize themselves on a national or federal basis, with a permanent office-holding hierarchy and full-time secretariat (as many of them already do). Although obviously distasteful to those who seek in the social movements a refuge from all forms of discipline and organization, nevertheless this seems to be the only way they can go if they are to exercise constructive influence. The office-holders then speak with the authority of an organized movement behind them, and can seek to establish the legitimacy of that movement through structured negotiations with other movements, with the trade unions, with SD/L parties, and with governments. The general framework for these negotiations is provided by the notion of a 'social contract' negotiated between the industrial and political wings of the labour movement. Opening up such a contract to an organized social movement seems to be the logical way in which to proceed to establish the broad coalition of interests that will be needed if the New Right is to be marginalized.

The social movements have much to offer such a coalition. They would represent the permanent counter-argument to the notion that the labour movement's project for the economy involves regimentation and suppression of diversity. It is the movements themselves which can bring an 'eco-feminist perspective' to the project of democratizing the economy—provided the appropriate framework is established within which this perspective may be expressed. On the other hand, the social movements themselves highlight problems, and mobilize protests, but they cannot transform the social and economic order themselves, other than through forging an alliance with the labour movement.

It is in providing a feasible and practicable means of expressing the common interests between the labour and social movements, that the paradigm of associative democracy can make its most important contribution. We have to go beyond rhetorical gestures that call for 'recognition of eco-feminist values' without specifying how this is to be done; and we need to apply some discriminating criteria to the social movements themselves, and to the currents within them, to identify which currents are contributing to a solution and which are exacerbating the problem. Meanwhile the social movements themselves will be writing their own script, and challenging the labour movement to keep up with them. Such plurality and diversity will remain the very lifeblood of the SD/L movement.

4.5 THE FUTURE FOR TRADE UNIONS

Of course, one of the key 'social movements' is the labour movement itself, organized in its trade unions. In so far as this movement maintains its autonomy from both SD/L parties and from the State, it is correct to characterize it as a 'social movement'. But it is a very special movement, because of its location at the heart of the productive apparatus. This has always been the strength and 'secret weapon' of the labour movement.

In this text, the unions have been assigned roles that they have only recently come to see as feasible, and they have been theorized as having a purpose and orientation that is quite different from that given them by many currents of the Left today. As against the New Right, which attacks unions relentlessly as being unnecessary, obstructive and inefficient, the associative democratic paradigm sees unions as the central organization of working people, into the foreseeable future. Their role is enhanced, rather than diminished, by economic democratization. They are theorized as the prime defence of associative democracy, and as the prime agencies of democratization.

Within the paradigm, unions preserve their role of protecting the associated interests of their members, but do so in novel ways. Among these, unions will:

- provide a means for workers to exercise collective control over investment and superannuation funds;
- act as election agents for worker directors on company boards, and provide an avenue for accountability of such representatives to the membership;
- act as the vehicle for workers collectively to co-determine with employers the details of work organization, production, trade and investment;
- provide a principal source of technical support to workers involved in financial, technical and other work-related negotiations with employers;
- provide a principal source of training for members, in the issues of democratization of work life and of the wider economy and polity.

The paradigm assumes that unions will seek to represent something broader than the sectional interests of their own membership; rather, through comprehensive social contracts with government and employers, it assumes that unions will increasingly come to represent the associated interests of workers as a whole (both employed and unemployed).

How then is all this to be done, and what changes are required in current practices? Above all, how does this approach differ from current theorizations of unions on the Left?

Unions arose in quite historical circumstances for specific purposes, to defend the associated interests of wage workers in the early years of the Industrial Revolution. They arose either as mutual benefit societies, pooling resources to tide over their members in the event of a strike, of personal sickness, accident or bereavement; or as 'combinations' of journeymen seeking to drive the price of labour above starvation levels. Since then, unions have evolved through a rich tapestry of social changes, but with the constant theme that they represent the associated interests of workers. Unions are constantly performing a balancing act between meeting the immediate needs of their members and seeking to expand their aspirations; between surviving in a hostile commercial environment and steering a course through changing political times; between being characterized in the press as power-hungry and greedy, and finding the few resources from their members just to stay alive.

Despite the obvious difficulties under which they labour, unions have not generally been received well by radical socialists in the past. They have been despised as 'economist', as being trapped in the capitalist system, as holding back workers' revolutionary consciousness. Socialists fondly imagined that a new society was just around the corner, and the unions that had so painfully been established would soon be surpassed. Today, I hope, we have more respect for the institutions that workers have formed, and are not so ready to airily dismiss their achievements in a world that is so relentlessly hostile.

Overcoming sectionalism

In the early 1960s, George Woodcock, then secretary of the TUC in Britain, exhorted the movement to make up its mind about its purpose: it had to decide whether it wanted to be the 'collective entrepreneur of labour, adopt the jungle ethics of the market and practise business unionism', or whether it wanted to play a significant part in the creation of a new society constructed on 'a morality of equity instead of greed'.

The formulation of the question shows the answer preferred by Woodcock, and by many commentators since—but *sectional interest* overriding equity or the general interest, continues to be the factor holding back the trade union movement.

This is partly a structural problem—the myriad number of unions that the movement is split into, each with their history and culture, arrayed like different regiments in the army, and constantly clashing with each other in the narrow pursuit of their own claims. To this structural problem there is a structural solution—greater and greater reliance on movement-wide campaigns and organizations. This does not mean one hundred per cent centralization, nor the dissolution of individual unions, but some real ceding of powers from these individual unions to central (peak) councils or creations of the central councils. One such initiative would be anti-New Right Fighting Funds, as well as the fostering of mergers and amalgamations.

But it is not just a structural problem. Years of social isolation imposed by mainstream capitalist society on the trade union movement, have taken their toll. There is amongst older unionists a 'catch as catch can' attitude, of 'looking after our own', that is entirely understandable, given the rigours these members have lived through, but which is entirely inappropriate for the interventionist trade unionism required in the future.

As Tony Lane says, 'in a society with democratic pretensions and where economic resources are patently not distributed according to any principles, least of all principles of equity', the unions 'might justifiably claim that without their presence the descent into barbarism would be swift and immediate, that it is they who impose what order there is. Such claims can readily be conceded.'[29] But their actions tend to be dictated by the needs of the moment, such as the defence of this or that job, or the contestation of yet another change foisted by a firm on a workforce without any thought as to its social consequences. This is the activist's dilemma. On the one hand, the broad membership harbour a deep-seated moral commitment to justice and equity, to a better way, and expect this of their union; on the other, they expect instant action when there is a particular problem to be remedied.

In my view this crisis of legitimacy will only be resolved by the unions moving beyond their current contradiction-fraught *defensive collectivism*, to seek to establish a new agenda for industry and the workplace. This will provide a real and progressive outlet for the genuine but frustrated moral energy that is locked up in the present structures of the movement. But to do so will involve a transformation of the practices of unionism, and a completely new conception of an active role for the membership in tackling their own workplace issues for themselves. The intra-plant collectivism will still be there, but the key contribution of the national union will be in channelling the resources and expertise to members when they need it, and in developing national and industry-wide policies for tackling issues in the workplace.

An obsolete model of trade unionism

To favour enterprise-level negotiation stands, in a sense, for a turn back in the direction of 'collective bargaining', but without all the pejorative overtones of this term. Collective bargaining, as practised by local union branches in America and Britain, has been at the heart of the *sectionalism* of the movement, and has frustrated attempts to formulate a genuine incomes policy founded on real 'comparative wage justice'. This model of unionism has been allowed to hold back the movement for far too long—but its days appear to be numbered. For example, according to successive Department of Labour surveys, union membership in the US is now down to below one-fifth of the workforce. US managements are starting to display a new, aggressive anti-unionism;

they scent that the unions are a spent force. Companies are moving to the Southern 'Sunbelt' where 'right to work' laws restrict unionism even more severely. In recent years unions have been forced into a 'concession bargaining' posture, giving up hard-won rights and conditions that were thought to be irreversible gains. The margin between wage levels in the unionized and non-unionized employment sectors is diminishing, and with it, the chief remaining incentive for workers to join unions. Now journals like *Business Week* are openly talking of a post-union industrial regime where the law protects individual workers in place of unions.[30]

The causes for this certainly cannot all be laid at the feet of the unions themselves. There have been adverse economic conditions; there has been a legislative assault on unions inspired by Reaganism, initiated by the now legendary attack on air-traffic controllers; there have been the adverse consequences of extensive deregulation. But the unions must bear some of the blame themselves. They have taken the model of 'adversarial collective bargaining' about as far as it can go.[31] This results in extremely complex local agreements—but oriented towards rights and grievance procedures, rather than to any strategic goal of worker influence over an efficient production system. The role of local stewards is confined to filing grievances under these collective contracts of employment, which started as one-page codes establishing mutual recognition, but have now become lengthy, legalistic documents specifying hundreds of rules for the conduct of the enterprise. For example, there could be pages covering how temporary assignments are to be made to cover for absent employees. Even so, any non-standard assignment can lead to a dispute, and find its way into a grievance procedure moving through one stage after another to an arbitration tribunal.

In one sense, this represents an important achievement on the part of the unions—the power of management to dispose of workers at will has been severely limited. But this achievement is bought at a price which unions are now coming to realize.[32] While the rules tie up managements, they can also tie the unions to a given work organization and technology, that may be overtaken by competitors not so bound. And as firms introduce new productivity-oriented management techniques, the complex agreements make it difficult for either side to accommodate them, and so the demands of efficiency provide an important and sometimes irresistible alibi for by-passing the agreed procedures altogether.

Similarly in Britain the unions remain attached to an ideology of 'free collective bargaining' long after it has lost its momentum and utility. The unions cling to their own autonomy, and apparently fail to see how this rigidly anti-centralist attitude has the effect of promoting sectionalism at the expense of a wider concern for those in other unions, let alone the unemployed and part-time employed. It also promotes a narrow concern for monetary wage gains at the expense of wider social wage issues and workplace democracy, and constrains the union movement as a whole through lack of effective central resourcing or central leadership.

The ideology that informs this now obsolete model of unionism is what I would call *abstentionism*. It abstains from getting involved in any substantive workplace issues, and keeps the membership in an essentially passive state. It is crippling the labour movement in its efforts to come to terms with the challenge of the New Right and with the demands of economic and industrial restructuring. But it is so tenacious because it is supported, tacitly, by a Left-Right consensus within the union movement itself. On the Right there is the familiar concern not to allow the unions to get too 'political' in their activities, and not to allow the membership to get too involved in issues that are 'best left to the leadership' to sort out. The bankruptcy of this approach to unionism is surely evident by now. But on the Left there is also a deep hostility to any involvement in workplace issues that smacks of being 'collaborationist'. This translates into insisting that a militantly oppositional stance be taken at all times: in practice it results in the agenda rarely being allowed to deal with other than the 'bread and butter' issues of wages and immediate conditions. Both approaches are condemned to a watching and waiting game; they abstain from all the real and complex issues that actually present themselves in the workplace, and that offer workers a means of exercising some real influence *if they can bring collective pressure to bear on these issues*.[33]

Edmond Maire, secretary-general of the French union federation CFDT, put the issue well when he stated in 1986:

> If the trade unions are to remain a force for social change, they can no longer be powered by a determination to defend collective guarantees but must be the agents of a new form of work and life.[34]

How is this renewal to move beyond the level of a rhetorical gesture? I would submit that the paradigm of *economic democracy* provides the framework for realistic advance.

Towards a new model of unionism

The democratization of economic and industrial life, by and through the unions acting in alliance with other social movements, represents an exciting challenge and a feasible goal that could regenerate the union movement. Abandoning the obsolete model of abstentionism, and focusing instcad on economic democracy, will mean that:

- Unions will become the principal promoters of high technology and efficiency in industry, bringing their resources to bear on a positive goal, and marginalizing the New Right employers who will be seen to be holding back productivity in the name of 'managerial prerogatives'.
- Unions will unleash the energy, creativity and imagination of their members, in a sustained drive for more productive and more democratic workplace structures, work organization, and management practices.
- Unions will concentrate their energies on the broad economic issues, and, by centralizing their resources, avoid allowing themselves to be weakened and distracted by pointless demarcation disputes and other forms of internal bickering.
- Unions will find their stocks rising in terms of general public perception, and they will make sure that the ground is carefully prepared, and the issues publicly explained, before they bring their collective might to bear against a recalcitrant employer or group of employers.
- Unions will find it more convenient to settle the issue of wage levels through central, political negotiation, and concentrate their resources on the myriad non-wage issues that affect economic performance and work experience.
- Unions will generate the means to direct or strongly influence the pattern of investment, through collective funds like superannuation or wage-earner funds, and through this be in a position to respond to and accommodate the concerns of their members for jobs as well as the concerns of the social movements (which include many of their members) regarding environmental, peace and gender issues.

The shift in emphasis can be described as a turn from fruitless *antagonism* to purposeful *protagonism*—with the unions becoming a leading force in the democratization of the social and economic order.

The attractive feature of this approach is that it provides a recipe for isolating the hard-line employers, and allowing them to be seen, correctly, as being concerned only with maintaining their own privileges and wealth. A sustained pursuit of economic democracy by the union movement would find many supporters among the ranks of employers, leading to a political split or series of splits among organized employer groups.

It needs to be stressed, because of the constant misrepresentations of abstentionists, that the emphasis on economic democracy is not 'a weak' option that shuns militancy. Militancy is not a quality that belongs to any particular view of trade unionism itself (apart from a few extreme right wingers in the movement who seek to undermine any genuine campaign). The *language* and *morality* of militancy, the culture of strikes, of blacklegs, the hard discipline of maintaining solidarity—*none of this is in question.* It all has to be called on, to some degree or other, by any collective, associative organization that is seeking to intervene in current events. It is not militancy itself, but *militancy in defence of abstentionism,* that I object to. Indeed, the union movement will need to call on all its resources of militancy if it is to succeed in breaking through to this next phase of its remarkable evolution, for the combined forces of the status quo will represent an immense obstacle. But it will need to call on these resources intelligently, and not just blindly call out the members and inflict widespread disruption on other citizens as well as on employers at the slightest provocation. The movement will have to treat the drive towards economic democracy as a decade-long campaign, and as such it will need strategic (long-term) and tactical (short-term) planning. Collective strength will be the key resource to be called on in this campaign—but must always be exercised in a controlled, responsible and publicly justified manner.

Strategy of transition

How are unions to start on this radically different trajectory? Experience over the past fifteen years, particularly in Scandinavia but also in other areas of Europe and in the Anglo-Saxon world, indicates that the key shift lies in the identification of broader social or industrial issues in which workers have a direct and immediate stake, and taking action over these issues, which culminates in the negotiation of specific enabling agreements that establish structures of co-determination. Such issues include:

- work organization and work practices;
- skills and work value;
- work measurement;
- health and safety;
- technological change.

Computerization of the workplace has stimulated many of the agreements negotiated on these issues, but it has not been the sole source of concern. Health and safety is an exemplary issue. In this most concrete of areas of concern to workers, unions have found that the key to successful intervention to curb hazards is at the point of technological change—before equipment is bought or processes installed. Through establishing workplace consultative structures, consisting of safety representatives and joint union-management committees, unions are able to insist that the likely hazards of new technologies be evaluated prior to their introduction, and in a setting of co-determination of the issues between management and workers organized collectively through their union. Unions have had great success in negotiating such agreements, and then in generalizing them to cover a range of work organization issues.[35]

In place of specifying thickets of defensive rules to cover every conceivable situation in the workplace, these agreements identify:

- the *issues* which will be the subject of co-determination;
- the *rights* of union representatives appointed to represent their members on these issues;
- the *goals* and *procedures* of the co-determination structures.

After that, it is left to the structures and procedures themselves to resolve the issues as they arise. This is the spirit embodied in the health and safety agreements negotiated over the past years, and it lends itself to all other workplace issues susceptible to joint determination. Worker representatives in these structures and procedures are not 'co-opted', because they remain accountable through their union, and they draw on technical resources through their union. This, of course, carries serious consequences for union resources and priorities, which we shall address below.

Single-issue co-determination agreements are effective only insofar as they involve members in a constructive and meaningful way. This implies that delegates be trained to be able to take initiatives for themselves. A feature of most health and safety agreements, and technological change agreements, is that they do in fact provide for paid leave for training of union-nominated delegates on union-sponsored courses. These courses can be a revelation for those who attend them. Issues which seemed to be best left to the concern of the 'experts', are suddenly seen in a new light as being susceptible to negotiation.

Training and resourcing of delegates to take up work organization and labour process issues, raises the question of the resourcing of unions themselves. Despite the rhetoric of the New Right accusing the unions of exercising too much power, they are in fact extremely precarious organizations. What power they have derives from the fact that they are located in the very heart of the production process, rather than being marginalized in the manner of most protest movements. But the broadening of the agenda of 'industrial issues' does not come cheap. The dramatic drive to involve workers in protecting their own health and safety, for example, is underwritten by huge national training programmes designed to give workers' health and safety delegates some modicum of technical confidence to tackle the issues. Substantive involvement of unions in questions of technological change requires the commissioning of consultants' reports and use of consultants in negotiations, together with further large training programmes for delegates. Entry into the field of superannuation again carries the need to secure financial expertise to set up trust deeds and manage funds that are established. It is unrealistic to expect unions individually, from normal membership fees, to be able to finance these sorts of activities.[36] Nor is it realistic to expect unions to be able to call on public funds to do so. Collective and centralised financing efforts are needed—as already undertaken in Scandinavia, Austria and West Germany, where union resources make their Anglo-Saxon counterparts look poverty-stricken. The establishment of multi-million dollar funds through levies, which would then generate substantial income each year, could finance a number of these sorts of initiatives. Unions have to move beyond the stage of financing all their activities from membership fees paid each year.

Public regulation of unions

A greater financial sophistication and strength on the part of the unions, in turn calls for a measure of public regulation. A lot of nonsense on this issue is still talked by the union movement. 'Freedom of collective bargaining' has been a rallying cry by trade unions for most of the twentieth century. It recalls the 'freedom of trade' slogans of the nineteenth century.

If as democrats we argue for social regulation of economic life, why should trade unions be exempt? Formulating the question in this way makes the answer obvious: they should not be.

Indeed, where unions have been to some extent free of external regulation, the results have been disastrous. (Witness the descent into gangsterism of the waterfront unions and teamsters in the US.) The reality is that the best efforts of idealists can be rapidly undone by ruthless power merchants who are enabled to take over an unregulated organization. So some form of advantageous regulation is necessary for the well-being of the organization, to provide a higher court of appeal if 'natural justice' is being flouted.

In Britain, unions have received a cold dose of regulation under the Thatcher governments's 'anti-union legislation', which includes such mild requirements as holding compulsory ballots before industrial action is taken, and draconian ones enabling employers to take punitive action against unions which do not conform to the new laws. The movement has repeatedly split over the challenge of formulating a response to these laws. Those who have proclaimed the perfectly reasonable position that some form of regulation is not wholly a bad thing, have been shouted down—but in the name of what? The legal isolation of the union movement is hardly a socialist aim. Worse—it plays into the hands of the New Right, who can point to such attitudes and argue that the unions are becoming a law unto themselves and therefore need to be destroyed.

In other countries, such as Australia, this debate does not resonate because the unions are in a very real sense the products of a highly regulated system established at the time of federation: the arbitration and conciliation system. The issue of *punitive* regulation was fought in Australia in the 1950s over the question of penal powers. The attempts by conservative forces to hold unions to no-strike agreements, imposed by the arbitration system, using the sanction of prison for union leaders, was defeated by a great show of strength when Tramways leader, Clarrie O'Shea, who had been jailed, was released. The penal clauses have been a dead letter ever since. Yet the question of social regulation surfaced again in Australia in 1985, with the deregistration of the Builders Labourers Federation (BLF) by the Federal government, and by the New South Wales and Victorian State Labor governments. This too was an agonizing experience for the unions, with many, particularly on the Left, supporting the BLF on what they saw as principled grounds, namely that Labor governments should not discipline trade unions. I would argue the converse: that it is a sign of the maturity of the movement if it can allow its political wing to discipline the industrial wing in the name of the survival of the whole movement. These are all stages on the unions' long journey from being seen as outsiders and marginal, through the stage of being recognized as the legitimate representatives of workers subject to certain norms, to eventually becoming protagonists of a new economic and industrial order.

Theoretical foundations of 'political' trade unionism

While unions remain the essential vehicles for expressing the associated interests of workers, the challenge identified here is one of swinging the unions away from their militant abstentionist postures—from what might be described as *sectional defensive collectivism*—to a posture of *pluralist interventionist collectivism.* 'Sectional' because unions have tended to present a single view and represent a single constituency on a narrow range of issues; and 'defensive' because they have tended to react to initiatives of employers, rather than seek to set the agenda themselves. An alternative posture, as sketched here, would be 'pluralist' in the sense that the union gives maximum encouragement and support to initiatives being taken by the membership; and 'interventionist' in the way that members are encouraged to intervene in the process of production, to co-determine with employers a wide range of industrial issues, but on a basis of collective accountability to the membership through union workplace structures. An interventionist union movement is constantly setting and resetting the social agenda, and never embarks on a campaign of industrial action without having first explained its aims, worked out its alternative proposals, and exhausted all reasonable avenues of discussion: it can then call on and expect to obtain maximum public support for its action against an isolated and intransigent employer.

A model of 'political' trade unionism is one which seeks to transcend the sectionalism that condemns unions to such fruitless wrangles as demarcation disputes, and that encourages the selfish pursuit of narrowly conceived interests against the wider interests of workers as a whole, whether employed or unemployed. It is a model that calls for conscious intervention at the political level, via negotiated agreements with governments, employers or both.

It is a model of unionism that sets itself conscious social goals, which must include: low unemployment, low inflation, social solidarity and social development.

I do not wish to be seen to be over optimistic in painting a rosy picture of the future. There will be times when the unions need to flex their muscles, and show, through determined strike action, that their membership is united on a certain question and determined to bring about change. There will be times when the unions will necessarily have to adopt defensive postures, and seek to maintain standards won against the efforts of employers or conservative governments to roll back those gains.

What I am attempting to depict is an image of the future of the movement that is *realizable* within the next decade or two, given determination and the tactical skill to achieve these strategic objectives. I do not for a moment imagine it will be easy. On the contrary, I believe that the unions' struggle against entrenched 'managerial prerogatives'—for that is what we are talking about—will be the greatest and most decisive struggle of their history. I would expect some unions and many companies to be destroyed in this process, and for Labour governments to be brought to office and to be deposed from office as the struggle waxes and wanes.

The setting for this model of political trade unionism will be 'social contracts' reached between the industrial and political wings of the labour movement, embodying at each stage more and more comprehensive issues and groups in the process of negotiation. Much of the debate within the Left over these agreements, conducted most recently in Australia over the ACTU-ALP Accord of 1983, stems not just from the point of view of its alleged 'corporatist' overtones, but over the timing and direction of its content. I would argue that the way to resolve these disputes is to agree on a set of minimal conditions that any social contract should satisfy, in order to make it *more likely* that it will work to politicise and strengthen the labour movement, rather than merely contain it and dampen wage levels. Threshold criteria that I would identify as needing to be met by any legitimate social contract include:

- an explicit method of agreeing the content and for adjusting it as circumstances change;
- clear lines of accountability built into the structures called up by the contract;
- no statutory sanctions;
- policies couched at macro, meso and micro levels, and in-

volving members of the contracting organizations at all these levels;
- the content to be broader than wages or incomes policy, and to encompass wider questions of industry and social policy.

In my view, a social contract that meets these criteria is well on the way to promoting or establishing a model of political trade unionism, capable of transcending the sectionalism that weighs unions down. It promises to take them off the treadmill of wages struggle and free them for more constructive social and economic activities. Note that these criteria are neutral as to the *actual content* of any contract, which will vary with the state of development of the parties and the options available.

If a proposed social contract does *not* meet these criteria, then there is a case for arguing that it will hold back the political development of the movement, and that unions will be used by a conservative government simply as a device to discipline their members.

Unions within the democratic economy

Contrary to many of the 'post-industrial' theorists, who seem to see unions as old-fashioned organizations belonging only to the 'industrial' era, the paradigm of associative democracy casts unions in a central role, now and in the foreseeable future. But this statement needs to be carefully qualified. The role of the unions, in my view, will always be that of providing a collective voice and means of action for their members, in the constructive sense as envisaged for the future, as much as in the destructive sense that has operated in the past. But they will *never*, in my view, become executive agents for the administration of productive functions or management tasks within the democratic economy. This would be to fundamentally misconceive their democratic role.[37] Thus I do not see unions evolving into, say, workers' co-operatives or public enterprises. These productive organizations will be formed within the space and on the terms laid down by the unions, but they will not be formed by the unions themselves. Unions will lay down policies and standards to be adhered to by democratic management, but they will not exercise management tasks themselves.

Trade unions are essentially organs of accountability, and this is the role that they will play in ushering in a democratic economy and in keeping it democratic once it is established. When unions get involved in actually running enterprises, disaster is never far away. The West German unions suffered catastrophic financial losses in 1986 when a whole series of businesses run by them collapsed; assets that had been accumulated over years were written off and sold for one dollar. Corruption is a constant temptation in such circumstances.

The paradigm of associative or economic democracy offers a vast and complex project for the unions: to effect the internal transformation of capitalist relations of industry, focusing on democratization, but always on the basis of collective accountability. There is no need to place more of a strain on the unions than is necessary. Changing the world is a task sufficient in itself; managing that changed world is a different matter entirely.

The future lies in workers and unions adopting policies and implementing constructive changes to work organization and, through that, to the organization of production and economic activity as a whole. Gramsci put it well, writing in the heat of the Factory Council movement in Turin in October 1919:

> Once the Councils exist, they give the workers direct responsibility for production, provide them with an incentive to improve their work, instil a conscious and voluntary discipline, and create a producer's mentality—the mentality of a creator of history. The workers will carry this new consciousness into the trade unions, which in place of the simple activity of the class struggle will dedicate themselves to the fundamental task of stamping economic life and work techniques with a new pattern.[38]

Seventy years later, these prophetic words can act once again as a guide to the movement, which is on the threshold of effecting a major historical transformation.

4.6 TOWARDS AN ASSOCIATIVE DEMOCRATIC POLITY

In the AD polity, politics will be a process of continual negotiation between organized groups or associations, within a framework laid down by governments at various levels. Associations will formulate their goals through their own internal democratic procedures, and then seek to achieve these in negotiation with each other and with the collective or public interest represented in 'the state'. In this process it will not always be sweetness and light. Groups will impose sanctions (such as withdrawal of labour, or withdrawal of support) which will frequently have serious social repercussions. The imposition of sanctions will be as much a test of the group's our coherence and solidity, as a threat to competing groups. Conflicts will be resolved through trade-offs, giving the groups involved partial satisfaction.

This has always been the style of competitive, negotiated relations between independent states. It has always been the style of competitive, negotiated relations between unions and employers (where it is called 'industrial relations'). It has always been the real-world style of operation of SD/L governments, who when elected to office quickly find themselves confronted by a host of organized associations seeking to influence the public agenda or obtain a share of public resources. These governments have in practice long abandoned the sense that they could 'rule', thrusting a doctrine or policy or even their entire manifesto down the throats of their political and social opponents. This notion of 'rule', as Paul Hirst has put it, is now dead: it lives on only as a myth in the heads of SD/L party activists who get impatient and frustrated with the tortuous progress of politics.

In many ways, Italy provides the paradigmatic case of such politics in action. In Italy the state is understood to be the arena in which 'associative concertation' takes place between negotiating groups, who enter into what the Italians graphically call 'political exchange' (*scambio politico*). Those who see only a succession of weak governments in the Italian political order, miss this feature altogether. Similarly in the US, the process of forming the Democratic Party manifesto is one of 'associative concertation' between various competing groups who form the party.

Westminster political systems with their 'winner take all' constitutions, particularly when combined with 'first past the post' voting systems, will become increasingly ill-adapted to this emergent politics of 'political exchange'. The formulation of party platforms for use in Westminster-style elections, which has been the major preoccupation of SD/L party activists in the past, will increasingly give way to the more immediate and challenging task of negotiating the terms of agreements/compacts/accords/contracts between the major associations affiliated with the party, and with those outside the party (such as employer groups). The AD polity will essentially be the site for such multiple agreements.[39]

Increasingly it will be the New Right that favours 'winner take all' electoral systems, for they are becoming the real 'radicals' who seek 'root and branch' restructuring of the social order in favour of unfettered market forces that benefit the wealthy, cutting through the plethora of democratic agreements and procedures that the SD/L movement has erected in support of social solidarity and responsibility.

A more stable polity based on a generalised system of 'political exchange' is consistent with the moves toward 'flexibility' in industry, as the formerly dominant mass production system gives way to a variety of 'post-Fordist' alternatives. The mass culture that was erected on the base of mass production is also giving way.[40] Much of the SD/L culture, with its own notions of mass unions, mass parties, and the membership marching in step behind the leadership—much of this, whether we like to admit it or not, has been fashioned within a Fordist, mass culture. Hence the culture of the SD/L movement is changing as well: its more rigid notions of a party platform winning 'mass support' and then being implemented to the letter, is giving way to a more flexible system of political exchange and agreements that will increasingly contain conditional clauses that enable them to accommodate to changing circumstances.

Another aspect of this change in the political culture of the SD/L movement is its new respect for the *values* associated with such issues as conservation and peace that have traditionally been seen as marginal within the dominant mass culture. This is, of course, linked with the new opening to the social movements as political forces to be reckoned with.[41] In turn, this brings us back to the question of constructing alliances, and the process of political exchange.

Through all this, what will distinguish the SD/L parties from their political opponents? Will there be anything at all to distinguish them in a general melee of interest groups fighting for competitive advantage? I maintain that what can distinguish them is precisely a commitment to a long-term vision, as expressed in a comprehensive *paradigm* , combined with a commitment to the promotion of *social solidarity* (as distinct from mass uniformity) as both a desirable end in itself, and as a means of cementing the political base of support for the SD/L movement. Projects of democratization of industry, of the economy and the social system, are conceived essentially in this light.

Provided these commitments remain intact, I see no reason to doubt that SD/L parties will be the dominant forces in an associative democratic polity. In the process, social democracy itself will change. What started out as pre-eminently a project of the *labour movement* in the nineteenth century, has become a joint project of the *labour and social movements* in the late twentieth century. In the nineteenth century, social democracy was equipped with a vision of labour as a class becoming the dominant social force and controlling production according to principles of social justice. Falling far short of that vision, it did succeed in sheltering the process through which workers were able to 'combine' in unions, securing their legal protection, and making the employment contract less subservient to the convenience of capital. In the twentieth century, with labour gaining political representation within the state, this influence was extended to build a more solid structure of support, encompassing: Keynesian macro-economic policies designed to sustain employment; industry policies designed to generate jobs in new sectors and regions; higher education policies to support skill formulation; and social concertation policies designed to consolidate the political influence of labour in industry. The thread linking all these policies is the desire to *minimize the arbitrariness of the employment contract*, and to foster social systems of family support that reduce the dependence of families on wages as sole source of income.

But at every step of the way, a tension has existed between reforms or benefits sought by the SD/L movement through the employment relation (such as industry-based health insurance funds, superannuation funds, on-the-job training schemes) and those placed on a social basis which transcends the employment relation—such as free and universal health care, or education, or income support measures.

I am suggesting that this tension has now reached breaking point. There is no future for the SD/L movement in clinging to the employment relation as the ideological and political *focus* of its policies and programmes. If the SD/L movement is to be truly the dominant influence in an associative democratic polity, it must broaden its concerns and influence to encompass the future of the social order as a whole, starting with two fundamental principles:

- that the basis of social organization is associations that regulate their own affairs within a framework laid down collectively;
- that democracy consists in the social arrangements through which associations negotiate with each other, subject to the rules laid down by public institutions governed by elected representatives.

The first of these principles gives due recognition to the

traditional culture of collectivism within the labour and social movements. It is the second principle that comes to terms with pluralism. It recognizes that there will always be social conflicts, and that democracy provides the best means of resolving these conflicts short of physical conquest of one group by another. Neither principle confines our notion of democracy to the narrowly interpreted 'political' domain. On the contrary, the principles work on the assumption that 'associative democracy' encompasses the entire social domain, including industry and the economy. It is in this manner that the AD paradigm fosters the shift in focus on the part of the SD/L movement from the employment relation to social and economic relations in general.

We are at a crossroads, or parting of the ways. One way leads the SD/L movement to continue its advance, speaking in the name of social solidarity and citizenship in a humane and democratic social order. The other leads to decline, where the SD/L movement becomes just another pressure group fighting for survival in an increasingly selfish, dispersed and violent society. This is the 'democratic divide'.

FIVE

KNOWLEDGE, ACTION AND POWER

In this text we have spent much time and energy seeking to hunt out from the labour and social movements' guiding principles a miscellany of abstractions that date from earlier, simpler and frequently discredited conceptions of the movements' prospects and historical trajectory. We have engaged, in short, in a conceptual purge, trying to exorcise the spell cast by such fugitive abstractions as the 'capitalist system' and the 'capitalist State'; the 'ruling class' and 'capitalist hegemony'. Too often in the past and indeed in the present, these abstractions have been used as an alibi to cover for the absence of specific policies and proposals, or for programmes that failed to ground themselves in real economic dynamics and failed to generate or mobilize their own support. Under those circumstances it is only too easy to fall back on the explanation that all our frustrations are due to the interventions of the 'capitalist State'—even if the argument is presented in bare-faced circular terms, that the State acts to safeguard the interests of capital (no matter how the SD/L party intervenes) *because* it is a 'capitalist State', and so on, and so on.

In contrast, we have posited an emergent politics of associative democracy that shifts the labour and social movements from their familiar culture of opposition, or protest, and challenges them to develop a culture of the responsible exercise of power within a democratic system. This does not imply any form of conservatism or maintenance of the status quo. On the contrary, I argue that SD/L parties hold power in government only for as long as they successfully mobilize their constituents, and continue to be radicalized and replenished by them—and, conversely, that the labour and social movements aim for government only as a means of orchestrating their projects for transforming their community, their workplace, and the wider economy, but not as an end in itself.

Such a shift carries important implications for theoretical work. In my view, too many on the Left have been content to develop a critique of each others' positions, and of 'the capitalist system' in yet another stage of its development, but fall short on specific proposals, or else announce their position in excessively general terms. For example, at the close of Przeworski's brilliant exposition of social democracy in Europe, he announces categorically that 'social democrats will not deliver the working class to socialism', and that we need to find a 'third way' between Lenin and Social Democracy—without giving the slightest hint as to how this 'third way' may be characterized.[1] This to me is to turn theory into the enemy of practice—it disables and undermines people's present activity, but gives them no vision or strategy to put in its place.

I would advance the proposition that perhaps the most significant obstacle to the realization of a genuinely democratic economic and social order, is the role of pessimistic theory in weighing down and weakening our goals and methods. Theory can come to weigh down the living forms of the labour and social movements, and imprison them in a series of predetermined behavioural slots that, in the end, are more deadly than media misrepresentation, economic sabotage, or the cudgels of riot policy. Before a movement can create a new order in reality, it must do so in imagination—and if it is imprisoned in imagination, then it will never break free in reality.

One lesson we must learn from the past is the damage caused by dogmatism. There is no point in putting forward proposals as the 'correct' solution to any set of specific problems. In this text, I have not put forward proposals for collective investment funds or guaranteed minimum income schemes, as a finished and perfect programme. On the contrary, I invite debate and argument. Above all, I would urge scientific analysis and testing of the proposals, in properly controlled experimental conditions and on adequately constructed and identified models; for what I have tried to create is not so much a finished product as a *paradigm* within which further theoretical development can take place. The associative 'model' or '*paradigm*' is one within which specific proposals for economic and social democracy may be tested and developed.

This approach implies a rather different conception of theory and theoretical work than is usual amongst Left intellectuals. I should like to close this text by elaborating this approach, for I see it as providing a positive role for theory that will bring it back into the vital relationship with practice that it has in many ways lost.

5.1 TOWARDS AN ALTERNATIVE CONCEPTION OF THEORY

We have theorized the labour and social movement project as one aimed at democratizing economic, industrial and social life, through the means of collective associations of workers and citizens; and suggested that such a framework of ideas, or paradigm, is suitable to guide the formulation of policy by the labour and social movements as they seek to define an identity for themselves that will carry them through to the year 2000 and beyond.

Such an approach has interesting implications for our notion of power, and for the related notions of knowledge and action. The French theorist Bruno Latour has developed a highly unorthodox account of power, but one which is strikingly similar to the approach taken in this text. As he puts it, power is paradoxical:

> When an actor simply *has* power nothing happens and s/he is powerless; when, on the other hand, an actor *exerts* power it is others who perform the action. It appears that power is not something one can possess—indeed it must be treated as a consequence rather than as a cause of action.[2]

Having set up the problem in these terms, Latour then deploys a 'translation' model of action as involving a chain of agents each of whom acts and translates a command in accordance with his/her projects. He contrasts this with a traditional 'diffusion' model of action, where a command is propagated to the extent that it overcomes resistance in the people to whom it is addressed. The translation model characterizes action as something which is composed in the here and now; it does not rest on some notion of stored inertia, or power, to account for its success. Success in fact depends on the number of actors who can be enrolled in a project, sharing the prime actor's outlook and *associating* together for a common purpose. As Latour puts it:

> In the translation model the study of society therefore moves from the study of the social as this is usually conceived, to a study of methods of *association*.

Latour introduced these ideas in the context of the study of science and technology, with the intention of shifting the focus of attention from the *social impact* of science and technology to the analysis of science and technology as expressions of social and political actors seeking to influence others. This indeed is the perspective we adopted in the section above on democratizing technology. But Latour's ideas are of wider relevance, as he himself now recognizes. His emphasis on 'methods of association' provides a striking link with the 'associations' that are discussed in this text as a means of effecting democratization.

Models and reality

Thanks to the work of a host of theorists in the realm of the study of science and technology, we now have through the formulation and testing of theories, a much more sophisticated understanding of knowledge and its translation into action than was available to earlier labour movement strategists.

In the rather more measured discourse of philosophy of science, we have now acquired a sophisticated understanding of the nature of scientific theories and how they enable us to make sense of the world and of our experience of it.[3] We can now appreciate theories as 'tools of thought' that enable us to intervene successfully in the world (e.g. to build a bridge, or launch a satellite), generalizing on the basis of experience, and taking leaps in imagination that mere repetition of technical procedures could never accomplish.[4] Above all, we now understand this disjunction between theories and the world of reality that they attempt to account for.

There was a naive view of science (taught to myself, and probably to most readers of this text, at school) that saw the 'world' and the laws of physics, such as Newton's laws of motion, as one and the same. Science, in this view, is a process of revelation of the 'true' structures and relations that make up the world—and the tension and excitement of 'doing science' derives from never knowing whether all has been fully revealed or not.

Now we understand better the conceptual tools we use to impose order on a world that is possibly orderless.

Take the case of Newtonian mechanics, which remains paradigmatic as a scientific theory. It is applicable to the whole or any part of the universe, and consists of a few basic concepts (force, acceleration, momentum, etc.) and the relationships between them, and is seen to provide a good approximation to the behaviour of bodies in the large. But at the atomic and subatomic level, where quantum effects are important, the model breaks down completely, and has no predictive value at all.

There is, in other words, a new appreciation of the *relative applicability* of theories. Depending on what we want to do or achieve, one theory may be more relevant than another. As a result of the work of such outstanding figures as Kuhn, Lakatos, and more recently Latour, Callon, or Feyerabend, there has developed a 'theoretical relativism' in the philosophy of science—a view and acceptance that different models and conceptual apparatuses may be employed to give different insights into the same phenomenon. There is now a profound rejection of the view that any one model provides 'the truth' about any aspect of reality. This is an epistemological position that has far-reaching implications.

Theories are tools for understanding and for intervention. They are conditioned by the real phenomena they attempt to account for, and their utility is tested by their ability to generate or predict new phenomena not yet observed. We now understand how scientific theories come into conflict with each other, and how these clashes may be resolved: partly through the institutional and social setting in which the theories are debated, but also through appeals to conceptual economy, elegance and power of generality. The notion that science is evolving through such a process to some closer and closer approximation of 'the truth' has long been abandoned. The 'truth' is now seen to be some mystic concern the pursuit of which is analogous to the pursuit of a single deity by the early Israelites in their incursion into the land of the Canaanites, surrounded, as the book of Genesis tells us so often, by false idols and charms.

So, theory is not concerned with 'truth', but with accounting for and explaining events. It provides a conceptual framework within which events may be given a meaning, and through which we may be able to intervene successfully to shape events in the way desired. Different theories will give different 'meanings' to events, but the arbiter is the success or otherwise of deliberate intervention to achieve a desired outcome.

We have, to put it plainly, lost our *epistemological innocence*. We can no longer claim to see science as generating some special *objective* knowledge that derives its power from its correspondence with *the truth*.[5]

I would argue that we must now apply these lessons in our approach to theory within the labour and social movements. Within the labour movement, we cannot fool ourselves that one specification for a social order is more 'scientific' or 'objective' than another. Politics, as Ernst Wigforss remarked, is a constant process of experimentation.

A utilitarian conception of theory

I see the responsibility of intellectuals as being to supply theory which gives meaning to current struggles, and to project a vision of an achievable alternative to the status quo. Theory must above all be concrete: it must engage with the real world, and not deal in abstract essences that are beyond human understanding. This is a utilitarian conception of theory.[6]

A good theoretical model of the economy, for example, will provide a means of testing different approaches to a structural issue like introducing a guaranteed income scheme. Tools for this process are available, in the form of econometric models. Like any other model used in science, an econometric model reflects a particular theoretical position, and has more or less of a 'purchase on reality' according to the soundness of that position. Most econometric models are used to churn out 'forecasts' of likely economic developments—yet this is not how they ought to be used.[7]

Forecasts are meaningless in the absence of an explicit listing of the assumptions that inform the predictions. Most econometric forecasts are published subject to the proviso that there will be 'no change' in policies. At best, then, they can be seen as offering us a picture of how bad things are likely to get unless there is a change in policies. But this is to take a charitable view of the activities of most forecasters, who in fact view 'policy change' as an interference in the validity of their predictions.

The point of modelling the behaviour of the economy is not to predict it, but to change it. This means using the model as a tool which allows one to think through the likely consequences of taking certain actions. In the case of a GMI scheme, different tax regimes may be tested, in order to 'tune' the scheme to a point where families on average weekly earnings are not worse off as a result of the scheme's introduction.

We can learn from the example of mathematics. In this domain, where human imagination has created its greatest works, wholly new and abstract systems are dreamed up, but they are exactly specified, and the 'facts' about them—the theorems that are true in any axiomatic system—are stated quite concretely. Where generalizations are made, they apply to all instances: *a counter-example disproves a theorem*. And theorems come to life when they are illustrated by specific examples.

This is an appropriate model for our approach to theorizing the future of the labour and social movements, and the prospects for democracy. We need to be imaginative, but specific; we need to cast formulations in general terms, but be able to provide concrete instances. Too often in Left discourse we find abstract generalizations that are never 'brought down to earth'. Rather than being the badge of 'high theory', this approach in my view spells weakness and insecurity. The striving for aphorism and verbal pyrotechnics needs to be tempered by the demands of intervention in the concrete circumstances of the real world.

5.2 A CULTURE OF ASSOCIATIVE DEMOCRACY

Przeworski concludes his 1980 survey of social democracy with the assertion that:

> Social democrats will not lead European societies into socialism. Even if workers would prefer to live under socialism, the process of transition must lead to a crisis before socialism could be organized. To reach higher peaks one must traverse a valley, and this descent will not be completed under democratic conditions.[8]

The better part of this text is devoted to a rebuttal of Przeworski's peremptory rejection of social democracy. Even so, I would not be so bold as to claim that social democrats *will* lead societies into socialism. I don't claim to know what a socialist society will look like, nor how we would know when we have achieved it. I do know that any sort of transition to a worthwhile alternative to capitalism will take decades of social ferment to achieve, utilizing a variety of institutional and organizational forms. After all, the transition from feudalism to capitalism took centuries to accomplish, just within Europe, and globally the transition to capitalism is not yet completed. Social formations just do not change overnight, nor in response to a single political ideology. Any illusions we might have had on that score should have been laid to rest by now.

Przeworski, and others like him, puts too great an historical burden on social democracy—and then, because it fails to deliver on his terms, he dismisses it as a political option. This is surely the height of illogicality. A more measured approach, and one that is favoured in this text, is to ask: what are the *preconditions* for worthwhile social advance? What social structures need to be in place before people can *choose* the sort of social organization they would like? I claim that the answer to this, more pertinent, question is: *democratization of economic and social life.* Without democratization, any notion that ordinary people can influence the debate on our social future as much as IBM or Exxon, is ludicrous. We need to implant a *culture of democracy.*

My conclusion is that democratization must now be seen as the prime strategic goal of the labour and social movements. It is the precondition for further social advance. Moreover, it seems to me to be the only viable response to the industrial challenge of effecting a rupture with Fordism, and the immediate political challenge posed by the New Right. Unless this challenge is met in an imaginative fashion, there will not be much of the labour or social movements left to be arguing about the future.

The goal of democratization of economic and social life will certainly not be easy. It, too, will take decades to accomplish—but a particular society could expect to see results within a ten-year period provided it is ideologically and politically mobilized to achieve it. I claim that the agencies of democratization already exist: they are the organizations of workers and citizens through which they may express their associative interests, and bring their collective pressure to bear on events. Those agencies are the trade unions, social movements, and SD/L parties. What they need is an effective mobilizing ideology to guide their actions—and this is what the paradigm of associative democracy offers them. What they *do not need* is the miscellany of ideologies and strategies inherited from the past, which may belittle or frustrate their efforts, or make claims that would render futile all their exertions. The need for a positive approach to theory is manifest. I claim that democratization is the social practice that will finally liberate social theory, and secure for the social and labour movements their rightful place in history.

Notes and References

1 Introduction

1 See Marshall (1981). Related treatises are *Social Policy in the Twentieth Century* (Marshall, 1975) and *Class, Citizenship and Social Development* (Marshall, 1977). For a particularly clear discussion of these ideas and their relevance to the present discussion, see Bryan Turner's recent study *Citizenship and capitalism: the debate over reformism*. (Turner, 1986).

2 On this Swedish strategy, see for example Walter Korpi (1978) *The working class in welfare capitalism*: and Gosta Esping-Andersen (1985) *Politics against markets: the social democratic road to power*. For a US view of the same process, see Samuel Bowles and Herbert Gintis (1986) *Democracy and capitalism: property, community, and the contradictions of modern social thought*. In light-hearted vein, Bowles calls this the 'Alligator Strategy': 'Alligators lie in a watering hole with just their eyes sticking out. The water buffaloes come down to drink. The water buffalo puts its foot in the water. The alligator grabs the foot. A tremendous struggle ensues. The water buffalo is defenceless if pulled into the water. The alligator, if pulled up onto the land, will get stomped... That's the game we're playing. We have to pull capital into the water. We have to understand that there are some terrains on which we are stronger than others.' (Wilson, 1985).

3 The German Social Democratic Party abandoned its nineteenth-century terminology (class struggle, dictatorship of the proletariat, etc.) and came to terms with pluralist democracy, in its Bad Godesberg programme of 1959. Similar moves in the British Labour Party were documented and expounded by Crosland (1956).

4 See my companion text, Mathews (1988) *Tools of change*, for an extensive discussion of these issues. The principles of Taylorism, embodied in the procedures of 'scientific management', were to fragment skilled jobs into semi-skilled components, and transfer the initiative of workers to the bureaucratic control of management. Such a system was perfectly adapted to the needs of mass production.

5 I employ the term 'paradigm' as an extension of its use by Thomas Kuhn in his pathbreaking text, *The Structure of Scientific Revolutions*. For Kuhn, most scientific work is 'normal science' carried out within a certain 'paradigm' of accepted theory, methodology, rules, or instrumentation. Occasionally a new theory threatens an established paradigm, and a struggle ensues over which is 'correct'. Familiar examples are the struggle in astronomy over the Ptolemaic vs Copernican view of the solar system; in mechanics over Newtonian vs Aristotelian dynamics; in chemistry over Lavoisier's theory of combustion vs the theory of phlogiston, and so on.

Kuhn described the emergence of a new paradigm as having two characteristics: the achievement is sufficiently unprecedented to attract an enduring group of adherents away from competing modes of scientific activity; and, simultaneously, it is sufficiently open-ended to leave all sorts of problems for the newly-formed group of practitioners to resolve. Kuhn noted that 'acquisition of a paradigm and of the more esoteric type of research it permits is a sign of maturity in the development of any given scientific field'. (T. Kuhn, 1970; p. 11).

For Kuhn, a paradigm shift was not a conscious development. It was the outcome of a fundamental tension in an existing theoretical and conceptual framework; these tensions would be resolved by a conceptual leap that opens the way to a new framework.

I am extending the use of this term to encompass a deliberate elaboration of a framework for sustained conceptual and practical work. By an 'associative democratic' paradigm I mean a set of principles and assumptions that would inform the practical activity of the labour movement, providing it with goals which transcend its current outlook and give new meaning to its existing institutions, such as trade unions, but which would also create a series of open-ended problems defining a programme of work to be carried out in the social sciences. The paradigm would allow this further scientific work to be distinguished from that carried out in competing paradigms, such as 'liberal', or 'neo-classical' or 'positivist' frameworks.

Others have extended Kuhn's notion of paradigm to the field of technological change. See for example R. Laudan, *The Nature of technological knowledge: are models of scientific change relevant?*. Boston: D. Reidel, 1984.

Kuhn's notion has met with a critical reception in philosophy of science circles, and he has modified it to meet some objections. See S.

Toulmin, *Human Understanding: the collective use and evolution of concepts*. Princeton University Press, 1972; and J. Lakatos and A. Musgrave (eds) *Criticism and the Growth of Knowledge*. Cambridge: Cambridge University Press, 1970.

In the light of these developments, it seems safer to use the term paradigm as a consciously imposed framework, as I am doing in this text, than as an unconscious framework within which it may be claimed that 'normal' scientific or technological work is conducted.

Note that my use of the term 'paradigm' needs to be carefully distinguished from the associated notions of *party*, *programme* or *movement*. I am not attempting to create or recreate any of these, but to suggest a framework of principles that might usefully inform the work of these existing entities. It is the task of the political activist to create the outline of a paradigm, and for the social scientist to fill in the details and test them with adequate methods.

6 See for example, David Beetham, 'Choose democracy: a new democratic order', *New Socialist*, May 1987, pp. 8–13; and Paul Hirst, 'Can socialism live?', *New Statesman*, 6 March 1987, pp. 6–10.

7 See the arguments advanced against democracy by Milton and Rose Friedman (1984) *Tyranny of the status quo*. London: Martin Secker & Warburg. Their basic argument is that elected representatives will seek to 'buy votes' by allocating public resources inefficiently. Such an argument has force only if the 'democratic system' is reduced to virtually a market in votes. In an associative democratic polity, with its much broader conception of democratic processes, the 'vote buying' argument is irrelevant.

2 The Social Democratic heritage

1 See E. P. Thompson (1968), *The Making of the English Working Class*. London: Penguin.

2 On the origins of early factory legislation, see Hutchins and Harrison, 1966.

3 On the history of socialism, see G. Lichtheim, 1970.

4 I do not want to be misunderstood. The rivers of blood have been set loose by the *opponents* of socialism, in one fascist coup or civil war after another. In a sense, both World Wars were fought fundamentally over the issue of socialism.

5 A. Przeworski, 1985; p. 16. Przeworski's essay 'Social democracy as a historical phenomenon', is alive with useful insights, but ultimately it

is unsatisfactory because Przeworski rejects the SD/L tradition, without stating his own position.

6 See R. Williams, 1976; p. 150.

7 J. S. Mill, *On Liberty*. There is, of course, an extensive literature on Mill and his liberalist doctrine, and some creative extensions as in H. A. L. Hart (1963) *Law, Liberty and Morality*. Oxford: Oxford University Press, where Mill's ideas are used to counter the traditionalist ideas of the English judiciary. Mill's text was recently re-issued in Italy (eds. G. Giorello and M. Mondadori, Il Saggiatore, Milan, 1981) as part of a socialist series of texts, *Lo Spazio politico*, creating something of a sensation in Italian progressive political circles, and indicating the new seriousness with which liberal traditions are being treated by socialists.

8 F. Castro, quoted in Hahn and Albert (1981), p. 372.

9 For example, it is stressed by Norberto Bobbio, a socialist senator and perhaps Italy's foremost political theorist, in his recent text *The Future of Democracy* (1984; 1987). In Italy the tradition of accommodation goes back further, to the notion of 'liberal socialism' propounded by Carlo Rosselli, a contemporary of Antonio Gramsci in Turin in the 1920s.

10 On the origins of German social democracy, see B. Hindess (1983), *Parliamentary democracy and social politics*. London: Routledge and Kegan Paul, and C. Schorske (1955, 1983) *German Social Democracy, 1905–1917*. Cambridge, Harvard University Press.

11 See Kautsky, 1964; 1971. For a useful review of the debates of this period, see Hindess, 1983, particularly chapter 1: Marxism and Parliamentary Democracy.

12 In Australia, the nascent Labour Party at the time of federation, in 1901, struck a deal with rural interests: it supported high tariff barriers, in exchange for rural support for statutory regulation of the labour market—a deal which lasted for half a century and more, and which exerted a profound effect on Australia's development. See S. Macintyre (1986), *The Oxford History of Australia: Vol. 4, 1901–1942 The Succeeding Age*. Melbourne: Oxford University Press.

13 See Przeworski, 1985; p. 13.

14 See Tingsten, 1973; p. 118–9.

15 Georg von Vollmar, leader of The Bavarian SPD, at the Erfurt

Congress; quoted in Peter Gay, 1970; *The Dilemma of Democratic Socialism*, New York; p. 258.

16 See K. Kautsky, op. cit.

17 See Bernstein, 1961.

18 See R. Luxemburg, 1900; p. 29.

19 For a refreshing account of the Bolshevik revolution as it was reported in the western press, see P. Knightly (1976), *The First Casualty: From the Crimea to Vietnam—the war correspondent as hero, propagandist and myth-maker*. New York: Harcourt, Brace, Jovanovich. The misreporting and miscomprehension of the Bolshevik strategy was almost total, and certainly had the unintended effect of romanticizing the Bolsheviks in western socialists' eyes.

20 I. Howe, 1985; p. 512.

21 For a somewhat acid commentary on the efforts of the German SPD at this time, exercised for example through its Committee on Socialization 1919, see Schumpeter's monumental *Capitalism, Socialism and Democracy*, especially p. 300 (1943; 1987).

22 See Przeworski, 1985; p. 33.

23 On the theoretical contribution of Ernst Wigforss to SD/L theory, see Tilton, 1979; and Higgins, 1985.

24 For a fascinating insight into the dilemmas of the European SD movement during the 1930s, see Adolf Sturmthal, *The tragedy of European labour, 1918–1939* (1944). This was written by the Austrian social democrat Sturmthal, who escaped to the US and went on to become a professor at the University of Illinois.

25 There is no 'ruling class' as such any more in a democratic order apart from some feudal throw-backs and the odd heir to a fortune. There are certainly people with power and influence far greater than that enjoyed by the average worker, but the point is that they reach these positions through the dynamics of the system, and not through any *predetermined* process, and their power and influence depends on the rules of the system operations. Let us take a concrete example: a redundancy struggle, where a takeover merchant acquires a company and seeks to dispense with the workers. The capitalist clearly has power and influence, but there are avenues open to the workers to defend themselves—through their union, through statutory severance arrange-

ments, through court action to enforce contracts of employment, through campaigns in the press and other media, and so on. To label the takeover capitalist as 'ruling class' adds nothing to our understanding of his or her position, and indeed positively hinders our ability to deal with the redundancy situation, for it discourages any sort of concrete action or negotiation.

26 Latin America provides a rich store of examples both of the collapse of democracy into fascist military dictatorships, and of the painful restoration of democracy. At the moment the pendulum is swinging towards a hesitant restoration of democratic liberties, with juntas having stepped aside over the past seven years in Ecuador, Peru, Bolivia, Argentina, Uruguay, Guatemala, El Salvador and most recently Brazil.

The experience of Peru is pregnant with lessons particularly with regard to the effects of ultra-leftists on a democracy. In the 1960s the democratic government of President Bealunde Terry was challenged by two leftist insurrections, from the Revolutionary Left Movement and the National Liberation Army, inspired by Cuban, Chinese and North Korean guerrilla warfare successes. Terry entrusted the suppression of these insurrections to the Army, which did the job in typically brutal Latin American fashion. No sooner were the leftist leaders executed, than the army commanders staged a coup of their own, in October 1968; they ousted the democratic government that had given them their head, and installed a military dictatorship that lasted twelve years. Under this regime the labour movement in Peru was cut to pieces.

With the restoration of democracy in 1980, Bealunde Terry was *re-elected* to the presidency. But at the same time, a new leftist insurrectionary movement, the *Sendero Luminoso*, was launched in Peru. It is understandable that in order to avoid a repetition of his 1968 experience, Terry did all in his power to keep the military from leading the fight against this neo-Maoist insurrection, and tried to contain it by civil guards and police (who had little effect on the insurgency, but left a disastrous record of murder, rape and pillage amongst the village peasantry—which only enhanced the reputation of the guerrillas). As a result, the democratic regime has been plunged into a civil war—very much in the same way as the democratic Philippines post-Marcos government is seeking to contain armed rebellion.

The *Sendero Luminoso* is an interesting case study in its own right of ultra-left infantilism of a deadly kind. It launched itself in the dying stages of the dictatorship by hanging dogs from the electricity poles in Lima. (This symbolized their disgust with the 'dog' Deng Xiaoping who betrayed the Maoist principles of the Chinese Cultural Revolution.) The group, known formally as the Communist Party of Peru, takes its name *Sendero Luminoso* (Shining Light) from a statement from an earlier Peruvian ideologist, Jose Carlos Mariategui: 'Marxism-Leninism will open the shining path to revolution'. The group is unique in not receiving any external help, and for being founded by a single fervent ideologue, Abimael Guzman, a professor in the 1970s at the University of San Cristobal in the region of Ayacucho.

This essentially intellectual and ideological movement has been foisted on a peasantry who barely know where China is, let alone the role that the 'dog' Deng Xiaoping plays in it.

The character of this insurrection has been brought out in a brilliant document written by the Peruvian novelist, Mario Vargas Llosa, who headed an independent commission of inquiry into a massacre of journalists in 1983. The military claimed that this had been done by Indians, following on the heels of a similar massacre of Senderistas— but such a claim met with universal disbelief. Llosa's inquest showed that it was in fact true, and it revealed how estranged the peasantry was from this urban movement that relocated itself from the city to the countryside in emulation of Mao's tactic of 'ringing the cities'. But Llosa went further and drew lessons for any democratic regime under threat:

> Perhaps this story helps to clarify the reason for the mind-shattering violence that characterizes guerrilla warfare in Latin America. These guerrilla movements are not 'peasant movements'. They are born in the cities, among intellectuals and middle-class militants who, with their dogmatism and their rhetoric, are often as foreign and incomprehensible to the peasant masses as Sendero Luminoso is to the men and women of Uchuraccay...
>
> Put simply, the peasants are coerced by those who think they are the masters of history and absolute truth. The fact is that the struggle between the guerrillas and the armed forces is really a settling of accounts between privileged sectors of society, and the peasant masses are used cynically and brutally by those who say they want to 'liberate' them...
>
> The story of the eight journalists [who were massacred] reveals how vulnerable democracy is in Latin America and how easily it dies under military or Marxist–Leninist dictatorship. It is difficult for people to defend a free press, elections and representative institutions when their circumstances do not allow them to understand, much less to benefit from, the achievements of democracy. Democracy will never be strong in our Latin American countries as long as it is the privilege of one sector of society and an incomprehensible abstraction for all the others.

One might paraphrase this conclusion of Llosa's, which I believe is accurate in the Latin American context, to state that democracy will never be safe in the west while it is confined to political institutions and remains merely an abstraction for most of the population in the area where it should count most: in the workplace and wider economy. The example is also cited as a *pathological* case, to illustrate the pressures to which all SD/L democracies are subject, though they are rarely revealed so openly in a typical western country.

(Source: Mario Vargas Llosa, Inquest in the Andes, reproduced in

The New York Times Magazine July 31, 1983, pp. 18–56, translated by Edith Grossman.)

27 See Claus Offe, *Disorganized Capitalism* (1985); and Scott Lash and John Urry, *The End of Organized Capitalism* (1987).

28 See A. Crosland (1956), *The Future of Socialism*, for a classic statement of this position. In 1980 the then leader of the Labour Party in the UK, Michael Foot, intervened in the selection process of a parliamentary candidate (Peter Thatchell) on the grounds that he had spoken out in favour of 'extra-parliamentary' campaigns. This shows how deeply rooted is this fundamentally flawed and misconceived doctrine.

29 On the 'rise and fall of full-employment capitalism' and the debates over SD/L strategy during this period, see Higgins and Apple, 1983.

30 See Esping-Andersen, 1986; p. 31.

31 See the French Socialist Party's manifesto for the May 1988 presidential elections; it includes a commitment to a GMI. Similarly, in New Zealand the tax and family package announced by the Treasurer, Roger Douglas, in December 1987, includes a Guaranteed Minimum Family Income (GMFI) Scheme—although its status at the time of writing is unclear.

32 See David Cameron (1984), 'Social democracy, corporatism, labour quiescence, and the representation of economic interest in advanced capitalist society'. In J. Goldthorpe, ed, *Order and conflict in contemporary capitalism: Studies in the political economy of West European nations*. Oxford: Oxford University Press, 1984. There is an extensive discussion of macro-economic strategies and their links with labour market policies, in the 1987 strategy document issued by the Australian Council of Trade Unions, *Australia Reconstructed* (ACTU/TDC, 1987). This document has had a major impact in Australia, swinging the labour movement away from its former Anglo-Saxon model to one more in tune with Austrian and Scandinavian strategies.

33 The term 'corporatism' is so ideologically loaded, with such obvious connotations of Italian fascism, that it is frequently used as a term of abuse for these developments. Some writers, like Wyn Grant, or in Australia, G. Dow, have attempted to use the term corporatism in a favourable sense, or have distinguished it from Italian fascist *Corporativismo* by calling the new developments 'neo-corporatism'. (Grant, 1985.) To my mind this is not satisfactory. Use of the term corporatism biases the discussion of these developments, and holds up serious analysis of them, e.g. in France, where the name itself has acted as a taboo.

Hence I propose in this book to follow up an idea of Schmitter and Streeck, and extend their use of the term '*associational*' to cover all such procedures and structures where interest groups come to form part of the political process in a binding framework. (Schmitter and Streeck, 1979.)

Terminology is always important, and in this case it is very important. I hope others will also see merit in this suggestion and engage in serious discussion of 'associational' political developments, without muddying the waters with terms that connote fascism.

34 A basic theoretical (and highly practical) deficiency in the discussion to date is the lack of any legitimizing principle for the 'associational' fusion of private power and political authority. Such structures are not sanctioned by any *constitutional* authority, as are, in theory, the operations of the State. So there is endless debate over *who* should participate; on *what* issues; according to *which* procedures; etc. In the absence of legitimation, what a *stable* 'corporatist' structure requires is a degree of consensus. Conditions for this would include a tradition of strong centralized unions and employer organizations; sanctions or deprivation of rights for organizations which depart from the associational structure; and goals of growth that make zero-sum conflict seem a less favourable choice for all parties.

What about voluntary forms of tripartite consultation, where decisions taken are not *binding* on the parties? Some authors have argued that this voluntary tripartism is 'corporatist'. Chubb, for example, holds that the state can 'build support for the enactment and implementation of its policies by granting privileged participation to a sectoral interest group sufficiently powerful to deliver the support of its benefiting constituency'. (Chubb, 1983; p. 26.)

But most of those who use the term argue that an associational mode is stronger than this. Wyn Grant, in a lucid survey of the literature, defines his use of the term 'corporatism' (or neo-corporatism, or liberal corporatism) as 'a process of interest intermediation which involves the negotiation of a policy between state agencies and interest organizations arising from the division of labour in society, where the policy agreements are implemented through the collaboration of the interest organizations and their willingness and ability to secure the compliance of their members'. (Grant, 1985; p. 34.) For him, this rules out voluntary tripartite structures without commitments, as well as arbitrary imposition of state policies through sham consultation—in particular, the practices of fascist states.

Fascistic, or state corporatism, is very different from the emergent associational principle of our time—and this is why the term 'corporatism' for these modern developments is so misleading. The characteristics of fascist corporatism were the creation of 'corporations' as auxiliary and dependent organs of the state'. The unions organized in these 'corporations' were sham. Hence it is completely misleading to use this term for modern 'social contract' arrangements.

35 C. Offe (1985); pp. 231–232.

36 See W. Streeck and P. Schmitter (1985), 'Community, market, state—and associations? The prospective contribution of interest governance to social order'. In Streeck and Schmitter (eds), *Private Interest Government? Beyond market and state*, London, Sage, 1985.

37 For an excellent overview of the literature on social concertation, see the Special Issue of the journal *Labour and Society* on '*Social Concertation*', Vol 12, No 3, Sept. 1987; and in particular the introductory overview: 'Social concertation: theories and trends', by Geraldo von Potobsky.

38 See Esping-Andersen *et al.*, Modes of class struggle and the capitalist state, *Kapitalistate* 4–5, p. 192. Quoted in Offe, 1985; p. 257. Note that Esping-Andersen's position has developed and in his 1986 text, cited above, he refers less frequently to the 'capitalist state', or to 'class struggle'. Both terms, of course, belong to an ideological era preceding 'associational' forms of organization.

39 See F. Stillwell (1986), *The Accord... and After?* Sydney: Pluto Press, Australia. For debate on the 'corporatist' features of the Accord, see D. McKnight, ed (1986), *Moving Left*. Sydney: Pluto Press Australia.

40 There is by now an enormous literature on the social movements, from the intensely theoretical, such as Habermas's works on the cultural contradictions within capitalism, to decidedly practical and action-oriented studies. See for example A. Touraine (1981) *The Voice and the Eye: An analysis of social movements*. Cambridge, Cambridge University Press.

41 See, for example, Poulantzas, 1968 (1973).

42 E. Meiksins Wood, 1986.

43 See Przeworski, *Material basis for consent*, in Przeworski, 1985; and the interesting papers by Kerry Schott, 'Investment, order and conflict in a simple dynamic model of capitalism', and Peter Lange, 'Unions, workers and wage regulation: the rational bases of consent', in J. Goldthorpe (1984).

44 Cited in Goldthorpe (1984); p. 146.

45 On epistemological pluralism, see Feyerabend (1975); Toulmin (1972); Latour (1987); and Charlesworth (1982).

46 See Jean-Francois Lyotard (1979, 1984) *The postmodern condition: A report on knowledge*. Manchester: Manchester University Press.

47 D. Selbourne (1986), *Against Socialist Illusions*, p. 121.

48 Geoff Dow puts the matter into perspective, when he notes:
These criticisms have historical precedent on their side. Incomes policies have, more often than not, brought reductions in real wages without the honouring of guarantees of expansion and job security that unions have had a right to expect. But against them must be cited a disregard for subtle shifts in class relations at different stages of capitalist development and an overt pessimism concerning the possibility of anything other than apocalyptic challenges to bourgeois prerogatives in production. (Geoff Dow, 'The case for corporatism', *Australian Society*, November 1984, pp. 14–16.)

49 Leo Panitch, 'Trade unions and the capitalist state', *New Left Review*, No. 125, January–February 1981; p. 28 (my emphasis).

50 See the discussion by Gramsci in his *Prison Notebooks*. Numerous commentaries are available, such as Alastair Davidson, *Antonio Gramsci: towards an intellectual biography*. London: Merlin Press; and Alastair Davidson (1982), *The Theory and Practice of Italian Communism*. London: Merlin Press.

51 A. Przeworski, 'Material bases of consent', in Przeworski (1985).

52 *Ibid*; p. 57 in original.

53 The SPD turned away from fundamentalist Marxism and neutralism in the 1950s, when it endorsed Keynesianism and gave up the idea of a 'class party' in the Bad Godesberg programme of 1959. The next major programmatic statement came in 1977 with the setting up of the 'Commission for Fundamental Values' and in 1984 a new 'Programme Commission'. In June 1985 an introductory statement of 'fundamental principles' was approved, with contributions from leading theoreticians Thomas Meyer, SPD Secretary Peter Glotz, Volker Hauff (author of a recent text, *Environmental Politics at a Crossroads*) and Peter von Oertzen (author of another recent text, *Towards a New Reformism*). See the survey article by Mario Telo, 'The Greening of Social Democracy: the SPD rethinks economics' (translated from the Italian by Michael Sexton), *Socialist Review*, No. 91 (Vol. 17, No. 1), January–February 1987. See also the manifesto by Peter Glotz, 'Forward to Europe: A Declaration for a New European Left', *Dissent*, Summer 1986.

54 See Harrington, 1970 (my italics). Harrington is notable not just for his emphasis on 'democratic collectivism', but for his radical insistence

that it is the growing divorce between ownership and control of the corporation that makes the case for socialization—in flat contradiction to Crosland's 1956 text, *The Future of Socialism*, which argued that ownership is now irrelevant.

55 Bowles, Gordon and Weiskopf, 1983.

56 See N. Bobbio (1976), *Quale socialismo? Discussione di un' alternativa*. Turin: Einaudi. (This is now available in English: N. Bobbio, *Which Socialism? Marxism, socialism and democracy*. Cambridge: Polity Press.) For a commentary see R. Bellamy (1987), *Modern Italian Social Theory*. Cambridge: Polity Press; and his Introduction to the English edition of *Which Socialism?* Bobbio's more recent text is Bobbio (1984), *Il Futuro della democrazia*. Turin: Einaudi. This has been issued as *The Future of Democracy*: Introduction by R. Bellamy (1987). Cambridge: Polity Press.

57 Richard Bellamy's Introduction encapsulates Bobbio's position in these words:

> To recapitulate, Bobbio seeks to adapt the foundations and institutions of liberal democracy to meet the demands and criticisms of socialists. He fully accepts the left's contention that the inequalities of wealth and influence, the growth of bureaucratic and corporative organizations and the increasing complexity, sophistication and specialization of modern societies have undermined the democratic accountability of governments and empowered other agencies that have never been subject to public scrutiny. The Marxist solution of simply identifying the individual's interests with those of the community has long been discredited, and Bobbio aligns himself with a prominent tradition of Italian socialist thought in rejecting it. Instead he suggests a reform of liberal justifications for civil and political equality to include social equality as the natural extension and partner of the other two. Following Rawls, he proposes a new social contract as the basis of a democratic society which places our social and political rights and duties on an uncompromising individualist ethical foundation. He complements this socialist reformulation of liberal theory with a number of proposals for restructuring the institutional framework of liberalism. He argues that we need to render not only the state but society democratically accountable. However, in order to avoid the counter-productive inflation of political activity and the particularist tendencies of traditional radical calls for participatory democracy, he maintains that a multi-party system operating within a strong legal framework guaranteeing citizen's rights provides the most practicable avenue for reform. (Bobbio, 1987; p. 13.)

58 Rosselli's ideas were expounded in the periodical *La Rivoluzione Liberale*, and were embodied in the anti-fascist movement *Giustizia e Liberta* (Justice and Liberty). See Carlo Rosselli (1929), *Socialismo liberale*. Einaudi, Turin, 1973, for his major writings. For an account of his life, see A. Garosci, *La vita di Carlo Rosselli*, (2 vols, Edizione U, Rome, 1946) and N. Tranfaglia, *Carlo Rosselli: dadl 'interventismo a 'Giustizia e liberta'* (Laterza, Bari, 1968), and the Introduction by Richard Bellamy

to Bobbio, 1987, *op cit*. The doctrine of liberal socialism combines the three elements: constitutionalism, parliamentarism and pluralism.

59 See D. Held (1987), *Models of Democracy*. Cambridge: Polity Press; p. 283.

60 Ibid, p. 289. Astonishingly, Held makes no reference to Rosselli, nor to Bobbio in advancing his term 'liberal socialism'. But his aims are clearly similar to my own in formulating the AD paradigm.

61 See R. Dahl (1985), *A Preface to Economic Democracy*. Berkeley: University of California Press.

62 Schmitter (1985); pp. 53–54.

63 See Paul Hirst (1987) 'Can socialism live?' *New Statesman*, 6 March 1987, pp. 6–10; and Hirst (1986) *Law, Socialism and Democracy*, London: Allen & Unwin. On this point see my pamphlet, *A culture of power* (1988a) and the commentary by Minson (1988), 'The new romantics'. For a more systematic development of this theme, see Paul Hirst (1988) 'Associational Socialism in a Pluralist State', *Journal of Law and Society*, 15, 1, pp 139–150.

64 The 1920s saw both liberal and socialist versions of 'associationalism' being developed as a foil against the overweening power of big government. In Britain, G.D.H. Cole's *guild socialism* envisaged the displacement of the State by a series of producers' associations, which could be left to manage themselves spontaneously. Hirst argues that it was their failure to comprehend the necessity for political and legal structures to regulate such associations that led to the decline of guild socialism. While I agree with this, I argue below that their greatest error was to see trade unions as the forebears of producers' associations, thus confusing fundamentally distinct functions of democratic management and democratic accountability. See G.D.H. Cole (1920) *Guild Socialism Restated*; and ibid (1920) *The Social Theory*.

In the USA at the same time, liberal bureaucrats in the New Era administration, led by Herbert Hoover, tried to create an 'associative state' based on coordination of business and community associations. For an account of this interesting experience, see Ellis Hawley (1974) 'Herbert Hoover, the Commerce Secretariat, and the vision of an 'Associative State', 1921–1928', *Journal of American History*, 61, pp 116–140. Hoover, as Commerce Secretary, vigorously pursued a vision of 'fundamental self-government' through a 'cooperative system' of 'self-regulating organisms' that would meet the needs of industrial democracy without statist interference: the phrases all come from Hoover memoranda cited by Hawley. While achieving successes in such areas as trade standardization, housing, and child welfare, the program wilted under the impact of the Depression, and was abandoned by the New Deal administration in the 1930s.

65 On Fordism, there is now an expanding and vigorous literature. For global overviews, see Aglietta (1979), Piore and Sabel (1984) and Lipietz (1987). For a creative exposition of a politics of post-Fordism, see Lipietz (1988; 1989).

66 For an account of debates between socialists over the nature of socialism, see for example, Nove, 1983; I. Howe, 1985; Albert and Hahnel, 1981; Hodgson, 1984.

67 Tilton, 1979; p. 507.

68 *Ibid*, p. 518. Wigforss produced no major statement of his philosophy that has been translated into English, but Tilton, 1979; and Higgins, 1985, provide excellent introductions.

69 Higgins, 1985; p. 242.

Chapter 3 Economic, industrial and social democracy

1 See C. Sirianni, 1980, for a superbly evocative account of this period.

2 Quoted in A. Benn, *Arguments for Socialism*, 1982.

3 On the development of mass production, see Piore and Sabel (1984); and C. Sabel (1982). I have written at length on these changes myself, in *Tools of Change: New technology and the democratization of work* (1989).

4 On the theorization of Fordism given by the French Regulation School, see Aglietta (1979) and Lipietz (1987).

For a creative application of the concept of Fordism to the problems of transition, see C. Perez (1985), 'Micro-electronics, long waves and world structural change: New perspectives for developing countries', *World Development*, Vol. 13, No. 3, pp. 441–463.

5 See H. Braverman (1974), *Labour and Monopoly Capital: The degradation of work in the twentieth century*. New York: Monthly Review Press.

6 On all these matters, see Mathews (1989), *Tools of Change*; ibid (1989) 'New production concepts', and Badham and Mathews (1989), 'The "new production systems" debate'.

7 See the ACTU/TDC report, *Australia Reconstructed* (1987).
On Australian 'Efficiency and Restructuring' agreements negotiated in a post-Fordist framework, see Mathews (1989b).

8 See Ralph Nader, Mark Green and Joel Seligman, 1976, *Taming the Giant Corporation* (New York, W.W. Norton). See also Christopher Stone, 1976, *Beyond the Law: the Social Control of Corporations*. (New York, Harper and Row).

9 F. Hayek (1960), 'The corporation in a democratic society'. In M. Anshen and G. Back (eds), 1960, *Management and Corporation in 1985*, New York: McGraw-Hill.

10 See Shann Turnbull (1988) 'The case for the corporate senate', *Journal* of the Australian Society of Security Analysts, September 1988, p 13. This article describes cases of companies where a corporate senate has been established through the articles of association, and functioned effectively. Turnbull's many innovative ideas regarding democratization of companies are expounded in his 1975 text, 'Democratizing the Wealth of Nations', Sydney, Company Directors Association of Australia.

11 Quoted in Carnoy and Shearer, 1980; p. 254.

12 On the Swedish experience, see Jan Holzhauser, 'Employee representation on company Boards', 1981, Working Paper, Swedish Centre for Working Life. On the Norwegian experience, and conclusions drawn from it, see Bjorn Gustavsen, 1984, 'A decade of employee representation on company boards: experiences and prospects for the future', Working Paper, Swedish Centre for Working Life.

13 E. Batstone, 1977: 'Industrial democracy and workers' represenation at Board level', in *Industrial Democracy—European Experience* (London, Her Majesty's Stationery Office); p. 35.

14 In their text, *Economic Democracy*, Carnoy and Shearer come to a similar conclusion:

> The danger of worker-directors, as is clear from the European experience, is not that they constitute a subversive force, but that they may be simply irrelevant and a sham. Such an outcome can be avoided only if worker-directors are seen as just one part of an overall strategy to democratize the economy. Democratic theory requires that the boardroom be opened to worker-directors and to 'special' directors representing components of the overall public interest—consumers, environmentalists, minorities, and women. 'Special' directors will be effective only under the conditions outlined by Batstone for worker-directors: they must come from a recognizable constituency—i.e. a consumer group, women's group, environmentalist group, or minority organization with a constituency to which they are accountable in some way; they must be provided with resources,

including a staff and research help; and they must, by law, have access to company information.

Over a period of time, the opening of boardrooms to such interests will affect to some degree the decision-making priorities of managers. Opening the boardrooms will not necessarily make the workplace itself more democratic, however, nor will it ensure that parties other than managers participate in business decisions. This is more likely, as the European experience shows, to come through aggressive collective bargaining and innovative labor legislation that introduces democratic participation into all levels of the firm, particularly inside the plant. (1980; p. 256–257.)

15 See S. Holland (1975), *The Socialist Challenge.*

16 Quoted in A. Benn, *Arguments for Socialism*, 1982.

17 *Ibid.*

18 These Boards are reviewed in a paper prepared in Victoria for the Melbourne City Council: S. Tregillis (1985), *A proposal to establish a Central Melbourne Enterprise Board*, Melbourne, Labor Resources Centre.

For an evaluation of the GLEB experience, see the papers from the Open University's Technology Policy Group: David Elliot, (1986), 'The GLC's Innovation and Employment Initiative', TPG Occasional Paper No. 11; and David Wield (1986), 'The politics of technological innovation', TPG Occasional Paper No. 10, Open University, Milton Keynes.

19 There is a flourishing literature on the role that such public enterprises can play in providing incubator or seeding facilities to employment-generating small companies. See, for example, A. Friend, 1986. *Local Employment Initiatives: Combating unemployment in an era of rapid structural adjustment.* Background Paper prepared for National Conference on Local Employment Initiatives, Canberra, July 1986. On incubators, see 'Technology Business Incubators and Tertiary Institutions'. Melbourne: Victorian Ministry of Education, 1988. The Cain Labor government in Victoria, elected in 1983, has established a number of companies limited by guarantee as democratic public corporations under its *Economic Strategy*, issued in 1983, and revised in 1987 ('*The next decade*').

20 See, for example, R. Mathews (1987). *Employee Ownership: Mondragon's lessons for Australia*, Melbourne: Australian Fabian Society, Pamphlet No. 47.

21 See 'Cooperative Monograph No. 1', 'Worker Cooperatives in France', A report produced under the direction of Hugues Sibille,

translated by Jim Asker, 1982; and 'Cooperative Monograph No. 2', 'Organization of the Cooperative movement in Italy', A report by Carlo Carli, 1985; both published by the Department of Employment and Industrial Affairs, Government of Victoria.

22 See R. Jackall and H. Levien, eds (1984). *Worker Cooperatives in America.* Berkeley: University of California Press. For experience in Australia, see the report, *Worker Cooperatives in NSW and Victoria: a policy review* (1984), prepared jointly by the Transnational Cooperative Ltd., Sydney, and the Labor Resource Centre, Melbourne, for the Victorian Ministry of Employment and Training.

23 We should note, however, that 'employee ownership' is a term open to abuse, and can be used to mean Employee Stock Ownership Plans or other forms of individualized share ownership by workers. Unless workers genuinely 'own' the company, through a majority shareholding and democratic constitution, it is incorrect to call such a company a co-operative. The Thatcher government, for example, has justified its privatization of nationalized industries through offering shares in these enterprises to the workforce. But this is a far cry from worker co-operatives or from *collective* worker ownership, as advocated in this text—even if Thatcher's methods have in some instances led to enhanced productivity.

24 See C. Cornforth (1983), 'Some factors affecting the success or failure of worker cooperatives: a review of empirical research in the United Kingdom', *Economic and Industrial Democracy*, Vol. 4, pp. 163–190. For an interesting case study of a women's cooperative, told with sympathy and insight, see J. Wajcman (1983), *Women in Control.* Milton Keynes: Open University Press.

25 For extended discussions of this point of view, see J. Mathews (1985a), *Health and Safety at Work*; and J. Mathews (chair), Occupational Safety, Health and Welfare Steering Committee, *The Protection of Workers' Health and Safety*, Report to the South Australian Ministers of Labour and of Health, 1984; and B. Creighton and N. Gunningham, eds (1985), *The Industrial Relations of Occupational Health and Safety.* Sydney: Croom Helm.

26 For description of the Swedish experience, see for example Korpi (1978); and W. Higgins (1986), 'Industrial democracy and the control issue in Sweden', in Davis and Lansbury eds, *Democracy and control in the workplace.*

On the Co-determination Act itself, and its working out in practice, see for example Bo Hedberg (1979), 'Worker participation in structural change: acting out the Codetermination Act in the Swedish steel merger',

Working Paper 1979: 2, Swedish Centre for Working Life, Stockholm.

27 This section is based on J. Mathews (1989), 'Democratization of capital', *Economic and Industrial Democracy* Vol. 10 No. 2.

28 See for example the useful discussion in M. Harrington (1986), *The Next Left*.

29 See G. Karlsson (1983) *Trade unions and collective capital formation*. Brussels: European Trade Union Institute.

30 P. Harbecht (1959); pp. 4–5.

31 Carnoy and Shearer (1980); p. 103.

32 See *Interim Report*, March 1981, of the Californian Governor's Public Investment Task Force, Sacramento (chair: John Harrington); p. 4.

33 See R. Barber (1982), 'Pension and wage earner funds in Sweden'. Report from IUD-AFL-CIO Mission to Sweden in Labour and Investments, Washington: AFL-CIO.

34 For an illuminating discussion of trade union and worker participation in the management of superannuation funds in Australia, see Diana Shaw: 'Trade union and worker participation in the control of superannuation funds', in E. Davis and R. Lansbury (eds) (1986) *Democracy and Control in the Workplace*, Melbourne, Longman-Chesire.

35 See Pontusson (1984) for a discussion of these points.

36 See M. Weitzmann (1984), *The Share Economy*. Cambridge, MA: Harvard University Press; and J. Meade (1982), *Stagflation, Vol. 1: Wage Fixing*. London: Allen and Unwin.

37 The Association for Employee Ownership in Australia has proposed a 'Compact' with the Labor Council of NSW, outlining a model Employee Share Ownership Trust which unions could negotiate with firms at enterprise level. The Association champions employee ownership, through Employee Buy-Outs (EBOs) and various leveraged stock ownership plans. Unions are learning that these techniques constitute a wholly new field of 'financial democratization'. Experience with worker-owned firms in Australia is reviewed in the article by Julie Lewis, 'Companies prosper after a buy-out by the employees', *Australian Financial Review*, Jan 11, 1989.

38 See J. Remus (1983), 'Financial participation of employees: an

attempted classification and major trends', *International Labour Review*, Vol. 122, No. 1, Jan-Feb 1983; pp. 1–21.

39 See Wallace Bell, D. (1980), *Profit-sharing and employee shareholding Report*. London: Industrial Participation Association.

40 See cover story by *Business Week*, 15 April, 1985.
The idea of the ESOP concept is credited to Louis Kelso, a San Francisco Lawyer, who in 1958 invented a credit mechanism to allow workers to buy stock in their own company. He helped employees of a West Coast newspaper take over their company, securing loan funds using an existing stock bonus plan as collateral. Since then Kelso has assiduously campaigned in support of his idea, as against the claims of conventional pension funds and profit-sharing schemes. (Kelso, 1967) He has had the support of Senator Russell Long, who has used his position on the Congress Finance Committee to secure various tax concessions for ESOPs.

41 For an exposition in German by the proponent, see Bruno Gleitze, 1968, *Sozialkapital und Sozialfonds als Mittel der Vermogens politik*. Cologne, Bund-Verlag.

42 Much to their chagrin — they sold off these enterprises, with assets of hundreds of millions of dollars, for $1 in 1986, because of mounting debts and corruption problems.

43 Stefan Wirlander (1967), *Perspektiven einer Einkommens-politik von morgen*. Vienna, DGB.

44 For an excellent narrative exposition of the Employee Investment Funds saga in Sweden, and its impact on the Swedish Social Democratic Party, see Hugh Heclo and Henrik Madsen (1987) *Policy and Politics in Sweden: Principled Pragmatism*. Philadelphia: Temple University Press.

45 This report has been translated into English, as R. Meidner, (1978), *Employee Investment Funds*. London: George Allen and Unwin.

46 Based on expert reports, the Department of Finance prepared a comprehensive report under the direction of P.O. Edin, so that the proposal for regional funds became known as the Edin plan (as distinct from the Meidner plan).

47 See W. Korpi (1978); pp. 332–333.

48 Two recent excellent international surveys are provided in the ILO's *International Labour Review*, by Meidner (1981); and Remus (1983).

Earlier surveys are given in English by Derek Robinson (1973): *Incomes policy and capital sharing in Europe*. London, Croom Helm. An overview of the situation in six European countries is provided by Hans Brems, 1973, *A wage earners' investment fund*, Economic Research Reports 15, Stockholm, Federation of Swedish Industries; and Hans Brems, 1980, *The economics of wage earners' investment funds*. Paper submitted to the seminar on capital and Economic Democracy sponsored by the International Centre of the Swedish Labour Movement (AIC), Stockholm, Sept. 1980.

A major report was issued by the Swedish National Commission on Wage Earners and Capital Formation, by Eidem and Ohman, 1979: *Economic democracy through wage earner funds*, Secretariat of Swedish National Commission on Wage Earners and Capital Formation, Stockholm. The Commission of the European Communities issued a memorandum in 1979 entitled: 'Employee participation in asset formation', Supplement 6/79, *Bulletin of the European Communities*, Luxembourg.

See also the Special Issue of *Economic and Industrial Democracy*, the journal of the Swedish Centre for Working Life, August 1980, (Vol. 1, No. 3) on 'Economic Democracy and collective ownership'.

A complete account of the Swedish experience is available in J. Pontusson (1984), *Public pension funds and the politics of capital formation in Sweden*. Stockholm: Swedish Centre for Working Life. Commentaries from other Anglo-Saxon observers are available: see B. Burkitt (1983), 'Post-Keynesian distribution theory and employee investment funds', *Economic Studies Quarterly*, Vol. 34, No. 2, pp. 124–132; and from the Right, see A. Fredborg (1984), 'Wage-earner funds: a statist experiment', *Economic Affairs*. Oct–Dec 1984; p. 45.

Experience across Europe has been reviewed in G. Karlsson (1983), *Trade unions and collective capital formation: a review of initiatives in Western European countries*. Brussels: European Trade Union Institute.

49 For the Swedish Renewal Funds, see R. Meidner (1987), 'Renewal Funds: a Swedish innovation', *Economic and Industrial Democracy*, Vol. 8, No. 2, pp. 237–242.

50 See Royal Norwegian Ministry of Foreign Affairs, *The press in Norway*, UDA 152/83, Oslo, 1983.

51 See James Curran and Jean Seaton, *Power without responsibility—the press and broadcasting in Britain*, 2nd edition, London, Methuen, 1985; p. 343.

52 In the UK, J. Curran and J. Seaton (1985) *op cit* propose a Media Enterprise Board which:

> would offer loan finance to under-financed groups with no prior ownership stake in the media, to bid for divested media companies. The Media Enterprise Board

should also provide financial support for under-resourced groups to start new media enterprises, providing always that these appear likely to succeed... It would be important to ensure that people from all the leading political parties are represented on the Board and that its activities are subject to proper parliamentary scrutiny. (p. 342–343)

Curran and Seaton suggest that the Board be financed from the Exchequer (i.e. out of consolidated revenue) but that its establishment could be accompanied by a levy of one per cent on all media advertising (yielding 35 million pounds annually).

For the Australian proposal, see J. Mathews and Dick Gross, 'Time for another media carve-up', *Australian Society*, June 1987, pp. 34–36. In this paper, an Australian Press Diversity Board is proposed, preferably established as a national body, to activate the ALP platform commitment to 'encourage diversity in the media'. This is now widely perceived as being a critical political issue, demanding some intervention. The proposed Board would be a tripartite body, funded by a tax on the media industry (either through a one per cent advertising expenditure levy, or a levy on newspaper turnover alone). It would use this revenue to:

- provide seeding capital to new ventures;
- provide subsidies under certain conditions to existing publications;
- establish public ventures, such as a distribution company.

For a comprehensive discussion, see J. Mathews (1988b), *The promotion of press diversity: options available to the Australian government.* Occasional Paper No. 4, Institute of Cultural Policy Studies, Brisbane, Griffith University.

53 This is one of the most significant applications of a general political principle, that it is strategically wiser to influence the flow of any category rather than the accumulated stock. I call this the 'Integration Principle' on the grounds that it is a strategy of transformation based on the point of change—just as integration is a mathematical process of forming a total value of a function from its differential. The term 'socialisation of the flow' has been used by S. Tsuru (1961), *Has capitalism changed?* Iwanami (cited in B. Burkitt, 1983).

54 R. Meidner (1978); p. 45.

55 The issue that such a course throws up for the unions is centralization of resources, and the power that comes from the control of these resources.

56 See Carnoy and Shearer, 1980. They note:

A number of the AFL–CIO building and construction trades unions have for many years used their pension funds to promote jobs for union members in residential and commercial construction. (p. 113)

The International Brotherhood of Electrical Workers puts forty to fifty per cent of its pension fund into government guaranteed home mortgages. To qualify for IBEW financing, homes must be built entirely with union labour.

Further examples of useful investment by pension funds were given in a series of reports produced by Governor Jerry Brown's *Public Investment Task Force* in California in 1981–82. See two key reports: the *Interim Report* of the Governor's Public Investment Task Force, California, March 1981 (chaired by John Harrington); and the follow-up first annual report of the Pension Investment Unit, *Targeting investment for economic development*, California, Dec. 1982. The Pension Investment Unit was rapidly disbanded after the election of the Deukmejian administration which defeated Brown in 1983.

57 W. Korpi (1978); p. 33. His proposal is in the same spirit as that for public as well as worker representatives on company Boards.

58 See A. Hamilton (1986), *The Financial Revolution: the big bang worldwide*. London: Penguin Books.

59 These developments have also created difficulties for those authors who have envisaged a step beyond capitalism as being the dissolution of the difference between debt and equity. For example, Mihailovic, in his *Democratic Socialism*, makes this point:

> Capitalism is transcended when wealth stops being capital, that is when it no longer generates profit and social power. This happens under two conditions:
> 1 when the return for an investment is no longer profit but a fixed interest...
> 2 when investment, into the means of production does not yield any management rights (in other words, when the stockholders, board of directors, or the corresponding supervising State agency, are replaced by a self-governing council democratically elected by all employees of the enterprise). (Mihailovic, 1960; pp. 68–69)

These neat formulations lose something of their appeal when capital itself ceases to make a fundamental distinction between debt and equity. In any case, the mechanism for converting equity to debt was never spelt out. The theoretical and practical relevance of collective funds is that they represent a quite explicit and concrete mechanism for transforming capitalism from within.

60 See B. Frankel (1983) *Beyond the State? Dominant Theories and Socialist Strategies*, p. 209.

61 See Esping-Andersen (1985), *Politics against markets: the Social Democratic Road to Power*. Princeton: Princeton University Press, for a systematic exposition of this notion. In brief, the argument is that the rise of capitalism was based on the creation of a market for labour, which

turned 'labour' into a commodity apparently like any other. This was 'commodification'. To the extent that working-class welfare can be provided for out of public revenues, rather than out of 'private' wage bargaining in the labour market, labour is 'decommodified'.

62 This conceptualization is fruitful, for it focuses attention on the arena in which the great battles have been fought this century by the SD/L movement, namely the public sector. However, it carries with it an unfortunate strategic implication, and that is that it views the welfare sector as 'separate from' and actually at war with the 'market sector', which is actually the rest of the economy. I argue below that this ghettoization of welfare will in the end pave the way to its destruction; on the contrary, it must be *integrated* with industry and labour market programmes if it is to survive. While it may seem that Marshall's perspective conforms with that of the Swedish SD party, which has long argued that workers' demands could not be met solely through negotiations with employers, but must involve a measure of public provision won through numerical control of the political domain, I would argue that the Scandinavian approach is actually one of integration of welfare with the requirements of restructuring, rather than a defence of 'social rights'.

63 For accounts of the 'crisis in the welfare state' see for example OECD, *The welfare state in crisis*, Paris, 1981; and Ramesh Mishra (1984) *The welfare state in crisis: social thought and social change.* Brighton: Wheatsheaf Books.

64 For a discussion of these strands, see G. Esping-Andersen and W. Korpi (1984), 'Social policy as class politics in post-war capitalism: Scandinavia, Austria and Germany'. In Goldthorpe, ed (1984).

65 See Francis Castles (1985), *The Working Class and Welfare: Reflections on the political development of the welfare state in Australia and New Zealand, 1890–1980.* Sydney: Allen & Unwin. Castles argues that the early strength and mobilization of the labour movement in Australia and New Zealand led it to adopt a strategy of social amelioration that was quite distinctive, and which he calls 'wage earner welfare'.

66 See David Plotke, 'The future of social policy: a response to the conservative critique of the welfare state'. Paper prepared for the Boag Conference on Democratic Socialism: Blueprint for the Future, October 1983, Vancouver.

67 For example, Belgium passed legislation in 1974 providing for the right to minimum means of subsistence; the UK enacted a scheme for Family Income Supplements in 1970; the Federal Republic of Germany

enacted the Social Assistance Scheme in 1961, and the Netherlands in 1963. More recently, Israel enacted an Income Guarantee system in 1980; Luxembourg established the right to a guaranteed minimum in 1986. For a discussion of these, and others, see C. Euzeby (1987), 'A minimum guaranteed income: experiments and proposals', *International Labour Review*, Vol. 126, No. 3, May–June 1987, pp. 253–276.

68 Claus Offe (1984), 'The future of the labour market', *Telos*, No. 60, pp. 81–96. Note that Offe does not actually employ the terminology GMI, but his argument clearly invokes it.

69 A. Gorz (1987), '(S)He who doesn't work shall eat all the same', *Dissent*, Spring 1987, pp. 179–187.

Earlier statements of Gorz's position were given in *Farewell to the Working Class* (1984, 1984) and in *Paths to Paradise* (1984, 1986). I discuss Gorz's ideas critically below.

70 On social credit, see C. H. Douglas (1922), *Credit power and democracy*; and C. H. Douglas, *Economic democracy: with the delusion of super-production.* Sudbury. Suffolk: Bloomfield Books, 5th edition, 1974; as well as C. M. Hattersley (1922), *The community's credit.* London: 'Credit Power' Press.

On the negative income tax, see M. Friedman (1962), *Capitalism and Freedom.* Chicago: University of Chicago Press.

71 R. Theobald (1963), *Freer Men and Free Markets.* London.

72 Keith Roberts (1983), *Automation, Unemployment and the Distribution of Income*, Second edition, Maastricht, European Centre for Work and Society.

73 For example, a number of American economists endorsed schemes for income maintenance in the 1960s, amongst them James Tobin, Robert Lampman, John Kenneth Galbraith and even Paul Samuelson. A presidential task force in 1966 endorsed the idea of a negative income tax on a limited basis, and led to the 1969 Heinemann Commission which delivered an influential report on income maintenance. However, these schemes have got no farther than some income-maintenance programmes tried in parts of New Jersey and Pennsylvania, which interestingly enough suggested that 'guaranteed income plans would not adversely affect work incentives'. (James Paterson (1981), *America's Struggle against poverty 1900–1980*, Boston, Harvard University Press; p. 189.)

74 R. Henderson (1975), *First Main Report of Commission of Inquiry into Poverty*, Canberra, Australian Government Publishing Service; Australian Council of Social Service, 1975, *GMI: Towards the Development of a policy*, Canberra.

The preferred Henderson option incorporated two levels of minimum income payments, with the higher one going to income units prevented from working (e.g. because of age or disability). With the fall of the Whitlam government, nothing came of this proposal although it has been adopted in principle in both ALP and ACTU policy. Since then there has developed a lively literature on GMI in Australia. The leading proponent today, Ian Manning, states in his recent *Incomes and Policy* (1985):

A guaranteed minimum income scheme can therefore be recommended as almost a pre-requisite for a workable policy of income. It has the virtue that it comes as near as any government device is likely to do to the reconciliation of the demands of justice in exchange and justice in distribution. It provides a floor of income for all—not merely for those eligible for pensions and benefits, so reducing the unfortunate incentive effects of making payments available only to people in particular circumstances—and at the same time straightens out the tax schedule so that all people including pensioners attract the same marginal tax rate. It therefore interferes less with the workings of exchange than the present tax and social security systems.

For further commentary in Australia, see Peter Saunders (1982), 'Henderson GMI scheme: a perspective from the 1980s', in R. Mendelsohn (ed) 1982, *Social welfare finance: selected papers*, Centre for Research on Federal financial relations, Australian National University; and Christopher Arup (1980), 'Structural problems for a GMI and a job guarantee scheme', *Federal Law Review*, Vol. 11, March 1980, pp. 19–39.

75 Ian Manning, for example, has departed from the original Henderson Commission proposals (on which he served as researcher) and has now advocated financing a scheme by a broad-based tax on expenditure. He states:

A value added tax has often been suggested in this context, but there are other indirect taxes which might work as well or better. The main difference between an indirect tax and income tax is that the deduction occurs at a different stage in business accounts—the former just after money has been received through sales, the latter just before it is put in the employee's pay packet. The difference is thus not as great as many think, and as a practical matter the choice between the two taxes turns on which imposes the smaller compliance costs on taxpayers, and is the least prone to evasion. The balance of opinion in the 1970s was in favour of indirect taxes, partly through exasperation with the income tax, and partly because such a tax could replace and consolidate a whole variety of taxes already collected through employers—PAYE income tax, company taxes, and some sales taxes. This would relieve most citizens of the burden of making out income tax returns. However, more recently the Federal government has shown itself willing to legislate against income tax avoidance (including the introduction of indexed retrospective payments in the more blatant cases) and the High Court has allowed the Tax Commissioner to win a few cases, so there is less pessimism about the ability to make income tax stick. Again, experience in the United Kingdom with the difficulties of a value added tax has shown that a great deal of care has to be put into the detailed design of any major revenue source. On grounds of familiarity, a guaranteed income scheme in Australia would probably be best financed by a linear income tax at least at first, but indirect tax might be substituted later. (1985)

Although this approach seems sound in principle, there is not much point in discussing it further until it has been exhaustively tested, validated and 'tuned' on econometric models of national economies by professional researchers.

76 Chantal Euzeby (1987) concludes her excellent survey of such GMI schemes with the observation:

In short, the principal danger of the liberal proposals lies in their excessive radicalism: abolition of social welfare services; replacement of an essentially horizontal form of redistribution, based on public and social transfers that take account of individual and family needs, by a form of distribution based solely on income differences and operated vertically through taxation; impossibility, in the case of the negative income tax, of making a satisfactory choice of level of benefit and exclusion threshold, the amount being either too small for effectively combatting poverty, or too large and hence apt to discourage work, saving and investment; excessive dualism between poor and non-poor . . . resulting from a too exclusively monetary approach to the fight against poverty. (1987; p. 267–268)

For Euzeby, the solution lies in making a less radical overhaul of the social security system, through a 'partial universal allowance' that leaves intact various existing supplementary and assistance schemes, combined with various funds to bring beneficiaries up to a designated social 'norm'.

Similar concern has been expressed by such theorists as the Canadian John Myles, in 'Decline or impasse? The current state of the welfare state', *Studies in Political Economy*, 26, Summer 1988, pp 73–107; and the French post-Fordist theorist Alain Lipietz, in his 'Alternative design for the twenty first century' (1988) and its longer French version, *Choisir l'Audace*, Paris, Editions La Decouverte, 1989. Myles makes the point that conservative proposals for a GMI (which he terms a GAI—Guaranteed Annual Income) would have the effect of encouraging the expansion of low-wage, low-skill service industries. These would crowd out high-wage high-skill service industries, unless these were provided by the welfare state acting as prime public sector employer. Lipietz for his part makes the point that any GMI scheme needs to be accompanied by a sharing in the gains of productivity through an increase in free time.

77 Asprey, 1975. *Full Report of Taxation Review Committee*, Canberra, Australian Government Publishing Service.

78 Gorz argues that a tax on automated production would have a

double role: it will prevent prices of automatically produced goods falling too low relative to goods and services produced by human labour, thereby replacing market prices by a system of *political* pricing. (This is akin to the system of fixing 'import parity pricing' on domestic oil production in several countries, or price-fixing in agricultural commodities, or taxing unhealthy products like alcohol and cigarettes. It is therefore hardly novel.)

Gorz argues that the disappearance of market laws of pricing, just like the disappearance of the law of value determining wage levels, is an inevitable consequence of automation. This may or may not be the case. (I personally think he overstates his argument.) But it is, nonetheless, a completely unworkable means of financing a GMI. It is hard enough to set a political price and tax level for something as simple as oil coming out of the ground—but for microchips, let alone the myriad of products they are going into, the problem would be insoluble. Gorz has committed the fallacy of seeing the advent of automation as *itself* breaking the work-wage nexus, and a system of GMI coming along in its wake. On the contrary, a GMI system must be *chosen* as a radical political act, by an advanced industrial society which already enjoys high incomes. The increased productivity offered by automation would be a favourable factor in reducing the overall quantum of work needed to be performed by a society to produce a certain quantity of goods. But the most productive sectors do not need to be taxed to peg them back to the economic level of labour-input goods and services; indeed this would have the economic effect of drastically slowing down the process of automation, and thereby allow the country to lose its competitiveness, and sink to a lower level—thus making it *more* difficult to finance a GMI. Gorz completely defeats his aim by his muddled financing proposals.

79 See Lipietz (1988, 1989) op. cit.

80 Technological determinism, in the words of MacKenzie and Wajcman, is 'the theory that technology is indeed an independent factor, and that changes in technology *cause* social changes. In its strongest version, the theory claims that autonomous changes in technology underlie all other changes in society'. (1984) Technological determinism holds that technical change is in some sense *autonomous*, proceeding according to its own technical logic of efficiency, and that although technical changes have an *impact* on society, there is no reverse impact of society, or social choice, on technology. On 'autonomous technology', see L. Winner (1977).

81 Recent detailed work has revealed how this process has worked in certain instances of productive technology. Tine Bruland, for example, has shown how industrial conflict served as a source of technical inno-

vation in the British textile industry in the nineteenth century—in particular, in the development of the automatic spinning mule, and calico printing machinery. (Bruland, 1984)

In the twentieth century, the development of numerically-controlled (NC) machine tools—the tools that produce all other tools—has been shown by David Noble to be a process dominated by social, rather than technical choices. (Noble, 1984) In this case, the early development of a 'record-playback', approach using magnetic tape—an approach built around workers' skills—was abandoned in favour of an alternative approach, based on programming, that by-passed workers' skills altogether. Noble was able to show that the NC approach, far from being more 'efficient' or 'economical', was in fact extremely costly and ridden with difficulties; it could survive only under the protective umbrella of the military budget. The option of NC was persevered with for purely political and ideological reasons.

More recent case studies are provided in W. Bijke (1987). These studies reveal how technology has evolved, not according to some inner technical logic or 'technological imperative', but through a series of social choices made for social ends.

82 Langdon Winner, 1977. *Autonomous Technology: Technics-out-of-control as a theme in political thought*. Boston, MIT Press; and Langdon Winner, 1986. *The Whale and the Reactor: a search for limits in an age of high technology*. Chicago, University of Chicago Press.

83 Winner's theme, of waking us from 'technological somnambulism' is similar to that of Jones' *Sleepers Wake*! (1982) in that both insist on our capacity to choose. In this sense, they would both be called 'technological liberals'. We explain in the text how the paradigm of AD goes beyond this position, in formulating a strategy of *collective* intervention in the process of technological change through associations of workers and citizens.

84 For an intelligent exploration of this theme, see the fundamental text by S. Toulmin (1972), *Human Understanding*. Toulmin refers to both technologies and legal systems as instances of *rational enterprises*, of which the paradigm is the body of intellectual disciplines we call 'science'.

85 Other examples include accounting systems with their different assumptions and conventions; markets and systems of exchange; or patenting systems and other means of identifying intellectual property.

86 A capacity to democratize technology draws for its theoretical justification on the now extensive literature characterizing technology as a social construct. See for example the case studies on: electric power

systems, synthetic dyestuffs, plastics, missiles, medical imaging technologies, electric vehicles and Portuguese vessel design in the fifteenth and sixteenth centuries, all in W. Bijker, T. Hughes and T. Pinch, eds (1987), *The Social Construction of Technological Systems: New directions in the sociology and history of technology*. Cambridge, MA: The MIT Press.

87 For an extended discussion of this issue see my recent text, *Tools of Change: new technology and the democratization of work* (Mathews, 1989) and the earlier texts, Mathews (1985a) (1985b).

For a Scandinavian perspective that draws on numerous case histories, see contributions to the recent text edited by G. Bjerkness, P. Ehn and M. Kyng (1987).

88 The introduction over the past two decades of electronic and computerized methods for text-entry, typesetting, layout and printing, has changed the whole newspaper industry. The work process has been revolutionized. Metal type is disappearing, giving way to digital storage of typefaces and their setting and manipulation through keyboards and screens using very sophisticated computer software and optical technologies.

In the face of these changes, the Scandinavian print unions, under the guidance of the Swedish Centre for Working Life (CWL) have developed a sophisticated counter-strategy aimed at placing workers' skills at the very heart of the new technology. Workers and technical specialists combined in a project called UTOPIA, a Swedish acronym for 'training, technology and products from a quality of work perspective', to develop a wholly new set of criteria to guide the design of page composition equipment—and they have followed through to ensure that these criteria are embodied in a product that has been brought successfully to the market.

The UTOPIA project was essentially a test bed for trying out different work organizations and designs for electronic page composition systems, bringing technical researchers together with workers on the job in a stimulating environment of interaction. It started as a simple mock-up workstation at the CWL, and graduated to a computerized workstation. The key criterion identified by the print workers as being desirable in the new technology was *full-page display* but this came up against immediate technical constraints. Even large screens were too small to show a full page in sufficient detail to allow composition work to be performed. The technical compromise developed was an 'electronic lens' capable of taking a part of the page and blowing it up on half the screen, the other half being reserved for full-page display with highly reduced text. (A similar approach has been adopted more recently in 'desktop publishing' in the 'pagemaker' program developed for the Apple Macintosh personal computer, for use with the 'Laserwriter'.)

These criteria came to life in the new system developed by Liber, the

Swedish state-owned printing house, based on technology generated at Sweden's University of Linköping. Liber offered UTOPIA a role in this project, and an agreement was signed ensuring that the new system would meet printworkers' specifications and criteria. Liber unveiled its Text and Image Processing System product in spring 1984, and has tested it successfully *in situ* at Sweden's daily newspaper *Aftonbladet* and on the Danish *Information*.

The UTOPIA project ran from 1981 to early 1985, involving an average of fifteen people, and public funding of $400 000 mostly from the Centre for Working Life, but also from other institutions and the print unions themselves. The key feature was the interface with Liber, with its $10 million development of a new Text and Imaging Processing System (TIPS). This shows the level of resources required to support a successful intervention in the process of technological change. The Liber/TIPS product is now being actively marketed in Scandinavia and the US, and is proving to be very successful.

See Robert Howard, 1985, UTOPIA: Where workers craft new technology, *Technology Review*, April 1985, pp. 43–49; see also the account of the UTOPIA project in its own publication, edited by project leader, Pelle Ehn, *Graffiti*, No. 7, 1985.

89 Interestingly, there is now a theoretical school that employs Kuhn's notion of *scientific paradigm* and applies it to technological constructs. *See* for example, Norman Clark (1987) 'Similarities and differences between scientific and technological paradigms', *Futures*, February 1987, pp. 26–42; and Rachel Laudan, ed. (1984), *The nature of technological knowledge: are models of scientific change relevant*? Boston, D. Reidel. I take these discussions to constitute support for my unorthodox tactic of extending Kuhn's term to apply to a framework of self-consistent political ideas and strategy. For further discussion of competing paradigms, see Badham and Mathews (1989).

90 The literature on these issues is growing rapidly. There is the work on new production systems, such as by Piore and Sabel (1984), Kern and Schumann (1984) and others, reviewed in Mathews (1988c) 'New production concepts'. There is the work of the French Regulation School, reviewed above, who categorize the Fordist system as an integrated model of a technical base, a regime of accumulation, and a mode of regulation. See Boyer (1988) or Lipietz (1988) for expositions. And there is the work on changes in 'technoeconomic paradigm' associated with the studies by Perez (1985) and Perez and Freeman. Mention should also be made of the 'Social Construction of Technology' school, which employs concepts from microsociology: see for example Bijker *et al.* (1987). For a critique that reimposes the macrolevel into the analysis, see S. Russell (1986), 'The social construction of artefacts: a response to Pinch and Bijker', *Social Studies of Science*, Vol. 16, pp. 331–346; and S.

Russell and R. Williams (1987), 'Opening the black box and closing it behind you: on microsociology in the social analysis of technology', Paper presented to the British Sociological Association Conference, *Science, Technology and Society*, Leeds, April 1987.

91 Stephen Hill, in his *Tragedy of Technology* (1989) develops a similar theme. He describes technology as providing a 'culture' for industrial societies, and beyond that, a 'grammar' or 'discourse' through which we are constrained to express ourselves in such societies. While this is a useful perspective, I cannot see that Hill's ideas give sufficient grounding for the program of democratization of technology advocated in this present text.

92 On 'market socialism', and associated terms, see A. Nove, 1983: *The politics of feasible socialism*, which is now the major statement on the concept; Selucky (1979); and W. Brus and H. Ticktin (1981), 'Is market socialism possible or necessary?' *Critique*, No. 14, 1981, p. 22.

See the debate between Alec Nove and Boris Frankel in *Radical Philosophy*, No. 39, 1985, pp. 24–35; and finally see Miller and Estrin, 1986.

93 For a general philosophical introduction to economic democracy, see Hodgson (1984); Green (1985); and Dahl (1985). An interesting perspective is provided by Allen Graubard (1984), 'Ideas of Economic Democracy: Workers' control and public rights', *Dissent*, Fall 1984; pp. 415–423. On the Swedish experience, see Sandra Albrecht and Steven Deutsch (1983), 'The challenge of economic democracy: the case of Sweden', *Economic Democracy*, Vol. 4, No. 3, August 1983, pp. 287–320.

94 Selucky, 1979; pp. 179–180.

95 Nove, 1983; p. 200.

96 The Yugoslav experience is highly relevant here, for it is the only society that has practised workers' self-management for some time. The positive aspect of that experience is that workers do not, when confronted by economic reality, vote themselves wage increases which will simply put their firm out of business. Any claim by conservatives that economic democracy is impossible on these grounds is thereby refuted. But Nove points to two negative aspects of the Yugoslav experience. One is the apparent lack of incentive that worker-controlled firms may have to take on new workers, at a time of unemployment, for fear of reducing their incomes. The other is the lack of long-term interest of workers in 'their' enterprise, since it is not in fact 'theirs'; they have no explicit shares in it.

Nove suggests dealing with the first problem by having a centrally negotiated set of wage rates which do *not* vary with the profitability of the firm, i.e. the system already operating in Sweden, where it is called a 'solidarity wage policy', or in Australia, where it is called comparative wage justice. Supplementary bonuses derived from 'profits' i.e. (value added) could then be added on to these wage levels, becoming in effect a profit sharing scheme. There is nothing wrong with this scheme in principle, although doubtless more financially complex schemes, like Employee Share Ownership Plans, could be dreamed up. The point is there would be no objection to individually-oriented bonuses *once a firm is democratized* (for example, through changes in Board structure and co-determination, and through collective ownership of the equity).

Nove suggests dealing with the second issue, by offering workers some kind of 'length of service bonus, linked with the long-term level of profits or the value of basic assets', to be paid to a worker who retires or transfers elsewhere. To my mind, this is a 'share' in all but name, and therefore ought to be called such. As I argue below, socialized capital is perfectly compatible with both individual and collective shareholdings, provided the rights of shareholders are carefully spelt out in company law as complementing but not over-riding the rights of workers.

For the definitive account of the Yugoslav economic system, see works by Branko Horvat, who is Professor of Economics at the Institute of Economic Sciences in Belgrade. See for example, B. Horvat (1982) *The Political Economy of Socialism: a Marxist social theory*. New York: M. E. Sharpe.

97 These two modes of planning can be formalized mathematically as optimization procedures in the primal space (target outputs) or dual space (shadow prices), which any student of linear programming will be familiar with.

I did my own thesis work on this issue, looking at abstract mathematical models of mixed centralized-decentralized planning schemes, to investigate what sort of information the peripheral nodes needed to be supplied with in order to develop system operations and trajectories that were optimal or nearly optimal with respect to certain specific criteria. See Mathews (1980b).

98 Miller and Estrin, 1986; p. 4.

However, Miller and Estrin go on to make the interesting observation that markets in products (and services) are *fundamentally different from markets in capital and labour*. Control over capital (i.e. investment) and over labour (wages and labour policy) cannot be left, in their terms, to 'the market'. Both 'products'—capital and labour—are 'special', and their allocation would fall into the hands of a small elite if performed by markets alone. This view tallies with my own proposals for investment decisions being taken by tripartite Boards of collective funds, while the labour market is regulated by centralized wage fixation and national agreements on conditions of work.

99 For example, Frankel in his critique of Nove argues that feminist values are blocked by markets:

> If enterprises were not threatened by bankruptcy or a drop in profits, a society committed to gender equality could pursue this objective in a manner which was free of the conflicting interests of market viability as opposed to central directives ... (Frankel, 1987; and the *Radical Philosophy* debate, Note 1. *op. cit.* Note 95)

Frankel's assumption seems to be that markets *essentially* make it impossible to express eco-feminist values in a democratic economy—a variant of the 'capitalist essentialism' line of argument criticized in chapter 2.

100 For a discussion of the democratization of econometric models, using them as an instrument to enhance public access to economic policy formation, see my pamphlet *Cybernetics and Economic Democracy*, Mathews (1982).

101 There is by now a well-developed theory of planning that these processes could draw on. This theory is in part derived from the cyberneticians in the Soviet Union, and in part from operation researchers in the West. Planning is now theorized as a decision algorithm utilizing information collected at different levels of aggregation, and involving different mixes between central and decentralized decision points.

The hardware explosion in microelectronics and telecommunications makes these algorithms very easy to implement in practice.

A particular application of these new procedures, utilizing Bayesian decision theory as its foundation, and formulated in an explicitly socialist context during the period of the Allende government in Chile, is discussed in my pamphlet, *Cybernetics and Economic Democracy*, Mathews (1982); and the account by the director of the project, Stafford Beer, in Beer (1974).

102 See Howard Wachtel (1986), *The Money Mandarins: The making of a new supranational economic order*. New York: Pantheon Books.

103 See Mathews (1976).

Chapter 4 The politics of associative democracy

1 Alex Carey (1986). In *7 Days*, Pilot issue, 20 June 1986, Melbourne.

2 Ibid. Alex Carey died tragically in 1989, having made fundamental contributions to social thought in Australia.

3 See Tom Baistow, *Fourth-Rate Estate: an anatomy of Fleet Street* (1985).

London, Comedia Publishing Group; and for the Australian case, David Bowman (1988), *The Captive Press*. Melbourne: Penguin Books.

4 Baistow, op cit, p. 96.

5 James Curran and Jean Seaton, *Power without responsibility — the press and broadcasting in Britain*, 2nd edition. London: Methuen, 1985; p. 343.

6 See J. Mathews (1988d), 'The promotion of press diversity: options available to the Australian government', Institute of Cultural Policy Studies, Griffith University.

7 I. Gilmour, 1977, *Inside Right*. London, Hutchinson; p. 211.

8 See D. M. Nuti (1985–86); pp. 377–378. Nuti defines these entities as 'legally binding unilateral commitments, on the part of the government, to adopt at a future given date or dates, a given parameter or parameters for that instrument (or package of instruments), *conditional on* a given state of the economy (say, a given level of employment, or the growth rate of income); such commitments would be irrevocable within a specified period of time, with a guarantee that they would not be nullified by subsequent off-setting measures within the time specified'. (Nuti in fact calls the entities *future contingent instruments* (FCIs). This is such an unattractive term that it almost kills the idea at the outset. I prefer the simpler and more transparent term *conditional commitments*.) As examples, Nuti cites the following:

> Let us suppose, for instance, that the government wishes to raise investment and employment, while workers would be willing to sacrifice wages but are distrustful of the uses to which their forsaken wages will be put by their employers. The government can guarantee this kind of pact by effectively indexing, through tax concessions, the lower level of wages to the rate of unemployment, simultaneously announcing that in a given number of months (equal to the expected average lag between investment outlay and employment) a capital tax will be levied also geared to the future unemployment rate unless this is on a pre-announced target consistent with the reinvestment of the wage cuts.
> Alternatively, the government could announce that next year in the event of unemployment reaching a critical level it would immediately step in with a given large-scale public works programme; this might by itself restore investors' confidence and lead to an improvement that might make that intervention unnecessary ... (p. 378)

9 See Frankel (1983), p. 11, for an exposition of this critique. For a longer version of the argument, see Boris Frankel (1982), 'Identifying dominant misconceptions of States', *Thesis Eleven*, No. 4, 1982, pp. 97–123.

10 See Marcuse, 1968; and the series by Michel Foucault: *Madness and*

Civilization — a history of insanity in the age of reason; The Birth of the Clinic — an archeology of medical perception; and *Discipline and Punish — the birth of the prison.*

11 On ISAs, see Althusser, 1968; Poulantzas, 1968. For a perceptive critique, much more effective than E.P. Thompson's blustering in *The Poverty of Theory*, see R.W. Connell, 'Complexities of Fury...a critique of the Althusserian approach to class', and 'The black box of habit on the wings of history: reflections on the theory of social reproduction', in Connell (1983), *Which Way is up?: Essays on Class, Sex and Culture*. Sydney: George Allen & Unwin.

12 See Hirst, 1988 for an account of the constitutional features of a pluralist socialism that has many features in common with the AD paradigm.

13 See Stretton (1987).

14 K. Wiltshire (1987), *Privatization, the British experience — an Australian perspective*. Melbourne: Longman Cheshire, in conjunction with the Committee for Economic Development of Australia; p. (viii).

15 See Christopher Jay, 'UK's share deals set a world model', *Australian Financial Review*, November 17, 1987; p. 10.

16 These proposals, contained in what became known as the 'Ridley report', were leaked to *The Economist* and published extensively in the edition May 27, 1978.

17 For general commentaries on privatization by its advocates, see M. Beeslay and S. Littlechild (1983), 'Privatization: principles, problems and priorities', *Lloyds Bank Review*, 149, pp. 1–20; S. Domberger and J. Piggott (1986), 'Privatization policies and public enterprise: a survey', *Economic Record*, 177 pp. 145–162; S. Littlechild (1981), 'Ten steps to denationalization', *Journal of Economic Affairs*, 2, pp. 11–19; C. Mayer and S. Meadowcroft (1985), 'Selling public assets: techniques and financial implications', *Fiscal Studies*, 6, pp. 42–56; C. Trengrove (1986), 'Privatization—a relevant word for Australia?', Centre of Policy Studies Discussion Paper D108, Monash University; and K. Wiltshire (1987), op. cit.

For critiques from the labour movement, see D. Heald (1983), *Public Expenditure: its defence and reform*. Oxford: Martin Robertson; Ruth Levitas, ed (1986), *The ideology of the New Right*. Cambridge: Polity Press; and D. Green (1987), *The New Right: the counterrevolution in political, economic and social thought*. Brighton: Wheatsheaf Books.

18 Details are taken from the series on privatization published in *Australian Financial Review*, Aug 31, Sept 1, 2, 1987.

19 The Australian historian, Hugh Stretton, has some sensible remarks to make in this context. Taking the case of South Australia, he offers three examples—one of good privatization, one of indifferent privatization, and one of bad privatization. His approach is interesting, and worth examining:

Back in the days when the public housing agency was building whole new towns and neighbourhoods in the outer suburbs [of Adelaide], it used to build their neighbourhood shopping centres and let the shops at low rents, to provide shops and services for the early residents before their numbers could attract private shop developers. Despite its low profitability, that was good public investment. Now that the neighbourhoods are full, the public landlord is selling the shops, mostly to co-operatives of the shopkeepers. That releases public capital for more urgent uses. If the original investment had been left to the market the residents would have suffered through the early years, and the shopkeepers would never have had the chance to become owners. The original public investment was sensible, and now the privatization is sensible.

One of the town centres—now a big centre of 60 000 people—was a public investment for the same reasons. Selling it now is more controversial. The town shops need extensive modernizing, thirty years after they were first designed. The public landlord could modernize them—but only by using the public loan money on which the federal government puts strict limits. There are more urgent needs for the capital, so the centre and its modernization have been long-leased to private developers. They choose the 'lock-up' method of modernization, turning a public town centre into a private shopping centre locked up at night and weekends: out of shopping hours, the citizens lost their town altogether. A number of their evening and weekend recreations have simply been stopped, their premises demolished. If the public landlord had raised the same capital from the same sources, and used it to modernize the centre more sociably, that would have made no economic difference: no difference to the national totals of saving, investment, employment or productivity. The federal government's Loan Council policies which force such things out of public into private ownership are simply irrational, except as favours to private wealth. But while those rules apply, the selling and locking up of Elizabeth town centre can be defended as freeing public capital for more urgent uses. An indifferent privatization.

We sold most of our land bank. For fifty years public enterprises, mostly unsubsidized, operating efficiently at cost in the public interest, supplied Adelaide with so much cheap land and housing that all Adelaide land, private as well as public, stayed comparatively cheap. Land prices and house rents were usually about two-thirds of their Perth and Brisbane levels, to the great advantage of industrial investors in Adelaide, and with economy and equity for the mass of Adelaide homebuyers and public and private tenants. But by four steps over the last twenty years federal and state Liberal and Labor governments have stopped or sold out the public land suppliers. The last step—begun by a Liberal government and completed by a Labor government—privatized a large part of the metropolitan land bank on terms which gave a super-profitable super-monopoly to a single private developer. The minor scandal is that the ANZ Bank, owner of the private developer, is virtually guaranteed a $75 million return for about $3 million investment. The major scandal is the wider effect on land and housing prices: in the five years it took to negotiate that final deal and put it into effect, Adelaide prices have raced past Brisbane and Perth to Melbourne and Sydney levels. So I am sorry to say that what used to be the home state of humane and imaginative land and housing policies has disgraced itself, and betrayed a mass of its poorer citizens, by a bit of pure Thatcher-style privatization.

(*Australian Society*, November 1986)

20 See Michel Crozier (1987) *État modeste, État moderne*. Paris: Editions Fayard. The 'modest state' is one that abandons many of its controlling and regulatory functions in favour of 'self regulation' by citizens, producers and consumers.

21 On the Dutch experience, see Kim Dovey, 'Un-common housing', paper delivered to Melbourne University seminar, 17 November 1988.

22 On the Swedish community service delivery arrangements, see Heclo and Madsden (1987) *Policy and Politics in Sweden*; and David Held (1987) *Models of Democracy*, p. 288.

23 See Streeck and Schmitter (1985).

24 See A. G. Frank and M. Fuentes (1987), 'Nine theses on social movements', *Thesis Eleven*, No. 18/19, pp. 143–165. For a recent and valuable critical review, see Carl Boggs (1986).

25 On socialist feminism, see for example Zillah Eisenstein, *Capitalist Patriarchy and Socialist Feminism*. Lydia Sargent (ed), *Women and Revolution*. Boston, South End Press; and on theory of sexual politics in general, R.W. Connell (1983), *Which Way is Up?*

26 On eco-socialism, see such recent texts as Weston (ed), (1986), *Red and Green: the new politics of the environment*, and the influential *Programme* of the German Greens, 1981. On the global Green movement, see Charlene Spretnak and Fritjof Capra (1984), *Green Politics: the global promise*. London, Paladin/Grafton Books. Many of the Red-Green (or eco-socialist) debates arose around the issue of nuclear power in the 1970s; see for example, Mathews (1980a).

27 Frankel (1987).

28 Albert and Hahnel (1981).

29 See Tony Lane (1982), 'The Unions: caught on the ebb tide', *Marxism Today*, September 1982, pp. 6–12.

30 John Hoerr (1985), 'Beyond Unions: a revolution in employee rights is in the making', *Business Week*, July 8, 1985, pp. 72–77.

31 This phrase is used by Charles Remus (1986), 'The future of industrial relations in the United States', *Labour and Society*, Vol. 11, No. 2, May 1986, pp. 149–158

32 D. Quinn Mills (1983), 'Reforming the US system of collective bargaining', *Monthly Labour Review*, March 1983, pp. 18–22.
As Mills puts it:

> An organization which depends upon adherence to a myriad of rules will always be vulnerable to competition from other organizations which operate in a more consensual and co-operative fashion, even when the latter have fewer resources...over time, rules tend to become increasingly costly and constraining as technology, materials, products, and other aspects of production change. Even rules which made great sense at first become out-of-date under changing conditions. But the rules are difficult to change, and particular employees may be further benefited the more outdated the rules become... The existence of the rulebook encourages both management and labour to assert their rights under the contract, rather than to attempt to work out problems... It fosters conflict and controversy.

All this is evident enough—but there are real costs for the unions themselves in allowing the situation to get out of hand. Mills goes on to say:

> In some instances, unions have created thickets of rules in which to immobilize management, just as spiders build webs to ensnare prey. But when the thickets of rules have crippled productivity, the unions have discovered themselves to be caught alongside management in the trap.

33 This is what the abstentionists do not or will not, understand. They think, for example, that if workers are to get involved in protecting their own health and safety, through electing a workplace delegate, that this will individualize an issue which they might otherwise be able to use to generate a strike. But it does *not* 'individualize' the issue: on the contrary, provided the union is involved at every step, it collectivizes the issue in the sense that members can now raise their grievances not individually, but through their health and safety delegate—and reserve their right to take collective action if there is no response. Collective militancy is the constant underlying thread to such an initiative—but the abstentionist cannot, or will not, see it. The real difference, and this is the crux of the matter, concerns the *source* of the militancy. For in the case of wage militancy, the role of the rank and file is to *support* their leaders' demands, and it is these leaders who become the heroes of a successful struggle. But in the case of health and safety militancy, the source is the members themselves, who understand their working conditions and their hazards better than their leaders, who have probably never been inside their workplace. Hence in any struggle there are unlikely to be heroes, unless it is a campaign that grows around an issue that is generalized across many plants, or firms, or industries.

34 Edmond Maire (1986), 'Some signposts for the future of trade unions', *Labour and Society*, Vol. 11, No. 2, May 1986, pp. 159–166.

35 On these issues, see my two previous books, Mathews (1989) and (1985).

36 Interesting experiments in boosting the intellectual capacity of unions through secondments have been tried in Australia (linking unions with the public service) and in Quebec, where unions have been able to undertake research with seconded academic staff. For a description of the Quebec scheme, see Carla Mummé (1988), 'A trade union based secondment scheme for academic researchers: the Quebec experience'. Sydney: Evatt Research Centre.

37 This was the principal error of the doctrine of 'guild socialism', as developed by G.D.H. Cole and others in the 1920s in Britain. Cole, in my view, made the fundamental mistake of seeing unions as evolving into administrative organs.

38 A. Gramsci (1977). The experience of translating Gramsci in the mid-1970s had a formative effect on my own thinking.

39 On this point I have been misunderstood by Jeffrey Minson (1988) in his otherwise excellent commentary on my pamphlet, *A Culture of Power* (1988a). Minson claims that I expect all the social movements to buckle under to the discipline imposed by the labour movement, within a single all-embracing 'Accord' that focuses on economic issues only. Nothing could be further from my intention. I envisage a multitude of such 'accords'. In the context of Australia I have suggested that this process needs to *start* by increasing the scope of the present ALP–ACTU Accord, by bringing in other parties such as the conservation movement.

40 The cultural expression of the mass production system was *modernism*. It is the break-up of the roots of mass culture that has generated a variety of expressions of *post-modernism*. See Frederick Jameson, 'The cultural logic of capital', *New Left Review*, No. 146, Sep–Oct 1984; Marshall Berman (1982) *All that is solid melts into air: The experience of modernity*. New York: Simon and Schuster; and Jean-Francois Lyotard, *The postmodern condition: a report on knowledge*. University of Minnesota Press, 1984.

41 On this issue, see for example Dennis Altman (1988) *A Politics of Poetry: Reconstituting Social Democracy*. Sydney: Pluto Press Australia.

Chapter 5 Knowledge, action and power

1 A. Przeworski (1985), *Capitalism and Social Democracy*. New York: Cambridge University Press; pp. 43–44. I wish to make it quite clear that this is a theoretical contestation of Przeworski's publicly stated dismissal of the prospects of SD/L parties, or what he calls 'electoral socialism'. It is not a personal attack on Przeworski; indeed, I have never met him. Privately, I have no doubt that he shares many of the aspirations elaborated in this text, such as a GMI. See his debate with Burawoy, 'Class, production and politics: a reply to Burawoy', *Socialist Review*, 89/2, 1989.

2 B. Latour (1986), 'The powers of association'. In J. Law, ed (1986), *A New Sociology of Knowledge*. London: Routledge and Kegan Paul.

3 See for example: Latour (1987); and 'The powers of association', in Law (1986); Callon, 'Some elements of a sociology of translation', in Law (1986); Law, 'Technology and heterogeneous engineering: The case of Portuguese expansion', in Bijker et al (1987); as well as Kuhn (1970); Lakatos (1976); and Feyerband (1975; 1978).

4 See C.H. Waddington (1977), *Tools of Thought*, London: Jonathan Cape.

5 For an enlightening essay on this topic, namely the fallacy of objectivity, see Randall Albury (1983), *The Politics of Objectivity*, Deakin University Press, Victoria. Albury discusses how this notion of objectivity becomes entrenched in popular attitudes and thereby obscures any understanding of the real power and methods of science.

6 I am indebted to Peter Beilharz for this term as characterizing my position (private communication).

7 For a fuller account of the politics of econometrics and the use of econometric models in the democratization of the budget process, see J. Mathews, *Cybernetics and Economic Democracy*, 1982.

8 A. Przeworski (1985); pp. 44–45.

BIBLIOGRAPHY

M. Aglietta (1979). *A Theory of capitalist regulation: the US experience.* London: NLB (Verso edition, 1987) (translated from the French edition, *Regulation et crises du capitalisme*, Calmann-Levy, 1976).

Michael Albert and Robin Hahnel (1981). *Socialism Today and Tomorrow.* Boston: South End Press.

Louis Althusser and Etienne Balibar (1968). *Reading Capital*, (translated by Ben Brewster from *Lire le Capital*, 1968). London: NLB, 1970.

D. Altman (1988) *A politics of poetry: Reconstituting social democracy.* Australia: Strategies for Renewal series, 2. Sydney: Pluto Press Australia.

P. Anderson (1983). *In the tracks of historical materialism.* London: Verso.

Aristotle. *The Politics.* London, Penguin Books, 1962.

R. Badham (1986) *Theories of Industrial Society.* London: Croom Helm.

R. Badham and J. Mathews (1989) 'The "new production systems" debate: conceptual reformulation of competing paradigms and strategies', *Labour and Industry.*

Rudolf Bahro (1982). *Socialism and Survival (articles, essays and talks 1979–1982).* London: Heretic Books.

Rudolf Bahro (1984). *From Red to Green: interviews with New Left Review.* London: NLB.

Stafford Beer (1974). *Designing Freedom.* London: John Wiley.

Stafford Beer (1981). *Brain of the Firm.* London: John Wiley.

P. Beilharz (1987). *Trotsky, Trotskyism and the Transition to Socialism.* Beckenham (UK): Croom Helm.

Daniel Bell (1960). *The End of Ideology.* Glencoe: The Free Press.

Daniel Bell (1976). *The Cultural contradictions of Capitalism.* New York: Basic Books.

Tony Benn (1982). *Arguments for Socialism.* London: Jonathan Cape.

E. Bernstein (1961). *Evolutionary Socialism.* New York: Schocken.

W.E. Bijker, T. Hughes and T.J. Pinch (eds) (1987). *The Social Construction of Technological Systems: New directions in the sociology and history of technology.* Cambridge, MA: MIT Press.

G. Bjerknes, P. Ehn and M Kyng (eds) (1987). *Computers and Democracy: The Scandinavian Challenge.* Aldershot: Avebury.

C. Boggs (1986). *Social Movements and Political Power.* Philadelphia: Temple University Press

Samuel Bowles, David Gordon and Thomas Weisskopf (1984). *Beyond the Wasteland: a democratic alternative to economic decline.* New York: Anchor Books. Revised British edition, London: Verso, 1986.

S. Bowles and H. Gintis (1986) *Democracy and Capitalism: Property, community, and the contradictions of modern social thought.* London, Routledge & Kegan Paul.

R. Boyer (1988) 'Is a new socio-technical system emerging?' in Proceedings of Conference *Structural change and labour market policy,* June 1988, Swedish Centre for Working Life.

Bullock (1977). *Report of the committee of Inquiry on Industrial Democracy,* chairman Lord Bullock. London, Her Majesty's Stationery Office.

B. Burkitt (1983). Post-Keynesian distribution theory. *Economic Studies Quarterly,* Vol. 34, No. 2, August 1983; pp. 124–132.

Marton Carnoy and Derek Shearer (1980). *Economic Democracy: the Challenge of the 1980s.* New York: M.E. Sharpe.

Martin Carnoy, Derek Shearer and Russell Rumberger (1983). *A New Social Contract: the economy and government after Reagan.* New York: Harper and Row.

F. Castles (1985). *The Working Class and Welfare: Reflections on the political development of the welfare state in Australia and New Zealand, 1890–1980.* Sydney: Allen and Unwin.

M. Charlesworth (1982). *Science, Non-Science and Pseudo-Science.* Geelong: Deakin University Press.

J. Chubb (1983). *Interest groups and the bureaucracy: the politics of energy.* Stanford University Press.

R.W. Connell (1983). *Which Way is Up? Essays on class, sex and culture.* Sydney: George Allen and Unwin.

C.A.R. Crosland (1956). *The Future of Socialism.* London: Cape.

R. Dahl (1982). *Dilemmas of pluralist democracy: autonomy vs control.* New Haven: Yale University Press.

Robert Dahl (1985). *A Preface to Economic Democracy.* Berkeley: University of California Press.

Ed Davis and Russell Lansbury (eds) (1986). *Democracy and Control in the Workplace.* Melbourne: Longman Cheshire.

J. Ellul (1980). *The Technological System.* New York: Continuum.

G. Esping-Andersen (1986). *Politics against Markets: the Social Democratic Road to Power.* Princeton, N.J.: Princeton University Press.

Paul Feyerabend (1975). *Against Method.* London: NLB.

Paul Feyerabend (1978). *Science in a Free Society*. London: NLB.
Boris Frankel (1983). *Beyond the State? Dominant theories and socialist strategies*. London: Macmillan Press.
Andre Gorz (1964). 'Strategy for labour'. In Branko Horvat et al. (eds) (1975). *Self Governing Socialism*. New York: International Arts and Science Press.
Andre Gorz (1980–2). *Farewell to the Working Class: an essay on post-industrial socialism*. First published as *Adieux au Proletariat*, Éditions Galilée, Paris, 1980. Published in English, translated by Mike Sonenscher, Pluto Press, London, 1982.
Andre Gorz (1983–5). *Paths to Paradise: on the liberation from work*. First published as *Les chemins du paradis*, Éditions Galilée, Paris, 1983. Published in English, translated by James Beveridge, Pluto Press, London, 1985.
Antonio Gramsci (1977). *Selections from political writings 1910–1920*, translated by John Mathews. London: Lawrence and Wishart.
Wyn Grant (1985). *The political economy of corporatism*. London: Macmillan.
Philip Green (1985). *Retrieving Democracy: in search of civic equality*. London: Methuen.
Adrian Hamilton (1986). *The Financial Revolution*. New York: Viking.
Paul Harbrecht (1959). *Pension Funds and Economic Power*. New York: Twentieth Century Fund.
Michael Harrington (1972). *Socialism*. New York: Saturday Review Press.
Michael Harrington (1986). *The Next Left: The History of a Future*. New York: Henry Holt and Company.
E. Hawley (1974). 'Herbert Hoover, The Commerce Secretariat, and the vision of an "Associative State", 1921–1928', *Journal of American History*, 61, pp. 116–40.
David Heald (1983). *Public Expenditure: its defence and reform*. Oxford: Martin Robertson.
H. Heclo and H. Madsden (1987) *Policy and Politics in Sweden: Principled Pragmatism*. Philadelphia: Temple University Press.
Agnes Heller (1982). *Why we should maintain the socialist objective*. Kooyong Federal Electorate Assembly, Australian Labor Party, Melbourne.
Winton Higgins and Nixon Apple (1983). 'How Limited is Reformism? A critique of Przeworski and Panitch'. *Theory and Society*, 12; pp. 603–630.
Winton Higgins (1985). 'Ernst Wigforss: the renewal of social Democratic Theory and practice'. *Political Power and Social Theory*, Vol. 5; pp. 207–250.
S. Hill (1989). *The Tragedy of Technology*. London: Pluto Press
Ulf Himmelstand and others (1981). *Beyond Welfare Capitalism—issues, actors and forces in societal change*. London: Heinemann.
Barry Hindess (1983). *Parliamentary Democracy and Socialist Politics*. London: Routledge and Kegan Paul.

P. Hirst (1986) *Law, Socialiam and Democracy*. London: Allen & Unwin.

P. Hirst (1987) 'Can socialism live?' *New Statesman*, 6 March 1987, pp. 6–10.

P. Hirst (1988). 'Associational socialism in a pluralist state', *Journal of Law and Society*, Vol. 15, No. 1.

Geoff Hodgson (1984). *The Democratic Economy: a new look at planning, markets and power*. London: Penguin Books.

S. Holland (1975). *The Socialist Challenge*. London: Quartet Books.

I. Howe (1985). *Socialism and America*. New York: Harcourt Brace Jovanovich.

B.L. Hutchins and A. Harrison (1903). *A History of Factory Legislation*. London: Frank Cass (Third edition, 1966).

I. Illich (1975). *Tools for conviviality*. London: Fontana.

R. Jackall and H. Levin (eds) (1984). *Worker Cooperatives in America*. Berkeley: University of California Press.

Barry Jones (1982). *Sleepers Wake! Technology and the future of work*. Melbourne: Oxford University Press.

Gösta Karlsson (1984). Trade unions and collective capital formation—European Survey, European Trade Union Institute, Brussels.

Karl Kautsky (1964). *The Dictatorship of the Proletariat*. Ann Arbor: University of Michigan Press.

Karl Kautsky (1971). *The Class Struggle*. New York: W.W. Norton.

Walter Korpi (1978). *The working class in welfare capitalism: work, unions and politics in Sweden*. London: Routledge and Kegan Paul.

W. Korpi (1983). *The Democratic Class Struggle*. London: Routledge and Kegan Paul.

T. Kuhn (1970). *The structure of Scientific Revolutions*, Second edition, University of Chicago Press.

I. Lakatos and A. Musgrove (eds) (1970). *Criticism and the Growth of Knowledge*. Cambridge: Cambridge University Press.

I. Lakatos (1976). *Proofs and Refutations*. Cambridge: Cambridge University Press.

S. Lash and J. Urry (1987). *The End of Organized Capitalism*. Cambridge: Polity Press.

B. Latour (1987). *Science in Action: How to follow scientists and engineers through society*. Milton Keynes: Open University Press.

J. Law (1986) editor, *Power, Action and Belief: A new sociology of knowledge?* London: Routledge and Kegan Paul.

George Lichtheim (1970). *A Short History of Socialism*. London: Weidenfeld and Nicolson.

Martin Linton (1985). *The Swedish Road to Socialism*. London: Fabian Tract No. 503.

A. Lipietz (1987). *Mirages and Miracles: the crises of global Fordism*. London: Verso.

A. Lipietz (1988) 'An alternative design for the twenty-first century'. In G. Pendse (ed), *Options in economic design*. Westport, NY: Greenwood Press.

A. Lipietz (1989). *Choisir l'Audace*, Paris, Editions La Decouverte.

Rosa Luxemburg (1900). '*Reform or Revolution?*' In Mary-Alice Waters (ed), *Rosa Luxemburg Speaks*. New York, Pathfinder Press, 1970.

Jean-Francois Lyotard (1979, 1984) *The postmodern condition: A report on knowledge*. University of Minnesota Press.

S. Macintyre (1985). *Winners and Losers: The pursuit of social justice in Australian history*. Sydney: Allen and Unwin.

S. Macintyre (1986). *The Succeeding Age 1901–1942*, Vol 4, Oxford History of Australia. Melbourne: Oxford University Press.

Donald MacKenzie and Judy Wajcman (eds) (1985). *The Social Shaping of Technology*. Milton Keynes: Open University Press.

David McKnight (ed) (1986). *Moving Left: the future of socialism in Australia*. Sydney: Pluto Press.

Ian Manning (1985). *Incomes and Policy*. Sydney: George Allen and Unwin.

H. Marcuse (1968). *Negations: Essays in critical Theory*. London: Allen Lane the Penguin Press.

T.H. Marshall (1975). *Social policy in the twentieth century*. London: Hutchinson.

T.H. Marshall (1977). *Class, Citizenship and Social Development*. Chicago and London: Chicago University Press.

T.H. Marshall (1981). *The Right to Welfare and other essays*. London: Heinemann Educational.

John Mathews (1972). *Ford Strike: the workers' story*. London: Panther Books/Granada.

John Mathews (1976). 'Scanner: The UN conference on the Law of the Sea'. *New Left Review*.

John Mathews (1980a). 'Marxism, Energy and Technological Change'. *Politics and Power*, No. 1, London: Routledge and Kegan Paul.

John Mathews (1980b). *The Optimal Regulation of Large-Scale Interconnected Linear Systems*, PhD thesis, London, Imperial College of Science and Technology.

John Mathews (1982). *Cybernetics and Economic Democracy*, Melbourne, Victorian Fabian Society, Pamphlet No. 38.

John Mathews (1984). Report of the Occupational Safety, Health and Welfare Steering Committee. *The Protection of Worker's Health and Safety*, 3 Vols., Adelaide, S.A. Ministries of Labour and Health.

John Mathews (1985a). Senate standing committee on Science, Technology and the Environment, Hearings of New Technology and Employment, submission: 'Technology, Trade Unions and the Labour Process', *Hansard*, Melbourne, Wednesday, 28 August 1985; pp. 1632–1813.

John Mathews (1985b). *Health and Safety at Work: a trade union safety representatives' handbook*. Sydney: Pluto Press.

John Mathews (1986a). 'The Politics of the Accord'. In D. McKnight (ed), *Moving Left*. Sydney: Pluto Press.

John Mathews (1986b). *The transformation of work: technological change and union strategies of intervention*, Deakin University working papers in the social studies of science, No. 2.

J. Mathews (1988a). *A culture of power: Rethinking labour movement goals in the 1990s*. Australia: Strategies for Renewal series, 1. Sydney: Pluto Press Australia.

J. Mathews (1988b). 'The promotion of press diversity: options facing the Australian government', Institute for Cultural Policy Studies, Griffith University, Nathan, Queensland.

J. Mathews (1989a). *Tools of Change: New Technology and the Democratisation of work*. Sydney: Pluto Press Australia.

J. Mathews (1989b). *Towards an 'Australian Model' of wages-linked regulated structural adjustment*. Stockholm: Centre for Working Life.

J. Mathews (1989c). 'The democratization of capital', *Economic and Industrial Democracy*, Vol 10, No 2.

J. Mathews (1989d). 'New production concepts', *Prometheus*, 7, 1, June 1989, pp. 129–49

J. Mathews, G. Hall and H. Smith (1988). 'Towards flexible skill formation and technological literacy', *Economic and Industrial Democracy*, Vol 9, No 4.

J. Meade (1982). *Stagflation. Vol. 1. Wage-Fixing*. London: Allen and Unwin.

Rudolf Meidner (1978). *Employee Investment Funds*. London: George Allen and Unwin.

Rudolf Meidner (1981). Collective asset formation through wage-earner funds. *International Labour Review*, Vol. 120, No. 3, May–June 1981.

E. Meiksins Wood (1986). *The retreat from class: a new 'true' socialism*. London: Verso.

M. Mihailovic (1970) *Democratic Socialism*. London.

J. Minson (1988). 'The New Romantics', *Australian Left Review*, No 107, Oct–Nov 1988, pp. 26–31.

R. Miliband *et al.* (eds) (1986). *Socialist Register 1985/86; Social Democracy and after*. London: The Merlin Press.

D. Miller and S. Estrin. 'Market socialism: a policy for socialists'. In Forbes (ed), *Market Socialism: Whose Choice?*, Fabian Tract, No. 516, November 1986, London.

R. Mishra (1984). *The Welfare State in Crisis: Social thought and social change*. Brighton: Wheatsheaf Books.

J. Myles (1988). 'Decline or impasse? The current state of the welfare state', *Studies in Political Economy*, 26, pp. 73–107.

David Noble (1984). *Forces of Production: A social history of industrial automation*. New York: Alfred A. Knopf.

Alec Nove (1983). *The Economics of Feasible Socialism*. London: George Allen and Unwin.

Alec Nove (1986). *Socialism, Economics and Development*. London: Allen and Unwin.

D.M. Nuti (1986). 'Economic planning in market economies: scope, instruments, institutions'. In R. Miliband *et al.* (eds) (1986).

J. O'Connor (1984). *Accumulation Crisis.* Oxford: Basil Blackwell.

Claus Offe (1985). *Disorganized capitalism: contemporary transformation of work and politics.* A collection edited by John Keane. Cambridge: Polity Press.

B. O'Meagher (ed) (1983). *The Socialist Objective: Labour and Socialism.* Sydney: Hale and Iremonger.

L. Panitch (1976). *Social Democracy and Industrial Militancy.* Cambridge: Cambridge University Press.

L. Panitch (1980). 'Recent theorizations of corporatism: reflections on a growth industry'. *British Journal of Sociology,* Vol. 31, No. 2, June 1980; pp. 159–187.

L. Panitch (1981). 'Trade unions and the capitalist State'. *New Left Review,* No. 125 (January–February 1981).

L. Panitch (1986). 'The impasse of Social Democratic politics'. In R. Miliband *et al.* (eds) (1986).

W. Paterson and A. Thomas, eds (1986). *The Future of Social Democracy: Problems and prospects of Social Democratic parties in western Europe.* Oxford: Clarendon Press.

J. Pontusson (1984). *Public pension funds and the politics of capital formation in Sweden.* Stockholm: Centre for Working Life.

K. Popper (1963). *Conjectures and Refutations.* London: Routledge and Kegan Paul.

N. Postman (1987). *Amusing ourselves to death.* London: Heinemann.

Nicos Poulantzas (1968). *Political Power and Social Classes* (translated by Timothy O'Hagan from *Pouvoir politique et classes sociales*). London: NLB, 1973.

Adam Przeworski (1985). *Capitalism and social democracy.* Cambridge: Cambridge University Press.

Michael Ruskin (1985). *For a Pluralist Socialism.* London: Verso.

P. Schmitter (1979). 'Still the century for corporatism'. In P. Schmitter and G. Lehmbruch (eds), *Trends towards corporatist intermediation.* London: Sage.

P. Schmitter (1985). 'Neo-corporatism and the state'. In W. Grant (ed), *The political economy of corporatism.* London: Macmillan.

J. Schumpeter (1943). *Capitalism, Socialism and Democracy.* London: Unwin Paperbacks, 1987.

David Selbourne (1985). *Against Socialist Illusion: a radical argument.* London: Macmillan.

Radoslav Selucky (1979). *Marxism, Socialism and Freedom.* London.

Harley Shaiken (1984). *Work Transformed: automation and labor in the computer age.* New York: Holt, Rinehart and Winston.

Carmen Sirianni (1980). 'Workers' control in the era of World War I: a comparative analysis of the European experience'. *Theory and Society,* 9; pp. 29–88.

Frank Stillwell (1986). *The Accord...and Beyond: the political economy of the*

Labor government. Sydney: Pluto Press.

W. Streeck and P. Schmitter (1985). *Private Interest Government: Beyond market and state*. London: Sage Publications.

Hugh Stretton (1987). *Political Essays*. Melbourne: Georgian House.

A. Sturmthal (1944) *The Tragedy of European Labor, 1918–1939*. New York: Columbia University Press; London: Gollancz.

E.P. Thompson (1968). *The making of the English Working Class*. London: Penguin.

Timothy Tilton (1979). 'A Swedish Road to Socialism: Ernst Wigforss and the ideological foundations of Swedish Social Democracy'. *The American Political Science Review*, Vol. 73, No. 2, June 1979; pp. 505–520.

H. Tingsten (1973). *The Swedish Social Democrats*. Totawa: N.J. Bedminster Press.

A. Toffler (1981). *The Third Wave*. London: Pan Books.

S. Toulmin (1972). *Human Understanding: the collective use and evolution of concepts*. Princeton: Princeton University Press.

Bryan Turner (1986). *Citizenship and capitalism: the debate over reformism*. London: Allen and Unwin.

H. Wachtel (1986). *The Money Mandarins: The making of a supranational economic order*. New York: Pantheon Books.

Judy Wajcman (1983). *Women in control: Dilemmas of a workers' cooperative*. Milton Keynes: The Open University Press.

Michael Walzer (1983). *Spheres of Justice: A Defence of Pluralism and Equality*. London.

R. Watts (1987). *The Foundations of the National Welfare State*. Sydney: Allen and Unwin.

Martin Weitzman (1986). *The Share Economy: conquering stagflation*. Cambridge: Harvard University Press.

Joe Weston (ed) (1986). *Red and Green: a new politics of the environment*. London: Pluto Press.

R. Williams (1976). *Keywords: A vocabulary for culture and society*. London: Fontana/Croom Helm.

D. Wilson (1985) ed. *Democratic Socialism: the challenge of the eighties and beyond*. Proceedings of a conference sponsored by the Boag Foundation. Vancouver: New Star Books.

Langdon Winner, (1977). *Autonomous Technology: Technics-out-of-control as a theme in political thought*. Boston: MIT Press.

Langdon Winner (1986). *The Whale and the Reactor: a search for limits in an age of high technology*. Chicago: University of Chicago Press.

INDEX